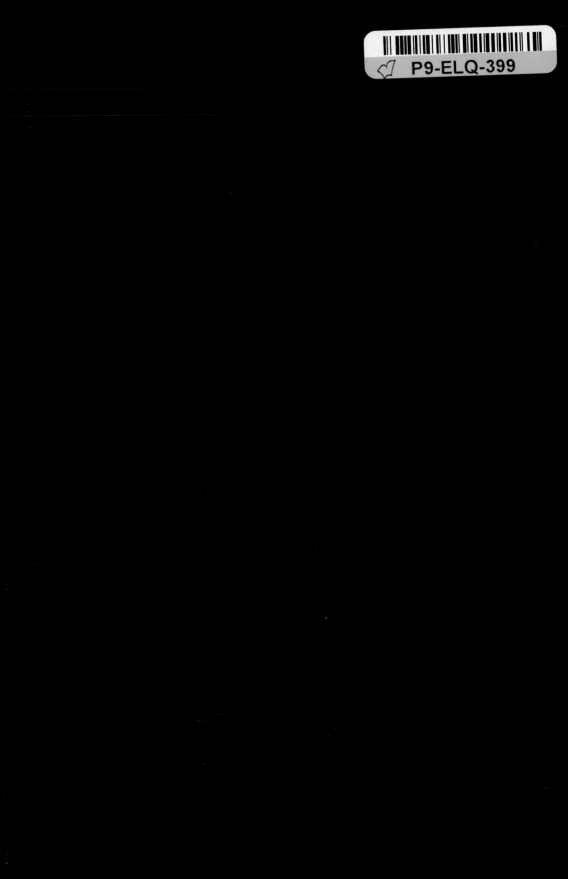

Political Bubbles

POLITICAL BUBBLES

Financial Crises and the
Failure of American Democracy

O O O O O O O O O O O O

Nolan McCarty
Princeton University

Keith T. Poole
University of Georgia

Howard Rosenthal
New York University

Princeton University Press
Princeton and Oxford

Published by Princeton University Press, 41 William Street, Princeton, New Jersey
08540
In the United Kingdom: Princeton University Press, 6 Oxford Street, Woodstock,
Oxfordshire OX20 1TW

press.princeton.edu

Jacket designed by Marcella Engel Roberts.
Illustration composite by Marcella Engel Roberts using stock diagram © Pincasso;
Capitol building, Washington DC © Orhan Cam; and bubbles © Marcel Jancovic.
Jacket photographs courtesy of Shutterstock.

Library of Congress Cataloging-in-Publication Data

McCarty, Nolan M.
Political bubbles: financial crises and the failure of American democracy / Nolan
McCarty, Princeton University, Keith T. Poole, University of Georgia,
Howard Rosenthal, New York University.
p. cm.
Includes bibliographical references and index.
ISBN-13: 978-0-691-14501-3 (cloth : alk. paper)
ISBN-10: 0-691-14501-6 (cloth : alk. paper)   1. Global Financial Crisis,
2008–2009—Political aspects.   2. Financial crises—United States—History—21st
century.   I. Poole, Keith T.   II. Rosenthal, Howard, 1939–   III. Title.
HB37172008 .M34 2013
330.973′0931—dc23   2012041583

British Library Cataloging-in-Publication Data is available

This book has been composed in Sabon

Printed on acid-free paper. ∞

Printed in the United States of America

1 3 5 7 9 10 8 6 4 2

CONTENTS

. . . .

CHAPTER 9
How to Waste a Crisis   251

ACKNOWLEDGMENTS

AT THE CLOSE OF OUR LAST BOOK *Polarized America: The Dance of Ideology and Unequal Riches*, we speculated about what might end the cycle of economic inequality and ideological polarization that the United States had witnessed over the past thirty years. Having carefully ruled out all the "small ball" solutions (e.g., open primaries, gerrymandering reform, campaign finance reform), we tried to go deep. One of the scenarios we laid out was a political realignment engendered by a financial crisis such as that of the 1930s, which ushered in the transition from a laissez-faire political economy to the New Deal.

We were chided by a few colleagues who found us unduly pessimistic. Surely the system could be changed short of financial calamity. And when the crisis did occur, the smart set was convinced that hope, change, and a new politics had arisen from it. But history has proven the conclusions of *Polarized America* to be downright Pollyannaish.

We had our crisis, but we didn't get much for it. This book aims to try to explain why we got so much right in *Polarized America* (or at least we think so) but got the conclusion so wrong.

This book was greatly improved by comments on our first draft from Adam Bonica, Patrick Bolton, Charles Cameron, Jean-Laurent Rosenthal, Joshua Thorpe, Chris Tausanovich, two readers for Princeton University Press, and an economist who wished to remain anonymous. Barry Sacks helped on the Employee Retirement Income Security Act. We also thank Tom Romer, who has been our excellent colleague at Carnegie Mellon and Princeton Universities for many years. Several ideas in this book were worked out when we collaborated with Tom on a 2010 article published in *Daedalus* (and a cheeky op-ed about Russ Feingold in the *Huffington Post*). None of these people is likely to be in complete agreement with the views we express. As nonideologues, we welcome debate.

Nolan McCarty would like to thank seminar participants at Princeton's Center for the Study of Democratic Politics for feedback on an early version of the book's arguments. Participation in a Russell Sage Foundation–funded collaboration on political responses to the crisis, headed by Nancy Bermeo and Jonas Pontusson, provided a large amount of feedback as well as the opportunity to write the first draft of the case studies on the economic stimulus plan and the Dodd-Frank Wall Street Reform and Consumer Protection Act. McCarty's discussions with Dan Carpenter, David Moss, and other participants in the Tobin Project on Regulatory Capture were very helpful in shaping the discussion of the politics of financial regulation.

Keith T. Poole would like to thank his colleagues Scott Ainsworth, Jamie Carson, and Tony Madonna for many useful conversations about the manuscript. He also received valuable feedback from students in two graduate courses and an undergraduate course on political polarization.

Howard Rosenthal's interest in the political economy of finance came about from visiting the European Center for Advanced Research in Economics and Statistics (ECARES) in Brussels in 1995. He had an exceptional group of colleagues, most notably Erik Berglöf, Patrick Bolton, Mathias Dewatripont, Ailsa Röell, and Gérard Roland. Berglöf realized that bankruptcy policy was historically a divisive political issue in the United States. An investigation of what could be learned about the conflict from roll call voting analysis was made possible by the DW-NOMINATE model that we had developed. Gérard Roland and Abdul Noury, the latter then an ECARES student, began to use NOMINATE to study the European Parliament and wound up writing, with Simon Hix, a book that won the Richard F. Fenno,

Jr. Prize from the Legislative Studies Section of the American Political Science Association. Playing off the joint work with Berglöf, Bolton and Rosenthal later wrote "Political Intervention in Debt Contracts," a paper that provides a rationale for government relief of debtors even in the shadow of moral hazard. The Bolton-Roland model of taxation was later used as a theoretical framework for our analysis of the politics of redistribution in *Polarized America*. The stop at ECARES was a career changer for Rosenthal.

Patrick Bolton deserves special thanks. He was an organizer of the meeting "Preventing Future Financial Crises" at Columbia University in December 2008. When the program was put together months before, no one realized that the American financial system was near collapse. Bolton asked Rosenthal to make a brief presentation on the politics of the crisis. Discussions after the conference led us to write *Political Bubbles*. As the book evolved, Bolton was always available to provide an economist's reality check to a trio of political scientists. In 2011–12, Bolton served as the first director of the Institute for Applied Social Science in Toulouse, France. He invited Rosenthal to give two talks drawn from the book manuscript. We thank those who were in attendance for numerous comments that influenced the revised manuscript.

Between the Columbia meeting and the Toulouse talks, Rosenthal was also able to present themes from the book as a plenary address at a political economy conference at Università Cattolica in Milan, as the William H. Riker Prize Lecture at the University of Rochester, and at the Priorat Workshop in Theoretical Political Science in Falset, Spain. Participants, particularly Larry Rothenberg and Guido Tabellini, are thanked for their comments. In addition to academic colleagues, Rosenthal owes a great deal to the undergraduate honors students who have taken his seminar Politics and Finance at New York University since 2006.

Rosenthal would also like to thank Luca Bocci and Nadia Bolognesi, who for the past thirteen years have provided a country home in Piemonte where a good deal of the work on both

Polarized America and *Political Bubbles* was carried out. Every year brings a reminder that there are many, many virtues to a country with a backward financial system, a corrupt political class, no babies, and mountains of debt.

The authors would also like to thank Michelle Anderson for very able research and editorial assistance. Our manuscript shares at least one similarity with the responses to financial crises: it was delayed. So special thanks goes to Chuck Myers, our editor at Princeton University Press, who was patient, persevering, and insightful.

Political Bubbles

○   ○   ○   ○   ○   ○   ○   ○   ○   ○   ○   ○

Prologue: A Bubble Couple

One of us was unfortunate enough to be caught up in the housing bubble in southern California. He was relocating to the San Diego area in late 2004. He and his wife had owned four homes in three states over the previous twenty-seven years. Typically, the couple would negotiate with sellers over price and then seek financing from a bank. They would also initiate contact with lenders for refinancing.

The couple went house hunting when the North San Diego County real estate market was frenetic. Their agent advised them to carry cell phones at all times because if anything came on the market potential buyers had less than a day to view a property and make an offer. Typically houses drew multiple offers. When they found a house a few days before Christmas, the agent advised making an offer close to the full asking price in hopes that the seller would accept it before an open house scheduled for two days after Christmas. Their offer was accepted.

The couple's real surprise came when they met with a mortgage broker who had an office in the same building as the real estate company. They were offered several different kinds of loans, several of which they had never heard of. The idea of an "interest only" loan seemed bizarre, and they opted for a 5-percent-down thirty-year mortgage. The first mortgage was with Genesis Mortgage Corporation, which resold it within a month to Wells Fargo. The second mortgage was with National City Mortgage of Cleveland, Ohio. Within two months National City, unsolicited, offered to extend more credit on the house.

A home equity line was provided that could be drawn on to make improvements to the house. Now the lender was throwing money at the borrower rather than the borrower trying to get a loan. Of course, the couple took the line. Owning a house in southern California was one of the best investments you could make. If you held on to a house for ten years or so you could sell at a big profit—so went the local lore. Things did not turn out that way.

National City was the epitome of the financial bubble. At one time a reputable bank dating back to the mid-nineteenth century, it got into subprime mortgages in 1999 by purchasing First Franklin Financial Companies.[1]

National City kept expanding. By 2003 and 2004 it was making $1 billion per year on its subprime business. In 2006 National City sold First Franklin to Merrill Lynch but had to hold on to $10 billion in subprime loans that Merrill Lynch did not want.[2] This was the beginning of the end. National City's subprime holdings tanked. The bank lost $1.8 billion in the second quarter of 2008, and it was forced to sell itself to PNC Bank in October of that year.[3] PNC used government money from the Troubled Asset Relief Program (TARP) to complete the acquisition. (Merrill Lynch was to meet its own end, even without that extra $10 billion in subprime loans.)

In 2007 the couple switched the second mortgage from National City to Wells Fargo. Wells Fargo let them make further draws on their "equity" to make improvements to the house. The housing bubble, the couple failed to realize, had already popped. The country was about to enter the Great Recession. Tax collections in California collapsed. Something had to give in the erstwhile Golden State, which for years had irreconcilable passions for low taxes, a prison gulag, and generous public-employee pensions. The author's employer, the University of California, cut nominal salaries through furloughs—unpaid vacations without the vacation. Public education, at all levels, became a victim of the collapse of the housing bubble. As for the couple, the salary cut put stress on their mortgage commitments.

The couple was more fortunate than most Americans. One day the phone rang. They were able to move to a much better job and a much bigger house in Georgia. They did lose a great deal of money on the California house. Getting caught up in the bubble set back the author's expected retirement date. But unlike National City, the couple survived, and unlike millions of other borrowers, they still have a home.

A Nation Bubbles Over

The financial system of the United States was close to collapse by the fall of 2008. On September 15, two of the four largest investment banks failed. One, Lehman Brothers, declared bankruptcy. Lehman failed to find a buyer, and the government decided not to guarantee some of its underperforming assets in order to facilitate a sale. The other, Merrill Lynch, the country's largest brokerage firm, was sold to Bank of America at a rock-bottom price.

The next day the Federal Reserve announced an $85 billion bailout of the nation's largest insurance company, American International Group (AIG). AIG's troubles were based on billions of dollars in swaps that it underwrote against defaults of mortgage-backed securities (MBSs) and collateralized debt obligations (CDOs).[4] A collapse of AIG would have destroyed the value of these securities and generated even greater sell-offs, losses, and insolvencies throughout the entire financial system. Three days later, on September 18, Secretary of the Treasury Henry Paulson went to Congress to plead for the enactment of the $700 billion Troubled Asset Relief Program (TARP). This sketchy plan, a virtual blank check from Congress to the U.S. Treasury, sought to reinject capital into the financial system. Government purchases of mortgage-backed securities and other distressed assets would, it was claimed, prop up markets and halt the financial crisis.

The dramatic failures of the week of September 15 capped a string of financial calamities that had begun with the government bailout of Bear Stearns in March 2008. Just a week before the collapse of Lehman and Merrill Lynch, the government took over the biggest players in the mortgage market, the government-sponsored enterprises (GSEs) Fannie Mae and Freddie Mac. Before the year was out, the federal government would also control AIG. The ensuing crisis hit an economy already in recession after the collapse of the bubble in housing prices. Unemployment pushed toward levels not seen since the early 1980s. The automobile industry, the traditional symbol of American manufacturing strength, almost collapsed before a government-orchestrated restructuring in which the American taxpayer became the owner of a majority of General Motors' stock. At the beginning of 2012, GM, Ally Financial (the successor to GM's long-time finance subsidiary GMAC), and AIG remained subject to government supervision; the future of Fannie and Freddie remains unresolved.

The financial crisis of 2008 was a truly traumatic event for Americans and affected almost everyone else in the global economy. But the causes of this calamity continue to be hotly debated.

The blame frequently goes to individuals such as investment bankers reaping huge bonuses on Wall Street, go-granny-go subprime mortgage originators in Pasadena, and house flippers in Las Vegas. Others focus on large structural factors such as the explosion of financial innovation and global financial imbalances that showered the United States and much of the industrialized world with cheap credit from China and the Middle East. Still others claim that the crisis was just one more instance of markets gone wild, a mass mania no different from the seventeenth-century bubble in the price of Dutch tulip bulbs.[5] We, however, do not reach a verdict of not guilty by reason of insanity.

We focus on the national government in Washington, D.C. To be precise, we put much of the responsibility for the crisis and the failure to undertake genuine reform of the American financial system squarely on members of Congress, on Presidents Jimmy Carter, Ronald Reagan, George H. W. Bush, Bill Clinton, George W. Bush, and Barack Obama and on those they chose to serve in their cabinets and in the Executive Office in the White House and to run regulatory agencies, including the Federal Reserve and the Securities and Exchange Commission (SEC).

We contrast their actions with those of the private-sector actors who indulged in "infectious greed" and "irrational exuberance." Political actors failed in their response to the challenges of financial innovation and the global "savings glut." They allowed the crisis to develop and inhibited response after the crisis was front and center in the public eye.

A notable culprit was Federal Reserve chair Alan Greenspan, the originator of these catchwords, venerated in his initial Senate confirmation vote and four reappointments, two by a Democratic president. Greenspan pumped up the housing bubble with easy credit and failed to exercise his responsibility to investigate and regulate deceptive "teaser loans" and outright fraud in the origination of subprime mortgages. His successor, Ben Bernanke, when appointed by George W. Bush in 2006, presented himself as a Greenspan clone (although one less prone to obtuse pronouncements) and was curiously passive until the September 2008 collapse of the financial sector. Bernanke's passivity may have reflected a Fed that is less "independent" than many imagine. Congress and the financial and housing sector would have been up in arms had Bernanke attempted to rock the boat.

The malefactors were bipartisan. They included Republican appointees like Greenspan and Republicans in Congress and the White House imbued with the mantras of "free markets" and "the ownership society"; Democrats were eager to have the poor in housing they could not afford. Both Franklin Raines, head of the White House Office of Management and Budget under Bill Clinton, and James Johnson, adviser to Walter Mondale, Al Gore, and Barack Obama, were grossly overcompensated as CEOs of Fannie Mae.[6] Clinton's chair of the Council of Economic Advisors, Nobel Prize Laureate Joseph Stiglitz, along with future Obama adviser and Citigroup employee Peter Orszag and Clinton adviser Jon Orszag, wrote a 2001 position paper for Fannie Mae claiming that there was only a one in 500,000 chance that Fannie Mae would go bust.

Perhaps of greater importance than the Democratic preoccupation with low income and minority housing, and with Fannie

Mae, was the acquiescence of the Democrats in financial deregulation, most notably by Clinton treasury secretaries Robert Rubin and Larry Summers. Rubin was in a Washington transition between Goldman Sachs and Citicorp; Summers did a stint at the hedge fund D. E. Shaw after his government service.

The financial crisis and the Great Recession it spawned have led to a spate of books on what went wrong. Ours is a late entry. What can we say that has not been said? We are certainly not the first to stress the influence of Wall Street on Washington. Others go so far as to imply that Wall Street has "captured" Washington and always gets what it wants and gets it right away. Such an account is far too simple.

Politicians and policy makers do often behave in ways that are not reducible to carrying water for Wall Street. For example, the Bush administration's Treasury Department, whose top officials had strong Wall Street ties, was reluctant to ask for congressional authority to address the financial crisis in early 2008. Later that year, perhaps because of congressional opposition to its role in saving the investment bank Bear Stearns, the administration allowed Lehman Brothers to go into bankruptcy rather than risk congressional reaction from a bailout. (It's worth noting that neither heavy campaign contributions from Lehman nor its CEO Richard Fuld's service as a director of the New York Fed saved Lehman from bankruptcy.) Possible Treasury Department fears about Congress, even Republican controlled, would have been well founded. Shortly after Lehman failed, the House of Representatives voted down the administration's first try to pass TARP.

As a second example, consider the difficulty the financial industry faced when it pursued "reform" of personal bankruptcy law. It took Visa, MasterCard, and other creditors seven years to force through the 2005 legislation that made consumer bankruptcy more difficult. The financial services industry is indeed powerful, but it does not always get what it wants. Moreover, the industry is competitive and not perfectly homogeneous. The demise of Bear Stearns, Lehman Brothers, and Merrill Lynch as independent firms may have been welcome news to the survivors, Goldman

Figure I.1. Financial collapse. Ben Bernanke, George W. Bush, Henry Paulson, and Christopher Cox after the bankruptcy of Lehman Brothers.
Source: Official White House Photo by Joyce N. Boghosian.

Sachs and Morgan Stanley. So it is important to sharpen our understanding of exactly how financial interests are represented in Washington and when those influences will be the greatest.

Our account provides a more nuanced understanding of the channels through which politics exacerbates financial crises. Whereas much of the discussion of the political underpinnings of the financial crisis has centered on the political interests of the financial sector, we stress the *Three I's*: ideology, institutions, and interests.

The actions of politicians reflect not only pressures from organized interests but also personal beliefs about the proper role of government in regulating the financial sector. As we document throughout this book, these ideological beliefs are rigid and are largely unresponsive to new information. Undoubtedly the manifest ideologies reflect some mixture of genuine personal belief, constituents' beliefs, and cronyism linked to personal venality.[7] What we hold to be important is not so much the recipe for this mixture but its rigidity. This rigidity, we argue, can impede measures that might prevent bubbles and limit the political response in a bust.

Political institutions such as elections, legislative rules and procedures, and regulatory structures affect the incentives and opportunities of elected politicians to engage in policy making that either exacerbates or mitigates financial crises. Our focus is on how the fragmented and supermajoritarian structure of U.S. political institutions makes it difficult for policy makers to keep up with financial innovation and to reform the financial sector in the bust.[8]

Groups and interests are the final ingredient. Well-organized, resourceful groups such as those in the financial sector are often able to exploit ideological allies and institutional structures to produce policy benefits for themselves. As we will show, powerful groups are able not only to push presidents and legislators for more favorable policies but also to stave off intruding regulators. Weak regulation, in turn, allows certain actors to push the boundaries of legality.

Washington failed to deal with three pillars of the financial crisis. The first pillar was the dramatic increase in risky residential loans known as subprime mortgages in which the borrower has an insufficiently good credit or work history to qualify for a lower-interest prime loan. The originators of these high-interest mortgages would often keep little or no "skin in the game" but instead would sell the mortgages to other financial firms. Some of the nation's largest financial institutions allegedly produced fraudulent documents and resold subprime mortgages as prime quality AAA paper.[9]

The second pillar of the crisis was the securitization of mortgages by bundling them into pools of loans that could be sold to investors. These mortgage securities were in turn sliced into tranches representing various levels of risk. The highest tranches maintained first claims on interest payments; the lowest tranche owned the lowest-priority claim, and therefore was the first one to feel the effects of defaulting mortgages.

Underwriters sought credit ratings for the various securities and their tranches. Despite the low quality of the underlying loans, credit rating agencies uniformly issued ratings at AAA, as safe as U.S. government debt.[10] (After the crisis, Standard & Poor's downgraded U.S. government debt but continues to give some MBSs AAA ratings.[11]) With the blessings of Standard & Poor's, Moody's, or Fitch, these securities were then marketed by financial institutions and peddled to investors around the world. Investment banks and large commercial banks such as Citigroup not only resold mortgage-backed securities but continued to hold many directly. In order to dramatically increase their leverage in these investments, they financed the purchase of MBSs and other CDOs with low-interest short-term loans in the "shadow" banking system formed by the overnight repo (sale and repurchase) market.

The third pillar was the use of credit default swaps (CDSs) to insure these mortgage-backed securities against default. The seller of a swap agreed to pay the buyer a predetermined sum in the event that the MBS defaulted. These insurance policies were designed to allow the holders of MBSs to hedge against risk. But other investors who did not hold MBSs also bought these swaps to place a casino-like bet against the MBS—the so-called naked credit default swap. The insurer AIG morphed into an investment bank and ran the biggest casino. Although CDSs are theoretically designed to spread risk, AIG's financial services division underwrote so many that a nuclear bomb of concentrated risk was created.

These three pillars, along with the easy-money policies of the Federal Reserve and the huge influx of foreign capital, promoted a housing market bubble. When the bubble popped, the first pillar collapsed with a wave of defaults on subprime loans. This took out the second pillar, as AAA securities based on mortgages began to default and lose value. The bank purchasing an MBS or CDO would turn around and use it as collateral for a short-term loan. When the housing bubble burst and defaults became probable, there were large increases in the collateral demanded to finance these short-term loans. Consequently, as mortgage defaults increased, holders of MBSs began to have difficulty refinancing their operations through the repo market as lenders feared defaults on these loans. Eventually, a full-fledged run on the shadow banking system started. Owing to a lack of transparency about holdings of "toxic" assets, the run spread through the financial system. Finally, the collapse of the second pillar caused buyers of CDSs to try to collect their insurance claims, taking out the third pillar and bringing AIG into insolvency.

Clearly, all three of these pillars are based on policy errors of commission and omission. Policy makers could have avoided the crisis by closely regulating or even prohibiting the products underlying any one of the three pillars. Subprime mortgages could have been curtailed by any number of regulations: interest rate regulation, restrictions on the types of mortgages available in the market; stricter supervision of lending standards, mortgage originators, and real estate agents; or higher total loan-to-value requirements on loans. The perverse incentives in securitization could have been curtailed by forcing mortgage originators to retain a substantial interest in the mortgages they sold. Both originators and securitizers could have been forced to "cover" the underlying securities and derivatives by retaining liability in the case of default. The conflicts of interest by ratings agencies could have been dealt with. Policy makers could have prohibited accounting gimmicks like special investment vehicles that allowed mortgage market investors to magnify leverage. Credit default swaps could have been restricted to those with "skin in the game," and issuers could have been required to hold more capital to protect against losses.

That regulatory measures might have avoided or ameliorated the crisis suggests the deep complicity of the White House, Congress, and federal regulatory agencies. The bubble that led to the crisis was stimulated by relaxation of mortgage market regulation in the 1980s, government pressure on both the GSEs and on private financial institutions to increase lending to low-income and minority borrowers, and by the protection of over-the-counter derivatives from regulation in the Commodity Futures Modernization Act of 2000. All these seeds of crisis were planted before George W. Bush took office and before the explosion of subprime mortgages and private-sector mortgage securitization. Corrective actions were not taken during the Bush administration despite the presence of many warning signals. The Bush administration throttled the SEC with the appointments of Harvey Pitt and Christopher Cox as chairs, while Republicans in Congress prevented action on attempts by Democrats to regulate predatory lending. If mortgages did indeed become Dutch tulips, Washington provided a superbly fertile flower bed.

But there is nothing unique about the recent crisis. The same types of policy failures occurred in both the savings and loan (S&L) crisis and the Great Depression. The S&L crisis was in full swing by 1985 and was ended only by the creation of the Resolution Trust Corporation in 1989. Similarly, the Great Depression was triggered by the stock market crash of October 1929, but major new policies waited for the first hundred days after Franklin Delano Roosevelt's inauguration in March 1933.[12] These policy innovations included the Glass-Steagall Act, signed by the president in June of that year. Glass-Steagall both separated commercial and investment banking and created deposit insurance. Notably, it also maintained restrictions on interstate branch banking that were lifted only with the Riegle-Neal Interstate Banking and Branching Efficiency Act of 1994. Financial market problems in the Great Depression were preceded by those that led to the Panic of 1907. The Panic, which took place in October of that year, drew no response from Washington. The objective of preventing a future crisis did result in the Aldrich-Vreeland Act of May 30, 1908, but a substantial response occurred only with the creation of the Federal Reserve in 1913.[13] Clearly, there is a recurring pattern of closing the barn door after the horses are long gone.

Why do such colossal policy failures and delays occur repeatedly? One argument is that recurrent financial crises are simply a reflection of capitalism, its cyclical nature and capacity for creative destruction. In this view, the lag in policy and regulation has more to do with the unpredictable nature of financial crises than with any political failures. But focusing solely on economic dynamics gives an incomplete picture of financial crises.

Many of the underlying causes of financial disorder were indeed known in advance. Yet attempts at reform were not just ignored but actively opposed. Such examples are easy to come by. We start with the 1990s.

In 1994, Askin Capital Management, a hedge fund heavily invested in MBSs, lost $600 million.[14] That December, Orange County, California filed for bankruptcy when derivative investments based on interest rates went south after a sudden rise in interest rates. In 1998, Merrill Lynch, which advised the investments, reached a $400 million settlement with Orange County. Congressional hearings on hedge funds and derivative securities were held in the aftermath, but no legislative correctives were proffered. A decade later, Merrill Lynch failed.[15]

In the late 1990s, a dozen small subprime lenders went bankrupt when, after several years of Ponzi-style lending, many of their outstanding mortgages defaulted.[16] In 1999, the hedge fund Long Term Capital Management (LTCM) failed; the Federal Reserve intervened to avoid further damage to the financial sector. Also in the late 1990s, Brooksley Born, the head of the Commodity Futures Trading Commission (CFTC), sounded the alarm about problems associated with the lack of regulation of derivative contracts including the CDSs that became central to the financial crisis of 2008. Yet her attempt to bring derivatives under the jurisdiction of the CFTC was adamantly opposed by President Clinton's economic team (most notably Robert Rubin and Larry Summers), chairman of the Securities and Exchange Commission Arthur Levitt, and congressional heavyweights such as Senate Banking Committee chair Phil Gramm.

The new century began with the pop of the dot-com bubble in 2001. Much attention was devoted to the role of misleading and fraudulent information that arose from accounting firms and market analysts. Merrill Lynch paid a $100 million fine for reports issued by its analysts. Citigroup, which later received billions in TARP funds, paid billions in fines and settlements over its role in the Enron and Global Crossing fiascoes. Nonetheless, the reforms of the Sarbanes-Oxley Act failed to prevent widespread accounting misinformation in the financial crisis.[17]

As the housing bubble got under way, concerns about the risky loan portfolios of Fannie Mae and Freddie Mac were repeatedly raised in the early part of the decade, but intense lobbying by these GSEs and their politically connected executives beat back any and all attempts at regulation. In particular, many state attorneys general sought to draw Washington's attention to the risks in the complicated mortgage products being marketed. They further sought to pursue predatory lending charges against banks but were "preempted" from doing so by national regulators.[18]

By 2005 and 2006, the Federal Reserve had collected unmistakable evidence of the mounting foreclosures and defaults on subprime mortgages yet it decided not to use its regulatory powers to raise lending standards. Prominent academics, such as Robert Shiller and Nouriel Roubini, were predicting a national housing crash. Moreover, policy makers simply ignored history: many recent financial crises such as those in Scandinavia, Japan, and Thailand were triggered by a collapsed real estate bubble. But Washington and Wall Street convinced themselves "This Time Is Different."[19]

So financial crises are not simply economic phenomena; they have a very important political dimension. As we argue in this book, behind every financial bubble there is a corresponding political bubble. Just as financial bubbles in markets are a combination of irrational exuberance and greed, political bubbles brew in their own mix of ideology, institutions, and private interest.

What Is a Political Bubble?

By *political bubble*, we mean a set of policy biases that foster and amplify the market behaviors that generate financial crises. Political bubbles are procyclical. Rather than tilting against risky behavior, the political bubble aids, abets, and amplifies it. During a financial bubble, when regulations should be strengthened, the political bubble relaxes them. When investors should hold more capital and reduce leverage, the political bubble allows the opposite. When monetary policy should tighten, the political bubble promotes easy credit.

In their causes, political bubbles bear a marked similarity to market bubbles. First, both types of bubbles rely on specific sets of beliefs. Economists stress the role of expectations in generating asset bubbles.[20] These beliefs are used to rationalize asset prices that depart strongly from their historical levels. For example, the belief that the excess returns that investors require for holding stocks (the so-called equity risk premium) had permanently declined helped fuel the stock market boom of the late 1990s. At the same time, the notion that a new information economy was emerging led to feverish public offerings. A firm selling dog food over the Internet, Pets.com, whose investment banker was none other than the bubbly, bullish-on-America Merrill Lynch, went to fourteen dollars a share after an eleven-dollar initial public offering in February 2000, only to be liquidated in November of that year.[21] Also in the first decade of the new century, the belief that globalization and a savings glut from the developing world could drive interest rates to permanently low levels fueled housing bubbles from Las Vegas to Latvia. Even investors who were more skeptical of these changes in fundamentals continued to buy inflated assets in hopes of selling them just before the crash.

Just as beliefs fuel a "this dance can go on forever" mentality of investors and speculators, the beliefs and ideologies of politicians and voters sustain political bubbles. First, the fact that politicians and voters may share in the investor's "irrational exuberance" makes them loath to support corrective policies. If a savings glut reduces the natural level of interest rates, it would be folly to use monetary policies to keep them artificially high. If the information economy is the wave of the future, it would be Luddism to tighten standards for either the public offerings that would capitalize the firms of the future or the pricing of stock options in accounting statements.

But beyond the beliefs that underpin a particular bubble, basic ideological beliefs about the nature of markets and the role of government also fuel bubbles. The *Oxford English Dictionary* defines *ideology* as a "systematic scheme of ideas, usually relating to politics or society, or to the conduct of a class or group, and regarded as justifying actions, especially one that is held implicitly or adopted as a whole and *maintained regardless of the course of events.*"[22]

Of course, ideological beliefs come in various flavors ranging from left to center to right. But the belief structure most conducive to supporting political bubbles is what we term *free market conservatism*. Like most ideologies, free market conservatism is based on a core set of principles. The absolute simplest form is the belief that government intervention in the economy is bad per se, no matter what. Markets are always better at allocating resources than bureaucracies are. Consequently, government intervention should be extremely limited. Government should engage only in the basic protections of life and property, and it should be specifically restricted to functions that cannot be provided by the marketplace (even free market conservatives disagree about what these are). Because markets allocate resources best, taxes and regulations should be as low as possible.

Beliefs associated with free market conservatism have advocates in both major political parties. Its influence has been especially pronounced in the Republican Party in recent years, serving as an important catalyst in the party's shift to the right and to the increased polarization of American politics.[23] But free market conservatism is not confined to the right side of the Republican Party. In fact, as we argue later, its adherents include many important Democrats.

Nonetheless, in recent years, some Republicans—especially those who have come to be identified with the Tea Party movement—have engaged in a virulent form of free market conservatism that we can term *fundamentalist free market capitalism*. The fundamentalist version sees no role for government under any circumstance. It can be contrasted with the view of earlier, prominent exponents of capitalism, ranging from the first treasury secretary, Alexander Hamilton, to the famous economist Milton Friedman, and even to Alan Greenspan, all of whom saw the need for government intervention, at least in exceptional circumstances. The fundamentalists severely hindered Treasury Secretary Paulson's efforts to stabilize financial markets, both in forcing the bankruptcy of Lehman Brothers and in opposing TARP.[24]

Although economic and political beliefs behave quite similarly in the rise of a bubble, there are important differences in the aftermath of the bubble's pop. Economic expectations can change dramatically and decisively over a short period of time when actors realize that economic fundamentals can no longer sustain the value of appreciated assets. But as the italicized clause of the *Oxford Dictionary* definition reveals, ideologues permit no such correction of their worldview. The rigidity of ideological beliefs inhibits the rational adaptation of policy to the circumstances of a financial crisis. Rather than concede that the old orthodoxy may be to blame, the ideologue searches for ways to blame perceived deviations from that orthodoxy. For adherents of free market conservatism, an apparent market failure is proof positive of government interference with the laws of economics. This suggests that policy making in the pop will exacerbate the crisis. The decisions will be delayed and distorted by ideological rigidity. The new policies are likely to contain the seeds of the next crisis.

The second commonality of financial and political bubbles is that both are strongly influenced by the institutions or the "rules of the game." These rules generate incentives to engage in social behavior that may be destructive. The incentives of economic actors are shaped by the structure of financial markets, the state of financial knowledge, and the presence or absence of government oversight and regulation. These factors determine to a large degree whether capital flows to society's most productive uses or, in contrast, feeds speculation and manipulation. Institutions similarly structure political decision making. The electoral system and campaign finance laws affect what policies politicians support. The structure of the federal government—bicameralism, the presidential veto, the filibuster, and the committee system in Congress—poses formidable obstacles to policy making. If these obstacles cannot be overcome, the government most likely will not be able to provide adequate oversight and regulation of financial markets.

In this way the political rules determine the economic rules. This political trump is important for understanding financial crises, as the entire set of hurdles imposes a status quo bias that inhibits governmental responses. The institutional hurdles that lead to gridlock are in turn exacerbated by ideological polarization.[25]

The final common feature of financial and political bubbles is the role of self-interest and greed. As we know from the Scottish economist Adam Smith in *The Wealth of Nations* and the American political scientist David Mayhew in *The Electoral Connection*, a lot of benefits flow from self-interested behavior in both the economic and political realms.[26] But, of course, there are limitations. Markets need a functioning invisible hand. Competition must be present and information must flow freely via the price system. Democracy requires competitive elections, free expression, and informed and engaged voters. When these conditions are not met, the social virtue of self-interest may cease, and opportunities for greed emerge.

Greed and interest are often what links finance to the political side of the bubble. Opportunist financiers will seek political alliances with opportunist politicians and compatible ideologues. Together such coalitions will exploit political opportunities to advance interests. A striking example of such alliances involves former senator Phil Gramm (R-TX) and his wife Wendy. From 1995 to 2000, Gramm was the chairman of the U.S. Senate Committee on Banking, Housing, and Urban Affairs. He was an author of the Gramm-Leach-Bliley Act, which repealed Glass-Steagall in 1999. Moreover, Gramm was instrumental in inserting the "Enron loophole" in the Commodity Futures Modernization Act of 2000.[27] Wendy Gramm was head of the CFTC from 1988 to 1993, and while she was head, Enron was granted exemptions pertaining to derivatives trading.[28] In 1993, Wendy Gramm became a member of the board of directors of Enron.[29]

When Phil Gramm retired from the Senate in 2002, he joined the Swiss banking firm UBS as a vice chairman. UBS was clearly troubled; in May 2004, the Federal Reserve fined the firm $100 million for illegally transferring funds to Iran and Cuba. In 2007, the SEC successfully pursued an insider trading case against a UBS executive.[30] In addition, UBS was in deep trouble in the financial crisis; it received $5 billion of the funds allocated to the AIG bailout. In 2009, UBS paid a $780 million fine for holding illegal bank accounts for Americans and agreed to turn over the names of 4,400 account holders.[31] In 2011, UBS lost $2 billion in a rogue trading scandal in its London office. For UBS, hiring a well-connected politician was an inexpensive investment.

Phil Gramm was known as an ardent advocate of free market conservatism. His ideology and his self-interest clearly overlapped. Phil and Wendy Gramm were beneficiaries not of competitive, but of crony, capitalism.

The UBS connection illustrates, moreover, that crony capitalism runs deep in both the Democratic and Republican Parties. In August 2009, President Obama played golf with one of his major fund-raisers, Robert Wolf, president of UBS North America.[32] The opportunism of the Gramms, Wolf, and Obama is striking. UBS is likely to draw benefits from its bipartisan connections. And these connections, we argue, are important to political bubbles.

Somewhat sadly, it can be difficult to disentangle the political influence of ideology from the influence of venality and greed.

Phil Gramm's free market conservatism was richly compensated. As free market conservatism has become an acceptable ideology to a large enough fraction of the mass electorate, personified in Joe the Plumber, who was hyped by the John McCain campaign in 2008, opportunistic politicians and crony capitalists can exploit this mass acquiescence for gain, contributing to increasing income inequality: Gramm's income increases much faster than Joe the Plumber's.[33] (Samuel Wurzelbacher, aka Joe the Plumber, is a Republican nominee for a House seat in 2012; if he wins, he may well realize the American dream and make his own way into the 1 percent.) Venality and free market ideology are complements in promoting a bubble. As Charles Kindleberger and Robert Aliber put it, "the supply of corruption increases in a procyclical way much like the supply of credit."[34]

Free market ideologies are not the only belief systems that can contribute to a political bubble. Even politicians on the left who subscribed to ideological beliefs rooted in economic and racial equality provided crucial support for policies that exacerbated the housing crisis. Executives of many real estate and financial firms exploited the political push to subsidize homeownership for lower-income and minority groups. In chapter 2, we point to a Fannie Mae annual report that establishes a direct link between Fannie Mae, Countrywide Financial's now discredited CEO Angelo Mozilo, and *redistributive egalitarianism.*

In this book, we show that a political bubble was at the center of the 2008 crisis. We also show that the dynamics of political bubbles played a central role in previous financial crises. Indeed, just as financial bubbles are endemic to capitalism, political bubbles are a permanent feature of capitalist democracy. Neither can be reformed away completely without forsaking the benefits of capitalism, of which there are certainly many.[35]

Nonetheless, American history has shown that some economic and political policies are preferred to others. After the Great Depression, the United States, until 2008, did not suffer any financial or economic dislocation that generated political pressure for substantial government intervention in the economy. Indeed, over the past thirty years, Washington has deregulated financial markets by law, executive order, budgetary cuts, and deliberate neglect. This contrasts with earlier historical experience. After the "panics" that occurred every twenty years or so during the nineteenth and early twentieth centuries, Washington produced short-run write-offs through bankruptcy laws and reductions in debts owed to the federal government as well as enduring legislation such as the Federal Reserve Act. In the wake of the Depression, institutional change occurred in the enactment of deposit insurance and the regulation of banking, securities markets, and public utilities. In our contemporary globalized, high-tech economy, the regulatory alphabet soup of the 1930s may not be reheated easily as the flows of capital and financial activity require much greater international coordination and cooperation. Nevertheless, a strengthening of government capacity for monitoring and intervention is clearly needed.

In the crises that have arisen since the New Deal, times have indeed been different. The opponents of change succeeded in limiting the legislative response to a crisis. Most notably, the Financial Institutions Reform, Recovery, and Enforcement Act of 1989, which responded to the savings and loan crisis of the 1980s, created a weak regulator, the Office of Thrift Supervision (OTS), and allowed for regulatory venue shopping by financial firms. AIG chose the OTS as its regulator. In the current crisis, the Dodd-Frank Wall Street Reform and Consumer Protection Act passed in July 2010 is a partial and overly complex act. We will see, in part 2, that it leaves ample opportunities for future bubbles.

We end the book by drawing policy conclusions that reflect our understanding of how political and economic bubbles interact. We favor a strong set of simple rules rather than regulatory discretion. The thirty-seven pages of Glass-Steagall are much to be preferred to the nearly three thousand pages of Dodd-Frank. Some may view us as Luddites. But we don't share their optimism about the benefits of financial innovation. Instead, we believe that the ever smaller increases in economic efficiency are undermined by ever increasing political risks.

We are skeptical about the unalloyed benefits of financial innovation for several reasons. First, economists do not agree among themselves. For example, Carmen Reinhart and Kenneth Rogoff nicely outline the broad academic disagreement about the seriousness of the U.S. current account deficit as the housing bubble grew.[36] Second, economists, even the smartest of the smart, often do not get it right. Joseph Stiglitz made a wrong call on Fannie Mae. Two other Nobel Prize Laureates, Robert C. Merton and Myron Scholes, were principals in LTCM, whose failure required a private sector bailout organized by the New York Fed. Third, judgment reflects financial incentives. The film *Inside Job* exposed how former Fed governor and current Columbia Business School professor Frederic Mishkin accepted a six-figure fee to coauthor a 2006 report titled *Financial Stability in Iceland*.[37] The Icelandic banking system crashed in 2008. Yale University professor Gary Gorton worked as a consultant to AIG before the crash, only to write a book later explaining how the emergence of a shadow banking system contributed to the crisis. The national and global financial systems are complex social systems. Within these systems, opportunities for economic and political manipulation abound. So it is naive to believe that markets always successfully self-regulate.

More broadly, we distrust arguments made in the name of economic efficiency that do not account for the political risks. Politics and markets alter new "products," ostensibly efficient, in a way that leads to inefficiency. For example, adjustable-rate mortgages (ARMs), allowed in the United States by the Garn–St. Germain Depository Institutions Act of 1982, make sense in that they allow lenders to avoid the interest rate mismatch involved in accepting short-term deposits but making long-term loans. They also make sense for assistant professors of finance, at the beginning of their life cycle earnings, to make smaller payments in the near term at the risk of making larger payments in the future. But the product quickly got distorted into "teaser" loans with low introductory interest rates that later reset to usurious levels. These loans were often made without verification of income or assets. Because Congress failed to sharply delimit the new product, the nation might have been better off without any ARMs.

We also argue for strong product regulation with a minimum of regulatory discretion because of Wall Street's ability to lobby on regulatory implementation. Until JPMorgan Chase's $5.8 billion trading loss in 2012, the implementation of the new Volcker Rule that prohibited commercial banks from speculating on their own account was likely to have been significantly weakened by lobbying by the firm's CEO, Jamie Dimon. Similarly, as the CFTC was deliberating rules for treating client money, Gary Gensler, the head of the CFTC, permitted himself to be lobbied by MF Global head and former Goldman Sachs colleague Jon Corzine. Clients, who are still waiting for their money back, deserved better from the former New Jersey senator and governor. Sharp legislation with severe criminal penalties for misuse of client monies might well have protected MF Global clients.

In theory, regulatory implementation after Dodd-Frank by the "best and the brightest" might lead to more market efficiency than a set of rules set in stone by legislation. But regulatory implementation is hardly a technocratic process that can be divorced from politics. As journalist David Halberstam recounted, "the best and the brightest" were deeply implicated in the American failure in Vietnam.[38] The elites and experts are no less implicated in our recent financial failures. Whether it was the LTCM failure, the Enron scandal, or the subprime crisis, graduates and faculty members of our elite educational institutions were on the scene.[39] The central characters of these debacles serve on the boards of America's leading philanthropies, cultural institutions, and public companies.

The composition of the board of directors of AIG vividly demonstrates the extent to which the American elite is implicated in the crisis. The outside directors between 2005 and 2008 included Obama- and Clinton-appointed diplomat Richard Holbrooke; Clinton defense secretary and former Maine Republican senator

William Cohen; Reagan White House adviser and Harvard University economist Martin Feldstein; Carla Hills, president Gerald R. Ford's Housing and Urban Development secretary and George H. W. Bush's trade representative; Ford "energy czar" Frank Zarb; American Museum of Natural History president Ellen Futter; and public television executive George Miles. Feldstein, Futter, Holbrooke, Miles, and Zarb served on the board for all or part of the years 2005–8. Over that period, their individual compensations as director ranged from $792,000 to $1,136,000. Perhaps those directors who served in government at low pay merited a subsequent private sector payout. But the AIG board failed to protect the public interest.

The moral of the story is that efficiency in the financial system has its limits. Efficiency should not be an end in itself because financial firms are inhabited by fallible people. The central goal of financial reform should not be efficiency but increasing the accountability of the financial system to the American public.

PART I

··

THE POLITICAL BUBBLE

Why Washington Allows Financial Crises to Occur

Introduction

At first glance, the financial crisis of 2008 appears to be the result of egregious, greedy actions in the private economy. The miscreants include the top management of financial firms, including Countrywide Financial, Bear Stearns, Lehman Brothers, Merrill Lynch, Goldman Sachs, American International Group, and Fannie Mae and of credit rating firms such as Moody's, Fitch, and Standard & Poor's. The scandalous behavior involved the misuse of innovations such as "sliced and diced" collateralized debt obligations, credit default swaps, and financially "engineered" strategies embedded in mathematical models. At the same time credit agencies with conflicts of interest issued misleading ratings of securities and lowered their credit standards for mortgage issuers.

Greed was rewarding. At the beginning of 2007, financial stocks were generally well ahead of where they had been in 1999 when Goldman Sachs became the last big investment bank to go public. Among the survivors of the crisis, Citigroup, Bank of America, and Morgan Stanley all outperformed the S&P 500 index during the run from 1997 to 2008 by about 50 percent. Goldman Sachs was up more than 150 percent.

The run-up in financial stocks was echoed by financial sector wages rising faster than wages elsewhere, by financial sector profits becoming a larger share of total corporate profits, and by human capital flowing into Wall Street. Ivy League graduates went into finance rather than into the "real" economy that provides health, technology, education, and public and private infrastructure.[1] Little trickled down to Americans working out-side finance. As we show in chapter 5, as of 2011 the innovations did not even benefit investors who bought and held the common stocks of the big commercial and investment banks.

Some greed is perfectly legal. Choosing to work on Wall Street strictly for the money qualifies. So does investing with Bernard Madoff in the belief of safely obtaining higher returns. Legal greed is taking a mortgage that one cannot afford in the hope of turning a quick profit by "flipping" the house. Legal greed is loan originators pushing such mortgages to receive higher fees. But greed also provides incentives to engage in illegal behav-ior. Ponzi schemes like Madoff's are one example. Another is the falsification of mortgage documents by loan originators in the hope of getting a better price by offering a risky mort-gage as a safe one. Another is the "robo-signing" of foreclosure documents.[2]

Major League Baseball has shown us how large parts of an occupational class can engage in illegal activity. Heroes like Mark McGwire, Barry Bonds, and Roger Clemens have been asterisked. According to ESPN's counts, the Mitchell Report identified eight-six players, including thirty-one All-Stars and seven MVPs, as having used steroids or other performance-enhancing drugs.[3] If misconduct in the financial and real estate sectors was as widespread as in baseball, financial steroids and performance-enhancing fraud contributed importantly to the crisis. We shall see that there is a political unwillingness to rec-ognize and punish widespread illegal activity.

Moreover, and more important, there is often a political will-ingness to facilitate a bubble by expanding the set of legal activi-ties firms can engage in. Adjustable-rate mortgages (ARMs), once banned, became legal financial products. It was a short step from a vanilla ARM to financial innovations of "teaser" loans, negative amortization loans, and predatory products that fed on the financial naïveté of many borrowers. In the savings and loan crisis, Congress relaxed accounting standards to obscure the insolvency of thrifts. Barriers between investment banks and commercial banks were relaxed by regulators and eventually abolished by Congress.

Indeed, if greedy financiers and their suspect innovations and business models were to blame, we can only ask, Why didn't the government do something to stop them?

The first element of our explanation is *ideology*, for which we emphasize two components. The first narrowly concerns the role of risk in financial markets. Many Americans and their political leaders accepted the idea that financial innovation contributed to greater prosperity by better managing risk and therefore extending credit to those who previously could not get it. Public beliefs about the benefits of modern finance were perhaps strengthened by the proliferation of 401(k) defined-contribution retirement plans that dramatically expanded the number of Americans who were directly linked to financial markets. But by 2008 it appeared that the touted benefits of risk management went primarily to Wall Street, and the 401(k) investors had taken it on the chin.

The second component is more general. Many Americans and their political leaders believe that government intervention in private markets is at best ineffective and at worst wrong. Why let government screw things up? Moreover, government is unnecessary because markets self-correct quickly. So bubbles cannot occur because asset prices never deviate from their true values for an extended time. This notion of self-correcting markets found no greater champion than Federal Reserve chair Alan Greenspan. If the housing market got out of whack, people would bet against it. Some individuals, such as John Paulson, did make a great deal of money betting against the market in 2007 and 2008, but, as we found out, these bets did not prevent a crash of financial institutions.[4]

Our second explanation has to do with *interests*. The executives of financial firms at the center of the bubble were getting rich. Clearly, they had an incentive to pressure the government not to intervene. Real estate developers gorged on the subsequent construction boom. The increased volume benefited real estate agents, mortgage brokers, title insurance companies, and construction workers, and, at least until 2008, investors in the stocks of financial firms. Loan originators were particularly important beneficiaries. They profited from the increased volume as relaxed lending standards fueled demand for mortgages. The most nefarious originators applied the most pressure through their lobbyists.[5] Homeowners benefited from the housing bubble as the rise in their equity made them richer. Some consumed their equity in the form of luxury goods.

Why should anyone in government do anything that would make so many Americans poorer? Interests, moreover, are a matter of perception. Federal Reserve governor Edward Gramlich called attention to the subprime mortgage market early on;[6] Commodity Futures Trading Commission head Brooksley Born sought to regulate credit default swaps. In a world of overconfidence, however, government intervention was opposed by borrowers who would eventually be foreclosed upon and especially by financial institutions that would eventually be bankrupt.

The final part of our answer has to do with America's governmental *institutions*. Even if many Americans recognized the problem and felt Washington should do something about it, it is not clear what the government could have done. Creating new regulatory structures requires Congress to pass a law, the president to sign it, courts to interpret it, regulators to faithfully enforce it, and Congress to continue funding for enforcement. Passing legislation is tough. The regulated have rights that the courts may protect. The large financial firms have access to talented attorneys and other legal resources that may overwhelm the prosecutorial resources of government. Moreover, faithful execution requires not only resources but also the willingness of a regulator to be tough on the industry that he may wish someday to work for. Even if all of these hurdles are overcome the effort may be undermined by other regulators at the federal or state levels. More aggressive intervention in mortgage markets by one or more of the fifty states could be undermined by federal preemption. For example, faced with regulatory action in Illinois, Wells

Fargo transferred a state-chartered branch to the supervision of the Office of the Comptroller of the Currency (OCC).[7]

The *Three I's*—ideology, interests, and institutions—are impediments to successful policy making and government performance in any number of areas. But as we argue, their effects are especially pernicious in the area of financial regulation. To borrow a metaphor from economics, the effects of ideology, interests, and institutions are procyclical. Rather than counteract the actions of private economic actors, these factors complement and exacerbate their effects. Because the links between the economic behavior and the political response are so tight, we argue that the *political bubble* is an intrinsic part of answering what went wrong.

CHAPTER 1
Bubble Expectations

The banks that survived the holocaust of the early
thirties probably differed from those that went under.
In addition, and very much likely more important,
they undoubtedly drew from their experience lessons
that affected their future behavior. For both reasons,
the banks that survived understandably placed far
greater weight on liquidity than the banks in existence
in 1929.

The shift in the liquidity preferences of banks was
destined to be temporary. To judge by the experience
of earlier episodes, the passage of time without any
extensive series of bank failures would have dulled the
fears of bank managers. . . .

—Milton Friedman and Anna J. Schwartz,
*A Monetary History of the United States,
1867–1960*

AN ECONOMIST DEFINES A "BUBBLE" as any situation in which
the price of an asset exceeds its "fundamental" value.[1] Therefore, bubbles pose a puzzle for standard economic theory. Why
would investors continue to purchase assets at prices for which
they are certain to lose money when the asset's price returns to
normal? Why wouldn't the market be flooded by offers to sell
the asset at the inflated price?

The "no-duh" answer is simple: investors believe that the fundamental value of the asset has increased. But where do such

beliefs come from, and how are they propagated? How do the beliefs become so widespread that buyers continue to buy and sellers won't sell as asset prices spike?

Economists are divided on the answers to these questions.[2] Behavioral economists like Richard Thaler, George Akerlof, and Robert Shiller have stressed the psychology of decision making. They argue that most investors are only *boundedly* rational.[3] In particular, they are not very good at distinguishing between fluctuations in prices and changes in underlying values. So if they see the price of an asset increase, they are likely to assume that its value has increased. Contrary to economic theory, they may buy more and sell less as the price increases. If most investors respond this way, asset prices may greatly exceed the underlying values— that is, until the price starts to drop and the same psychology leads to plummeting values.

Other economists are less likely to stress the irrational aspects of the bubble. After all, because the value of an asset is what someone is willing to pay for it, it is not irrational to pay the market price for an asset whose price has risen. One only needs to expect to be able to sell later for a higher price. As former Citigroup chair Chuck Prince put it, "when the music stops, in terms of liquidity, things will be complicated. But as long as the music is playing, you've got to get up and dance. We're still dancing."[4] But the musical chairs explanation just moves the question back one level: why do investors believe that other investors believe that the fundamentals have changed?

So, regardless of whether one views a bubble as a reflection of rational or irrational behavior, the driving force is overoptimistic beliefs about the value of assets. The consequences of such exuberance are far reaching. First, investors overinvest in the bubble asset, diverting resources from assets whose price-to-true-value ratio may be lower. Just as market capitalizations for Internet start-ups skyrocketed during the dot-com tech boom, there were huge increases in residential real estate investment that could not be justified by an increasing demand for housing. Second, investors borrow additional funds to buy more of the bubble asset, using the asset as collateral. Investors also borrow to take cash out to finance consumption. Because the asset prices are inflated, these loans are naturally highly leveraged (the ratio of the loan to the true value of the asset is very high). But the belief that the price of the bubble asset will rise even further leads to even laxer lending standards, magnifying leverage and risk even further.

What happens when the bubble pops? The economy survived the pop of the dot-com bubble without a great recession. The pop of the housing bubble was different. When the residential real estate bubble popped, falling prices led to increased expectations that underwater borrowers would not pay the basic mortgages. This led to a fall in the price of securitized mortgage loans. Financial institutions became less willing to accept these securities as collateral. Highly leveraged owners of these assets were forced to seek liquidity by selling other assets, spreading the crisis throughout the economy. The crisis is worse if optimism is replaced by pessimism and asset prices fall below fundamental values.

Because beliefs and expectations are crucial, the most obvious government intervention would be to cool down these expectations or to counteract their effects. But that is much easier said than done. The biggest hurdle is that key government officials and regulators often share the beliefs on which the bubble is sustained.[5] For example, one of the principal beliefs that sustained the recent housing bubble is that innovations for securitizing mortgage debt could be used to package together bits and pieces of the very risky subprime mortgages into almost riskless securities that could be sold to investors in exchange for a reasonable rate of interest. Consequently, lending standards could be lowered, more buyers would be brought into the market, and rising home prices would be the natural response to this shift in the way that risk was "spread out." This innovation made it appear that high-risk securities were "diluted" by being poured into an "ocean" of low-risk securities.

Did this view justify the complex and far from transparent instruments that were created in the bubble? On the one hand, there are sharply diminishing returns to risk management by diversification. In his famous book *A Random Walk Down Wall Street*, Burton Malkiel makes the point that one gets almost as much diversification by owning twenty stocks as by owning two thousand.[6] On the other hand, massive defaults of purportedly "dilutable" no-income-verification loans are economically harmful—perhaps even more so when risk management strategies carve up the original loan into pieces owned by a multitude of owners.

Nonetheless, there was, in the expression of Warren Buffett, a "mass delusion" about the benefits of financial innovation in the mortgage market.[7] Market actors were by no means the only ones who believed that securitization of subprime mortgages could sustain large growth in the housing sector.

Politicians of all stripes shared the industry's enthusiasm for financial innovation. Upon signing the Gramm-Leach-Bliley Act that repealed the Glass-Steagall firewall between commercial and investment banking, President Bill Clinton declared, "This historic legislation will modernize our financial services laws, stimulating greater innovation and competition in the financial services industry. America's consumers, our communities, and the economy will reap the benefits of this act. . . . Removal of barriers to competition will enhance the stability of our financial services system. Financial services firms will be able to diversify their product offerings and thus their sources of revenue. They will also be better equipped to compete in global financial markets."[8] Alan Greenspan told a Federal Reserve Conference in 2005, "Innovation has brought about a multitude of new products, such as subprime loans and niche credit programs for immigrants. Such developments are representative of the market responses that have driven the financial services industry throughout the history of our country. . . . The mortgage-backed security helped create a national and even an international market for mortgages, and market support for a wider variety of home mortgage loan products became commonplace."[9]

Put simply, when the policy makers share the bubble beliefs, they must also believe there is no rationale for intervention.

Willem Buiter, now the chief economist at Citigroup, has dubbed this phenomenon the "cognitive capture" of financial regulators: "It can be called *cognitive regulatory capture (or cognitive state capture)*, because it is not achieved by special interests buying, blackmailing or bribing their way towards control of the legislature, the executive, or some important regulator, like the Fed, but instead through those in charge of the relevant state entity internalizing, as if by osmosis, the objectives, interests and perception of reality of the vested interest they are meant to regulate and supervise in the public interest instead."[10] That private investors and policy makers share beliefs is not terribly surprising. There are tight social and professional links between the regulators and the regulated. In many cases, today's regulator is tomorrow's regulated. Moreover, government officials are influenced by the same economic research and financial journalism that informs market actors.

Even if government officials did not share the enthusiasm of the market participants, it would have been politically difficult to intervene given that the bubble euphoria extended well beyond Wall Street to the general public. According to the Gallup Organization, in May 2005, 70 percent of Americans believed that the average price of houses in their area would increase over the coming year.[11] This follows a decade in which housing prices grew at astronomical rates.[12] Even at the top of the market in 2006, 60 percent still believed that prices would push higher.[13] Given such beliefs, it is little wonder that millions of Americans bought new homes and refinanced existing mortgages in the hope of profiting from increasing home values.

As we now know all too well, the consequences for popping the bubble were traumatic: defaults, foreclosures, and huge financial losses. Yes, these losses would have been mitigated if the government had intervened in 2005, 2004, or 2003. But in a democracy, one can hardly expect elected officials to take direct responsibility for costly actions running so counter to public opinion. To paraphrase Abraham Lincoln, most people fool themselves most of the time. Career politicians, even if they know better, have to go along. They want to be reelected. There are not enough "profiles in courage." Most are loath to "take away the punch bowl during the party." It is much better for them politically to let the bubble run its course.

Governments are often themselves the cause of bubble beliefs. Asset values may inflate simply because market participants believe that government will step in to offset the losses if things go bad. For example, during the bubble, many market participants believed that their downside risk was hedged by the "Greenspan put." In other words, there was a widespread belief among investors that if financial markets were in trouble, the Federal Reserve would use its various policy tools to calm the markets and prevent losses. Thus, government policy worked exactly like a put option in which the investor has the right to unload a security at a prespecified price if its value declines too far. Such beliefs clearly promote risk taking by investors. Another example of policy beliefs inflating a bubble was the widely believed, but never explicit, government guarantee of the debt of Fannie Mae and Freddie Mac. This belief substantially lowered the government-sponsored enterprises' cost of borrowing and allowed them to dramatically ratchet up their holdings of mortgage-backed securities. It is hard to count on government to counter bubble beliefs when it is often the underlying source of them.

When the bubble pops, there will be greater divergence in beliefs between the financial services industry and government officials. Policy makers and their constituents are naturally going to be more suspicious of information and analysis coming from the industry. Similar to investors whose pessimism deepens, policy makers and voters may become overskeptical of the benefits of unregulated financial markets and practices. As we discuss in chapter 8, busts often lead to populist backlashes against financial services firms.

A prime example is the firestorm that erupted over the payments of retention bonuses to many American International Group (AIG) employees after the government bailed out the firm following its losses on credit default swaps. Government-selected CEO

Edward Liddy argued that the retention bonuses were necessary to keep key personnel in place to liquidate AIG's positions at minimal cost to the taxpayer.[14] But voters and their representatives in Congress were outraged that bonuses would be paid by a firm that had received a bailout of well over $100 billion of taxpayer money. They believed that the bonus payments were essentially a looting of the U.S. Treasury; they did not accept that the bonuses were a business necessity given the compensation practices in the financial services industry and the need to retain expertise in a company now owned by the taxpayers. The House quickly passed legislation (of dubious constitutionality) taxing the bonuses at a 90 percent rate. The House engaged in cheap populist theater, knowing the Senate would never go along. And the Senate did not.

Although the malleable and procyclical expectations of investors and politicians play a very important role in generating financial crises, we argue that they are far from the only beliefs that matter. As we discuss in chapter 2, the rigid and inflexible beliefs emanating from political ideologies are perhaps even more important in generating and sustaining the political bubble.

CHAPTER 2
Ideology

There are no atheists in foxholes and no ideologues in financial crises.

—Ben Bernanke, quoted in Peter Baker, "Administration Is Seeking $700 Billion for Wall St."

ALTHOUGH BUBBLE EXPECTATIONS are important for generating the public and private sector behavior that leads to financial crises, there is another more important source of the beliefs that influence the government response to the bubble and its collapse: ideology. An ideology is a set of basic beliefs about how the world works and about what is right or wrong. We distinguish ideologies from bubble expectations primarily in terms of the rigidity of the beliefs. Because they are deeply held and often rooted in basic principles, ideological beliefs are much less responsive to new information, persuasion, or context. Consequently, we distinguish the ideologue from a pragmatist, who would be more open to information and arguments. The pragmatist agrees with Lord Keynes's famous quip, "when the facts change I change my mind."[1]

To see the differences between ideologues and pragmatists, consider beliefs about the appropriate level of tax rates. In certain contexts, pragmatists and ideologues alike might agree that lowering tax rates is a good idea. But a pragmatist would want assurances that such a policy change would deliver specific benefits, such as more incentives to work, invest, or save, and minimize unwanted costs such as deficits and reductions in government services. After taxes were lowered, a pragmatist would want to see actual evidence that benefits were delivered and costs avoided. The pragmatist would also understand that context matters. Lowering taxes when taxes are high is quite different from lowering them when they are low. Conversely, an ideologue may want to lower taxes simply because she believes that lowering taxes is inherently a good thing to do. Of course, she may argue that lower taxes stimulate more work, investment, and savings and that tax cuts pay for themselves. But ultimately, her position is unlikely to change if in fact the tax cut leads to declining investment and runaway deficits. She is just as likely to support tax cuts the next time they are offered. And context doesn't matter. The fifth tax cut is just as valuable as the first four.

Even when they respond to new information, the way ideologues adjust their views is tempered by their preexisting beliefs. In other words, ideologies are also the framework for how people interpret new data.[2]

Consider an example of this phenomenon. To ameliorate the recession brought on by the financial crisis, President Barack Obama and the Democratic majorities in Congress passed a $787 billion stimulus plan with little support from Republicans. The administration's economic team forecast that this stimulus plan would prevent the unemployment rate from exceeding 8 percent. But by July 2009, the unemployment rate was at 9.5 percent and showed no signs of retreat. Democratic leaders and advisers interpreted the news as an indication that the stimulus plan had not been large enough. Laura Tyson, a member of President Obama's Economic Recovery Advisory Board, said that the unemployment situation proved that the stimulus plan was "a bit too small."[3] Democratic majority leader Steny Hoyer declared "[W]e need to be open to whether we need additional action [on economic stimulus]."[4] The Republican response was—no surprise—sharply different. Republican House leader John Boehner complained on Fox News that "[the stimulus plan] was supposed to be about jobs, jobs, and jobs. And the fact is, it turned into nothing more than spending, spending, and more spending on a lot of big government bureaucracy."[5]

So the new information revealed in the employment numbers led to far less, rather than more, consensus on the effects of the stimulus package. This was all the more true of academic economists. Nobel Prize winners could be found on both sides of the debate, predictably located by their inflexible positions on government intervention in the economy.[6]

A strong ideological challenge to free market capitalism did not follow the pop of 2008. On the contrary, the financial crisis and the Obama administration's response were followed by, as we said in the introduction, the flourishing of fundamentalist free market conservatism, embodied in the Tea Party.

Of course, all policy makers and citizens must rely on ideology to some degree. Without a preexisting belief structure, it is hard to make sense of the world. Alan Greenspan told a congressional panel that "ideology is a conceptual framework . . . the way people deal with reality. Everyone has one. You have to. To exist, you need an ideology."[7] We do not disagree with Chairman Greenspan; but we also sympathize with Representative Betty McCollum (D-MN), who responded, "if we need an ideology, if we need a philosophy to govern, as Mr. Greenspan suggested, I would suggest we give pragmatism a try, we give common sense a try."[8]

Ideologies and doctrines are a poor substitute for intelligence, reason, and evidence. Beliefs in socialism and Marxism impeded economic development in much of the world for most of the twentieth century. But more recently, doctrinal beliefs that government regulation is always inappropriate and that markets are infallible abetted the crisis of 2008, much as the same beliefs did in 1929. In the introduction, we defined these doctrines as free market conservatism.

The role of ideology in the political response to crises was recognized by Federal Reserve chairman Ben Bernanke in a 2002 testimonial address in honor of Milton Friedman. In describing President Herbert Hoover's administration's reaction to the onset of the Great Depression, then professor Bernanke wrote,

"The problem within the Fed was largely doctrinal: Fed officials appeared to subscribe to Treasury Secretary Andrew Mellon's infamous 'liquidationist' theory that weeding out 'weak' banks was . . . harsh but necessary."[9]

Mellon's views in the early 1930s were echoed in the financial crisis by former Senate Banking Committee chair Phil Gramm (R-TX). Gramm was present when President Bill Clinton signed the Gramm-Leach-Bliley Bill in 1999. He celebrated the signing by proclaiming, "We have learned government is not the answer."[10] Later, when the financial markets failed in 2008 and housing foreclosures exploded, Gramm, at the time a campaign adviser to John McCain, appeared not to update his beliefs about government. In Mellonesque fashion, he famously declared that the United States was a "nation of whiners."[11]

The rigidity of ideological beliefs contributes to the procyclical nature of political bubbles. After the collapse of Wall Street, Alan Greenspan confessed that his strong belief in the self-regulation of financial markets had prevented him from intervening in the early days of the bubble.[12] His exchange with House Oversight and Government Reform Committee chair Henry Waxman is illustrative:

> GREENSPAN: I made a mistake in presuming that the self-interests of organizations, specifically banks and others, were such as [sic] that they were best capable of protecting their own shareholders and their equity in the firms. . . .
>
> WAXMAN: In other words, you found that your view of the world, your ideology, was not right, it was not working.
>
> GREENSPAN: Absolutely, precisely. You know, that's precisely the reason I was shocked, because I have been going for 40 years or more with very considerable evidence that it was working exceptionally well.[13]

We argue, in contrast, that over Greenspan's forty-year period, "evidence" was pretty useless because of the toxic changes that intertwined deregulation and financial innovation. Looking at the past would fail to anticipate the unintended consequences of freeing up markets. Greenspan had the good fortune to leave

the Fed before his "shock" arrived. He reportedly collected a
$250,000 fee for meeting with Lehman clients just a couple
of weeks after leaving the Fed; the Lehman stint was followed
by a long string of post-Fed affiliations with Wall Street firms.
Free market conservatism indeed worked exceptionally well for
Chairman Greenspan.[14]

Before the crisis of 2008, free market conservatism had
plenty of support from Democrats as well as Republicans. Bill
Clinton twice reappointed Alan Greenspan as Fed chair,[15] and
signed—with the endorsements of Larry Summers and Robert Rubin—Gramm-Leach-Bliley. Only eighty-six representatives opposed passage of the bill in the House, although a large
majority of Democrats did oppose passage in the Senate. Only
a handful of the most liberal Democrats voted against Greenspan's reappointments.

We are far from the first to suggest that free market conservatism contributed to the financial crisis. Nobel Prize Laureate
Joseph Stiglitz went so far as to claim that this ideology was the
root cause of the crisis of 2008. In January 2009 he wrote in
Vanity Fair, "Was there any single decision which, had it been
reversed, would have changed the course of history? . . . The
truth is most of the individual mistakes boil down to just one: a
belief that markets are self-adjusting and that the role of government should be minimal.[16]

Free market conservatism had been reinforced by "the great
moderation," a period that roughly corresponds to the forty
years when Greenspan's ideology worked—a period in which
central banks tended to become independent and limited their
policy interventions to targeting inflation. Theoretically, limited
intervention was reinforced by the rational expectations school
in economics that led to the efficient markets hypothesis in
finance. Rational expectation models predicted that government
intervention has no beneficial long-term effects on markets.

Free market conservatism's belief in market efficiency,
though, was far from the only ideological doctrine related to the
2008 crisis. A related set of beliefs concern the extent to which

government bailouts and moratoriums promote *moral hazard*. The basic idea of moral hazard is that insurance leads people to engage in riskier behavior. For example, insuring someone against all medical costs dulls his incentives to refrain from smoking, overeating, and bungee jumping. In financial markets, the concern is that financial institutions who expect to be bailed out, either because they are "too big" or "too politically connected" to fail, take on excessive risks knowing that taxpayers will pick up the tab on the downside. Ideologues concerned with moral hazard may want some firms to fail in order to signal to others that they will not be bailed out in similar circumstances.

This book's introduction noted that congressional beliefs about moral hazard may have led Treasury secretary Henry Paulson to let Lehman Brothers file for bankruptcy. Similarly, some Republican officials opposed government assistance to struggling mortgagees for fear that government assistance would exacerbate moral hazard in the mortgage market. Although moral hazard is certainly a valid concern for policy makers under a number of circumstances, we argue in later chapters that rigid adherence to a "no bailout" policy can be counterproductive.

Strong ideological commitments to markets and fears of moral hazard explain the behavior of politicians on the right, but the *egalitarian* ideology on the left was also important in setting the stage for the crisis. Specifically, egalitarianism fueled some of the excess in the mortgage market. Subprime and prime mortgage lending, especially to racial and ethnic minorities, was seen by many as an effective tool for redistributing income and wealth.

The administrations of both Bill Clinton and George W. Bush pushed the idea of maximizing homeownership (though for rather different reasons). In doing so, each promoted policies that further distorted the incentives away from renting and toward owning. One of the major pushes during the Clinton administration was to require that Fannie Mae and Freddie Mac increase the share of their loan portfolios dedicated to mortgages for low- and middle-income families. In 2000, Andrew Cuomo, then the Department of Housing and Urban Development (HUD) secretary with oversight responsibility for these government-sponsored enterprises (GSEs), increased the required percentage of low- and middle-income mortgages from 42 percent to 50 percent of the portfolios. Moreover, he dramatically increased requirements for the GSEs to buy mortgages from underserved areas and those of "very-low-income."[17] Partly as a result of this policy, Fannie Mae's portfolio of subprime loans grew to $15 billion in 2002 from a level of just $1.2 billion in 2000. To diffuse any potential political backlash against GSE purchases of risky loans, Cuomo's HUD also exempted the GSEs from additional reporting requirements on their high-risk loans.[18] The GSEs also purchased private-label subprime and close-to-subprime Alt-A residential mortgage–backed securities to the tune of $253 billion.[19]

These policies were continued during the administration of George W. Bush, but with different ideological objectives. For President Bush, increasing homeownership rates was a central component of his "ownership society," the philosophical thrust of which was that homeownership and asset accumulation promoted less reliance on the government. The more government policy could be used to promote investing and homeownership now, the less demand there would be for government in the future.[20]

The congruence of "egalitarian" and "ownership society" ideologies was encapsulated in Fannie Mae's 2003 annual report, which featured a full-page color photograph of Angelo Mozilo, the later-to-be-discredited CEO of Countrywide Financial. Mozilo is quoted as stating, "Everybody wins if we can increase minority homeownership, so together we're taking on the challenge of getting more people into homes." The report stated directly, "So as long as there is a gap in minority and non-minority homeownership rates, Fannie Mae and Countrywide will continue to make sure all Americans have the chance to realize the dream of homeownership."[21] The policy was a complete bust. In the first quarter of 2012, the homeownership rate for whites was 73.5 percent, while for blacks it was 46.3 percent (see fig. 5.1).

As problems mounted in the early years of the new century, competing commitments to free market conservatism and egalitarianism generated a polarized debate over reining in the GSEs. Conservatives argued that the GSEs represented an unwarranted government intrusion into the housing market. Moreover, they argued that the belief in the implicit government guarantee lowered Fannie and Freddie's capital costs and gave them an unfair advantage in the mortgage securitization market. Liberals viewed any attack on the GSEs as an attempt to undermine homeownership for the poor.[22] The result was a severely delayed and tepid response that was not sufficient to stave off the collapse of the GSEs in 2008 and the subsequent government takeover. The bailout cost for Fannie and Freddie is likely to be on the order of $300 billion.[23] This is large in comparison to $162 billion, the estimated cost to taxpayers of ending the savings and loan crisis of the 1980s.[24]

Tracking Ideology

To flesh out our argument that ideological rigidity was central to the financial crisis and its aftermath, we need to explain how we conceptualize and measure ideology.

Although our discussion of ideology has emphasized attitudes and beliefs, we are unable to measure these systematically for individual policy makers. Instead, we work with a *behavioral* definition of ideology. The most important feature of our definition is consistency. Ideological behavior of an individual is manifest in consistency over time and across issues. In other words, a politician who maintains consistent positions year after year and whose position on each issue is strongly related to positions on other issues is ideological. One whose positions change with some regularity or who takes unpredictable positions is not.

To make these definitions concrete, consider the primary ideological division in American politics: liberalism and conservatism.[25] Most observers of American politics recognize that members of Congress can be thought of as occupying a position on a liberal-conservative spectrum. Bernie Sanders is a liberal, Dianne Feinstein a moderate Democrat, Ben Nelson even more so; Olympia Snowe is a moderate Republican and Jim DeMint is a conservative Republican. Few would quibble with these characterizations.

The reason that perceptions of liberalness and conservativeness are commonly shared is that politicians' behavior is predictable. "Roll call" is congressional lingo for votes on bills and amendments to bill. Ted Kennedy consistently voted for liberal positions on roll calls over the course of a forty-seven-year career in the Senate. Jim DeMint can likewise be predicted to vote as a conservative. Moderates like Nelson and Snowe may split their votes between conservative and liberal positions, but they are also consistent in that they do so year after year. Moreover, moderates who are ideologically close will tend to split their votes identically. So when Democratic moderate Max Baucus (MT) voted on the conservative side on a Senate roll call, Blanche Lincoln (AR) and Ben Nelson (NE) typically did so as well.

Consistency across issues is also important. If we know a senator or representative's position on tax cuts, we can make fairly confident predictions about her positions on financial regulation, fiscal stimulus, the minimum wage, and cap and trade. We may also have a fairly good idea where she stand on abortion, gay marriage, and federal funding for stem cell research.

It is not hard to discern that Bernie Sanders is more liberal than Dianne Feinstein, who is in turn more liberal than Jim DeMint, but we would like to have more objective and refined measures. One approach is represented by the ratings of interest groups such as Americans for Democratic Action (ADA), the League of Conservation Voters (LCV), or the U.S. Chamber of Commerce. Groups construct ratings by choosing the roll call votes that are important to their legislative agendas and by determining whether a yea or nay vote indicates support for the group's goals. Indices are then constructed from the proportion of votes a member casts in favor of the group. These indices are highly similar across groups.[26] The similarity reflects two factors. The first is that members' votes are quite consistent across different policy areas, and the second is that the interest groups themselves are polarized along liberal-conservative lines. Any two liberal groups, such as the ADA or LCV, have ratings that are highly correlated, and their ratings are mirror images of any conservative group such as the Chamber of Commerce or the National Taxpayers Union.

Interest group scores are limited in that they assess differences among the legislators only in a single congressional term. Therefore, they do not provide any direct information about the differences between legislators serving at different times, or even the behavior of the same legislator over the course of her career. An additional problem is that all group ratings are based on small, selective samples of roll calls that, in particular, tend to clump lots of legislators at the extreme scores of 0 or 100. This clumping tends to obscure real differences among legislators.

Given these problems, we can create much better measures of ideology from a method that uses all of the roll call votes. The method assumes that legislators make their choices in accordance with the *spatial model of voting*. To understand the spatial model, the analogy of a geographic map is helpful. We commonly think of Boston in the Northeast, Miami in the Southeast, Seattle in the Northwest, Los Angeles in the Southwest, and Kansas City somewhere in the middle of the United States. Thinking in the two dimensions of north-south and east-west is fine for automobile drivers, but perilous for space shuttle pilots docking with a three-dimensional object rotating and orbiting through space. But this book is not rocket science (nor is it financial engineering). We are car drivers. We seek a simple representation that helps us to understand political processes. We ignore higher-dimensional, less important, complexities.

Indeed, American politics is not two-dimensional, like the United States, but nearly one dimensional, like Chile, with Arica in the north, Punta Arenas in the south, and Santiago in the middle. Chile is a long, narrow strip, and for some purposes one can regard east-west differences as of negligible importance.

Our analogy to a one-dimensional map of Chile is the liberal-conservative continuum in American politics. In political science jargon, we use a *spatial model*. The spatial model is a representation of political conflicts and preferences where the positions of not only politicians but also policies are presented as points on a map, technically a geometric space.

The SAT test that American high school students take furnishes another analogy that is useful in understanding how we measure ideology. Being a math whiz may involve many different facets of neural activity, but the SAT math score assumes that math ability can be reduced to a single, unidimensional score. The test is designed to differentiate students (or in our case, legislators) by ability, and the test items (roll calls) are chosen to have different levels of difficulty. The best students answer all the items correctly and get that elusive 800 score. Middling students answer some relatively easy items correctly but miss the more difficult ones. And low-ability students get only the very easiest questions right. So the test runs from low ability to high ability. In our roll call "test," low, negative numbers are associated with liberals and high positive ones with conservatives, but we intend no aspersions on the ability of liberals.

In the liberal-conservative continuum, politicians can be arrayed on a horizontal line from liberal to conservative. Liberals like Bernie Sanders and Nancy Pelosi would be placed on the left end, moderates like Olympia Snowe and Ben Nelson in the middle, and conservatives like Jim DeMint and Rand Paul on the right. We call each member's position on the line his *ideal point*. Policies can be similarly arrayed with single-payer health care on the left, employer mandates for health coverage in the middle, and health care savings accounts on the right. More simply, a twenty-dollar minimum wage might be on the left, an eight-dollar minimum wage in the middle, and no minimum wage on the right.

In principle, we could draw one such map or line for each political issue. Some politicians might be liberal on abortion, moderate on labor relations, and conservative on taxes and minimum wages. Indeed, American politics might not be one-dimensional, like Chile, or even two-dimensional, like the United States, but very highly dimensional. Nevertheless, our research has shown that, for most of American history, just one liberal-conservative line can account for a very large proportion of congressional roll call voting.[27] There were times at which race and sectionalism generated important second dimensions of political conflict. These regional conflicts were clearly subordinate to the liberal-conservative or left-right conflict, with the exception of the Era of Good Feelings and the Civil War. Since 1980, it's all left-right conflict.

How do we find the left-right line and where politicians are located on it? Think of the 111th Senate, during which the Dodd-Frank Wall Street Reform and Consumer Protection Act was passed. We observe that Bernie Sanders and Tom Coburn always (or almost always) cast opposing roll call votes. Whenever Sanders voted yea, Coburn voted nay, or vice versa, so it is natural to think of them as anchoring the ends of a dimension. Arbitrarily and innocuously we can label Sanders as left or liberal and Coburn as right or conservative. We also observe that Russell Feingold, although usually voting with Sanders, voted a bit more with Coburn (and other conservatives) than did Sanders. So Feingold is placed slightly to the right of Sanders. Dianne Feinstein voted even more with Coburn than did Feingold, so Feinstein is placed to the right of Feingold. And Feinstein is still to the left of Olympia Snowe, who frequently, but not always, voted with Coburn. And Snowe is to the left of Jim DeMint, who almost always voted with Coburn.

Our method, the widely used DW-NOMINATE procedure, actually takes into account the entire voting pattern of a senator—not just how she stands relative to Coburn. Moreover, it accounts for mistakes or errors. Feingold, as was the case with his vote on Dodd-Frank, votes with Coburn at times when Feinstein and DeMint cast opposing votes. This kind of mistake causes us to move Feingold's position just a bit toward the right. How much so depends on whether the mistake is a big one or a little one. If Feingold votes with the Republicans on what is otherwise a party-line vote, he moves less than if he votes with the minority on a 90–10 split in which the other nine voters in the minority are the most conservative Republicans.

We can also see how Feingold and other legislators change their liberal-conservative positions over time. To simplify, if Feingold voted more frequently with Coburn in the 110th Congress than in the 109th, we would find that he has become less liberal. But our main finding is that individual legislators have remarkably stable ideologies over time. Their liberal-conservative positions change very little. The one exception is that the position shifts if the legislator shifts party affiliation.

We can link all the Congresses because legislators overlap. The overlap allows us to compare the positions of Barry Goldwater and Rand Paul even though they never served together. Goldwater overlapped with Strom Thurmond, who overlapped with Dianne Feinstein, who now serves with Rand Paul. These overlaps in congressional service allow us to claim that Congress has become more polarized over the past forty years.[28] (A brief chapter appendix provides a bit more of the intuition behind our measures of positions on the liberal-conservative scale.)

During most of the period treated in this book, a single liberal-conservative dimension does an excellent job of accounting for how members vote, be it on minimum wages or the shopping list of issues represented in party platforms or a presidential State of the Union address. One way of directly measuring the predictive power of the liberal-conservative dimension is to compute the percentage of votes on which a legislator actually votes for the roll call alternative located closer to her on the dimension. This classification success exceeds 87 percent across all Congresses since 1980.

Over the past thirty years, the explanatory power of the ideological model has increased dramatically. Consider figure 2.1. For each chamber and each biennial session, it plots the percentage of roll call vote choices that can be accounted for by a single, liberal-conservative dimension. For comparison purposes, we

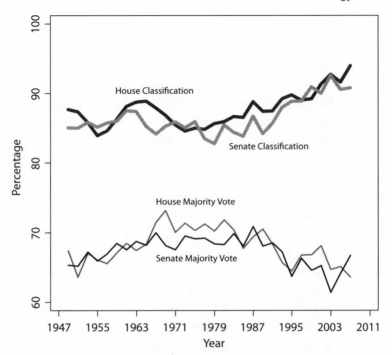

Figure 2.1. The predictive power of the ideological model. The figure shows that a liberal-conservative dimension correctly classifies about 90 percent of all individual roll call decisions although the percentage voting on the majority side is typically below 70 percent. Moreover, the classification percentage has increased steadily since 1980 while the majority percentage has been decreasing. That is, ideological voting is increasing and consensual voting is decreasing.

plot the average votes on the winning side. The figure shows that our liberal/conservative model is very good at predicting congressional voting behavior. In the most recent Congresses, the model accounts for more than 90 percent of the votes cast. Moreover, this success is not merely a consequence of more lopsided votes that increase the size of the winning coalition. Over the past two decades, the number of legislators voting on the winning side has declined, while the classification success of the spatial model has increased. In a nutshell, there is less consensus and more ideology.

It is also important to stress that we are picking up far more than the simple effects of more disciplined parties. Although we do find that fewer Democrats vote with Republicans over time, our method does a very good job of identifying exactly who are the most likely moderate Democrats to cross over and support conservative measures. Similarly, the method does a very good job of distinguishing moderate from conservative Republicans.[29]

Our liberal-conservative placements allow us to identify those legislators who are most likely to support or oppose particular financial regulatory policies as well as those moderates whose support would be pivotal. To illustrate, table 2.1 lists for each chamber the most liberal legislators, the most conservative, and the moderates. Roughly speaking, negative numbers large in magnitude go with liberals, positive ones with conservatives, and numbers near zero with moderates. Not surprisingly, all the liberals are Democrats, and all the conservatives are Republicans. Even the moderates are now split on party lines, with the Democrats being somewhat more liberal (lower scores) than Republicans. The table shows that we place Mike Enzi as slightly more conservative than John Barrasso, but they are in a virtual tie; the small difference is not of statistical significance. Just as Enzi is adjacent to Barrasso, James Inhofe is adjacent to John Ensign. But the difference between Ensign and Inhofe is more significant. Of course, the difference between a conservative like Ensign and a liberal like Barbara Boxer is very large.

Table 2.1 contains few surprises to close observers of American politics and thus illustrates how well our technique can capture the underlying ideological divisions. As the table shows, there is now no ideological overlap between the parties. The most conservative Democrat is more liberal than the most liberal Republican. This has not always been the case. In the 1960s, Southern Democrats like Georgia senators Richard Russell and Herman Talmadge compiled considerably more conservative voting records than liberal Republicans like New York's Jacob Javits or Massachusetts's Edward Brooke.

President Obama and several members of his administration served in Congress. Their ideology scores are shown in table 2.2.

TABLE 2.1.
Ideology scores from the 111th (2009) Congress

The House, 2009				The Senate, 2009			
Representative	Party	State	Ideology Score	Senator	Party	State	Ideology Score
The Liberals							
McDermott	D	WA	−0.83	Sanders	I	VT	−0.69
Stark	D	CA	−0.76	Kaufman	D	DE	−0.66
Kucinich	D	OH	−0.76	Boxer	D	CA	−0.60
Miller	D	CA	−0.71	Feingold	D	WI	−0.58
Woolsey	D	CA	−0.69	Burris	D	IL	−0.58
Lee	D	CA	−0.69	Gillibrand	D	NY	−0.57
Waters	D	CA	−0.68	Merkley	D	OR	−0.57
Filner	D	VA	−0.68	Brown	D	OH	−0.57
Olver	D	MA	−0.68	Lautenberg	D	NJ	−0.56
Conyers	D	MI	−0.66	Durbin	D	IL	−0.56
The Moderates							
Griffith	D	AL	−0.01	Carper	D	DE	−0.27
Bright	D	AL	0.02	Landrieu	D	LA	−0.24
Hill	D	IN	0.02	Bayh	D	IN	−0.22
Childers	D	MI	0.02	Baucus	D	MT	−0.20
Minnick	D	ID	0.11	Nelson	D	NE	−0.04
Jones	R	NC	0.24	Snowe	R	ME	0.01
McHugh	R	NY	0.29	Collins	R	ME	0.05
LoBiondo	R	NJ	0.29	Voinovich	R	OH	0.24
Smith	R	NJ	0.30	Lugar	R	IN	0.24
Lance	R	NJ	0.30	Murkowski	R	AK	0.25
The Conservatives							
Hensarling	R	TX	0.84	Burr	R	NC	0.58
Deal	R	GA	0.85	Barrasso	R	WY	0.62
McClintock	R	CA	0.86	Enzi	R	KY	0.62
Franks	R	AZ	0.87	Bunning	R	KY	0.63
Shadegg	R	AZ	0.90	Kyl	R	AZ	0.64
Broun	R	GA	0.91	Vitter	R	LA	0.65
Lummis	R	WY	0.94	Ensign	R	NV	0.69
Flake	R	AZ	0.97	Inhofe	R	OK	0.76
Sensenbrenner	R	WI	0.98	DeMint	R	SC	0.81
Paul	R	TX	1.30	Coburn	R	OK	0.87

TABLE 2.2.
The Obama administration

Officials with Past Congressional Service	Ideology Score
Hilda Solis, Sec. of Labor	−.45
Hillary Clinton, Sec. of State	−.36
Barack Obama, President	−.34
Joseph Biden, Vice-President	−.33
Rahm Emanuel, White House Chief of Staff	−.32
Ken Salazar, Sec. of the Interior	−.22
Ray LaHood, Sec. of Transportation	+.27

Note that almost all of these people have ideal points considerably more moderate than the liberal wing of the Democratic Party. This fact is notable given our discussion below of the intraparty conflict generated by Obama's response to the financial crisis.

An important question, however, is to what extent we can characterize our estimated positions as reflecting ideology. If these positions reflect ideological commitments, we would expect them to be very stable across issues and over time. That there is consistency across issues is clear. Despite the fact that the congressional agenda contains hundreds of issues spanning economic, social, and environmental policy domains, a single left-right dimension accounts for 90 percent of the voting behavior. This is precisely because positions on taxes are very good predictors of preferences about regulation, which are good predictors of views on welfare, global warming, and so on.

A related question asks which of the many issues confronting Congress is most closely related to our left-right continuum. While many observers might stress the importance of racial attitudes and social issues as the defining cleavages of American politics, our own research documents that it is economic issues and debates about the role and scope of the federal government that map most closely onto our continuum.[30] Therefore it can be expected that financial regulation will be a liberal-conservative battleground. The explanatory power of the ideological model has increased because positions on racial and social issues have become more like the divisions on economic issues, not the other way around.[31] That racial issues morphed into economic policy conflicts is strikingly illustrated by our quote from the Fannie Mae annual report concerning minority housing.

Ideological positions are also quite stable for politicians throughout their careers. Of course, there are a few prominent examples of politicians whose positions changed, such as the right-to-left movements of Oregon's Wayne Morse or the left-to-right movements of Richard Schweiker (R-PA) or the right-to-left-to-right meandering of John McCain. A very, very small number of politicians have been erratic, such as William Proxmire (D-WI). But for the most part, legislators' positions on our scale move significantly only if, like Morse and South Carolina's Strom Thurmond, they switch parties (though, of course, party switching is quite rare).[32] Even a member whose constituency changes quite dramatically, either by elevation to the Senate or through major redistricting, rarely changes positions in a significant way. The assumption that legislators maintain the same ideological position throughout their careers performs just as well statistically as the assumption that legislators are able to change positions in each biennial term.[33]

Moreover, the behavior of legislators deviates in large and systematic ways from the preferences of their average or median constituent. For example, senators from the same state do not vote identically. Most obviously, senators from the same state but different parties, such as John Kerry (D) and Scott Brown (R) of Massachusetts, pursue very different policy goals. The difference is picked up in their polarized ideology scores. If the two senators are from the same party, they are, of course, more similar. Even here, however, there are differences. Consider California Democrats Dianne Feinstein and Barbara Boxer. They not only represent the same state but were first elected by exactly the same electorate on the same day in 1992.[34] In the most recent Senate term, Boxer's ideology score of −0.60 makes her the third most liberal member of the Senate. By contrast, Dianne Feinstein's −0.38 score makes her the thirty-seventh most liberal.

Moreover, this California duo is not unusual. Four other states had pairs of senators from the same party in 2009 with at least as great a difference in their ideology scores.[35]

House districts, being single-member, do not allow the natural experiment that is possible for the Senate. It is possible, however, to compare the voting behavior of a member to her successor. Even the same-party replacements of House members can have ideology scores that are different from those of their predecessors. True, a liberal Democrat is likely to be replaced by another liberal Democrat. But the variation in the scores between same-party predecessor and replacement is quite large. It is about half as large as the total variation of positions within the party.[36] In other words, the ideological score of the outgoing incumbent is at best a crude predictor of the position of the new member even if they are in the same party. The takeaway is that a representative has a great deal of latitude in either building a coalition of supporters or expressing his or her personal ideology. Of course, the scores do pick up many factors other than personal ideology; these include some constituency effects, interest group influence, and pressure from party leaders and activists. Moreover, the ideological scores are not perfect predictors of behavior on a given decision so these other factors may be especially important in some contexts. Just how much these other factors matter—especially for regulation of financial markets—is an issue we take up below.

This consistency of ideological behavior has important consequences for the timing of policy changes. Because the individual behavior of legislators is so stable, political shifts in ideology occur mainly through the replacement process of elections. This feature of American politics had important ramifications in previous financial and economic crises. During the Panic of 1907 the American financial system was saved primarily because J. Pierpont Morgan had the power and influence to act as a de facto central banker. Morgan's personal achievement, however, was hardly evidence that the private sector on its own would head off or resolve future crises. But in the aftermath of the Panic, ideological opposition to a federal government central bank precluded its establishment. Congress did no more than pass the modest and temporary Aldrich-Vreeland Act whose only substantive reform was to allow groups of national banks to issue emergency currency.[37] Only after the Democrats picked up a net gain of 118 seats in the House, 19 Senate seats, and the presidency in the elections of 1910 and 1912 was there a majority sufficient to pass the Federal Reserve Act. Similarly, the market-oriented and "associationalist"—voluntary cooperation of private individuals and groups—ideologies of President Herbert Hoover and the Republican Party limited the use of federal authority in response to the stock market crash of October 1929. Consequently, the most significant policy changes (summarized in chapter 4) occurred only after Franklin Delano Roosevelt took office over three years later, in March 1933.

Ideologically driven politics continues to shape responses to financial crises. Much of the response of the George W. Bush administration, particularly with regard to the bankruptcy of Lehman Brothers and to the handling of the $700 billion Troubled Asset Relief Program (TARP) fund reflected ideological biases in Congress related to fears of moral hazard and opposition to direct government intervention in banks. The 2008 elections resulted in the Obama presidency and the increased Democratic congressional majorities. These events were followed both by the stimulus package and the Dodd-Frank Wall Street Reform Bill. The midterm elections of 2010, however, resulted in numerous replacements, with the Republicans gaining sixty-three House seats. The ideological change suggests that any policy changes engendered by the crisis are likely to be curtailed. In contrast, the Roosevelt era changes, such as Glass-Steagall, were ideologically consolidated by the midterm elections of 1934. Policy change under Roosevelt was also facilitated by an absence of ideological polarization.

Polarized Politics

As politics became more ideological over the past few decades (recall figure 2.1), the ideological gap between the political parties widened. In figure 2.2, we plot the average difference in

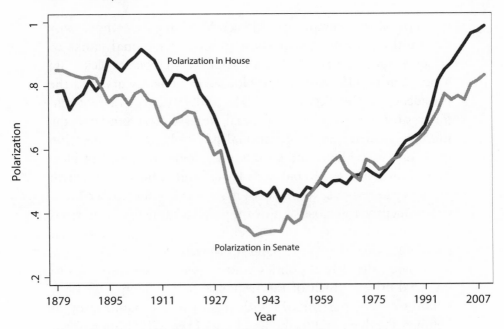

Figure 2.2. Polarization in Congress. The two graphs trace the difference in the position of the average Republican and the average Democrat. The graphs for the House and Senate are largely parallel, indicating that the substance of politics, not the institutional rules of the chambers, determines polarization. The liberal-conservative dimension is constructed to have a minimum value of −1 and a maximum value of +1. Consequently, the recent differences between the parties cover about half the length of the dimension.

ideological scores between Democrats and Republicans in the House and Senate going back to the end of Reconstruction. As one can see, this difference, which we label *polarization*, has recently reached an all-time high, exceeding even that found in the original Gilded Age of the 1890s.

There are many reasons to believe that it is not mere coincidence that ideological polarization in our own Gilded Age looks like that of the 1890s. Both periods featured little regulation, overheated economies, substantial immigration of unskilled labor, and increasing concentrations of income and wealth. In both eras, the Republican Party was the defender of the free market gospel and limited government regulation of markets. It was also an era of frequent financial crises and panics with major crises in 1893 and 1907.

In *Polarized America: The Dance of Ideology and Unequal Riches,* we argued that there are strong linkages between economic inequalities and political polarization.[38] There are at least two mechanisms at work. The first is a causal effect of economic inequality on political polarization. As we have argued, the primary ideological dimension of American politics is the role of the state in regulating the economy. So in periods in which there are huge economic rewards to unfettered markets, support for free market conservatism increases—especially among those individuals and groups who benefit the most. The political scientist E. E. Schattschneider argued that the moneyed interests rule as long as an issue fails to become salient with the mass public, proclaiming, "Since the contestants in private conflicts are apt to be unequal in strength, it follows that the most powerful special interests want private settlements because they are able to dictate the outcome as long as the conflict remains private. . . . It is the weak who want to socialize conflict. . . ."[39] That is, if the arena is Congress and regulatory agencies, money prevails unless the conflict is viewed as having become sufficiently public to engender electoral consequences.

What if, however, the losers attempt to use the power of the state to capture some of those economic rewards outside the market? Yet, as we argue in more detail below, the structure of American political institutions makes it difficult to create new laws to regulate economic behavior. This effect leads to the second mechanism whereby political polarization increases inequality and the concentration of wealth. As we discuss, political polarization leads to political gridlock that makes economic reform difficult. Not only can the economic losers not form a coalition to redirect the allocation of resources, but the government cannot effectively respond to those economic shocks and crises which in turn further increases polarization.

Polarized America did not specifically address financial policies and regulations, but there is plenty of evidence to support links between political polarization and the concentration of wealth and resources in the financial sector. The economists Thomas Philippon and Ariell Reshef have compared the wages of employees of the financial sector relative to the wages of equally skilled workers in other sectors of the economy from 1908 to 2006. The wage ratios ranged from a low in the 1970s of 1.05 indicating financial workers enjoyed a 5 percent premium to 1.7 in 2006 when financial workers made 70 percent more than comparable workers in other parts of the economy.[40] In their statistical analysis, Philippon and Reshef find that the main determinants of the financial sector wage premium are financial deregulation and corporate activities related to initial public offerings and credit risk.[41] Similarly, Jon Bakija, Adam Cole, and Bradley Heim have found that the finance sector employed twice as many of the top 1 percent of earners in 2005 as it did in 1979. Moreover, among the top 1 percent of earners, incomes from the financial sector grew the fastest.[42] Consequently, finance has played a very large role in the dramatic increase in the share of national income going to top earners.[43]

Consistent with our previous arguments about polarization and inequality, the cycles in financial sector wages closely match our measure of polarization over the past century. In figure 2.3, we plot the wage premium in finance and polarization in the House. Both polarization and wages in finance are high at the beginning and end of the twentieth century. But both indicators are at a low for much of the middle of the century following financial market reforms and the middle-class political economy created by the New Deal.

There are important differences in the timing of the series. In particular, political polarization appears to be a leading indicator of rising wages in the financial sector. (Although the contemporaneous correlation between polarization and wages is only 0.65, the correlation with polarization lagged ten years is 0.90.) This is consistent with the argument we develop below: government gridlock (i.e., the inability of government regulation

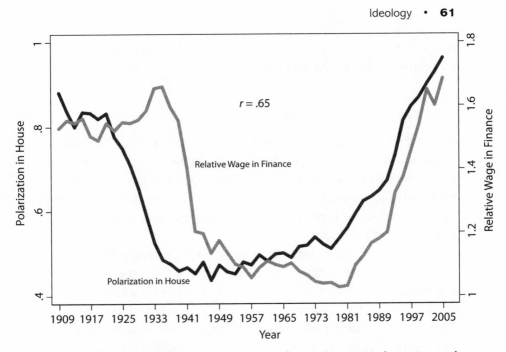

Figure 2.3. Polarization and wages in the financial sector. Polarization and wages in the financial sector follow similar paths through time, with changes in polarization preceding those in wages by 10 years. Relative wage shows financial wages with respect to wages elsewhere in the economy. *Source*: Philippon and Reshef (2009). Source for House polarization: authors' computations from DW-NOMINATE scores posted at voteview.com.

to keep up with financial innovation) was a driving force behind the crisis of 2008.

That polarization has had such effects on policy making might be less troubling if politicians were simply responding to greater and greater divisions among the public. But political scientists have found little evidence that mass polarization can account for polarization of the magnitude we see in Congress. Although Alan Abramowitz and Morris Fiorina debate whether voters have polarized at all, there is little evidence that the public has polarized as much as the elites.[44] It is true that voters who identify with the Democratic Party have policy preferences that are increasingly distinct from Republican identifiers. But much of this effect is the response of voters sorting themselves into increasingly distinctive partisan camps.[45]

Ideology and Voting on Financial Issues

We now turn to a demonstration of the extent to which our measures of ideology can explain the voting behavior of members of Congress on financial legislation. Our illustrations in this chapter pertain to votes during the bubble. In the second part of the book, we discuss votes in the "pop" period that followed the Lehman Brothers bankruptcy.

We illustrate the impact of ideology on financial regulation roll calls with three histograms of votes taken in the House of Representatives before the collapse of Lehman Brothers in September 2008. The horizontal axis in each figure represents the liberal-conservative positions of the representatives. Histogram bars on the left end represent liberals, the middle moderates, and the right end conservatives. Each plot also shows the "cutting line" for the bill. If a bill fell perfectly on the liberal-conservative dimension, the cutting line would separate those members who voted yea from those who voted nay. For example, if there was a roll call where the eight most liberal senators in table 2.1 voted yea and the ninth most liberal, Frank Lautenberg (D-NJ), and the other ninety-one senators all voted nay, the cutting line would be between Sherrod Brown (D-OH) and Lautenberg. More generally, the cutting line corresponds to the point on the liberal-conservative dimension where a legislator should be indifferent between voting yea and nay. The spatial model often makes incorrect vote predictions for legislators with ideal points close to the cutting line. Because their ideology leaves them close to indifferent, they are more likely to be swayed by constituency pressures and other factors.

The first histogram, figure 2.4, shows the House vote to pass the bill to regulate accounting firms sponsored by House Financial Services Committee chairman Michael Oxley (R-OH). The House passed Oxley's bill (H.R. 3763) on April 24, 2002, by

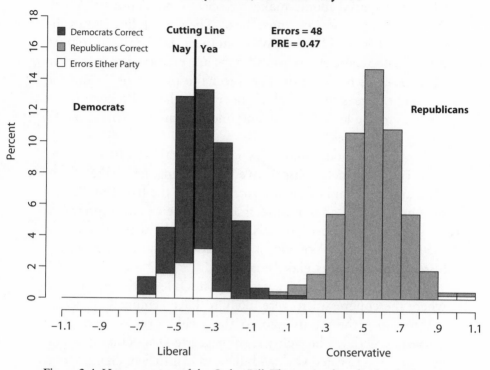

House: Regulation of Auditors
24 April 2002, Yea = 334 Nay = 90

Figure 2.4. House passage of the Oxley Bill. The cutting line divides the Democrats, with the most liberal members voting against the bill. Prediction errors for the liberal-conservative dimension appear in white. The errors are concentrated near the cutting line. There are also two errors at the conservative end of the dimension. The two representatives, Flake and Paul, were likely voicing a fundamentalist free market conservatism objection to regulation in any form.

a vote of 334 to 90. (The House named the bill the Corporate and Auditing Accountability, Responsibility, and Transparency Act; this bill was then merged with a bill sponsored by Senator Paul Sarbanes (D-MD) and the result became the Sarbanes-Oxley Act.) The vote shows a liberal-conservative split with the division within the Democratic Party. Liberals viewed Oxley's bill as an inadequate response to the Enron and other accounting scandals. The dark shading shows Democrats who voted "correctly" and the light shading shows Republicans who voted "correctly." The white areas at the bottom of the bars are cases where the spatial model makes erroneous predictions. We call these "voting errors" or "mistakes." The cutting line shows the point that best divides the nays from the yeas. On the histogram we indicate where the yeas and nays are predicted to locate. In figure 2.4, the nays are predicted to be to the left of the cutting line and the yeas to the right. Conversely, the white portions of the bars to the left of the cutting line indicate yea votes, and to the right nay votes.[46]

The spatial model makes two big "mistakes" on the Oxley vote. Two extremely conservative Republicans, Jeff Flake of Arizona and Ron Paul of Texas, voted against the bill. Ron Paul is such an extreme conservative that he is one of two representatives in the rightmost bar. His nay vote is the white portion of the bar. The white portion of the second rightmost bar in the histogram represents Flake's nay vote.

The two conservative votes against Oxley's bill are a case where the congressmen were likely to have genuinely preferred not to move the status quo to the weak form of regulation offered by Oxley. The eighty-eight negative Democrats stood on principle and rejected Oxley's bill as an insufficient change from the status quo. Such odd cases of "both ends against the middle" are very rare in practice and rarely generate more than a few "mistakes" that are inconsistent with a liberal-conservative split.

The second histogram, figure 2.5, shows a November 15, 2007, roll call on legislation designed to further regulate mortgage lending.[47] Note that the voting patterns are very consistent with the liberal-conservative positions of the representatives. All Democrats voted in favor of the new reforms but the roll call divided moderate Republicans from conservatives. All of the "mistakes" of the model are moderate Republicans near the cutting line. Voting on this bill was not "both ends against the middle." Out of the 421 representatives who cast a vote on the bill, only 32 were incorrectly classified.

The third histogram, figure 2.6, shows a roll call vote on July 23, 2008, to pass the American Housing Rescue and Foreclosure

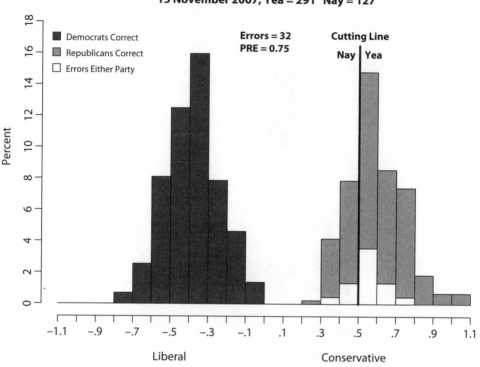

House: Reform Mortgage Lending
15 November 2007, Yea = 291 Nay = 127

Figure 2.5. A roll call on mortgage lending reform. On this vote, the Democrats are unanimous and are joined by moderate Republicans. As in figure 2.4, the classification errors cluster around the cutting line.

Prevention Act of 2008. The bill responded to spiraling foreclosure rates on home mortgages, and provided $300 billion for refinancing mortgages and an unlimited line of credit to Fannie and Freddie. This vote, like the previous illustration, split the Republicans internally. These internal party splits allow us to measure the shades of liberalism or conservatism that exist within each party.

The takeaway from these examples is that ideology is a powerful predictor of legislative action in financial and economic crises. Our estimates of ideal points, which are generated from voting across the whole panoply of congressional votes, do an

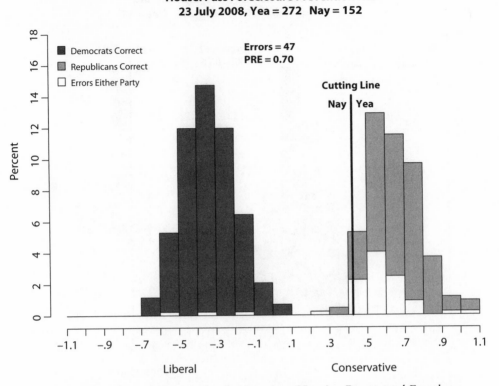

Figure 2.6. The passage vote for the American Housing Rescue and Foreclosure Prevention Act. This vote shows a high degree of support among Democrats and a high degree of opposition among more extreme Republicans. More moderate Republicans are split.

exceptional job of explaining congressional behavior in three very distinct aspects of financial regulation. This might not always be the case. The bankruptcy bill died in 2001 when the House rejected the conference report with "both ends against the middle" voting. The report included the amendment from Charles Schumer (D-NY) designed to protect abortion clinics. Liberals voted against it because they saw the bill as anticonsumer. Conservatives voted against it because they saw it as prochoice. Similar failures of a one-dimensional model occurred more frequently in the mid-twentieth century when the granting of civil rights for African Americans was a distinct issue from economics. Our examples illustrate, however, that a single ideological dimension accounts for many varieties of financial regulation.

Of course, ideology can hardly account for every vote cast. Legislators often defy the predictions on account of any number of factors ranging from constituency interests to party pressure to interest group influence. These factors not only result in deviations from pure ideological voting but also influence the content of the legislation that is put to a vote. Lobbyists were active in formulating the TARP stimulus package and Dodd-Frank. Moreover, what legislation is voted on and what becomes law reflect not only ideologies and interests but also the way agenda control is exercised and whether legislation can clear the hurdles inherent in bicameralism and the presidential veto. Consequently, we take up the impact of interests on political bubbles in chapter 3 and of institutions in chapter 4.

We pause to end this chapter with a caveat, obvious but worth stressing: sometimes ideology cannot be differentiated from venality. Did Phil Gramm really believe "government is not the answer," or was he influenced by the lucre from UBS and Enron? Was Angelo Mozilo a committed egalitarian, or just implementing part of his corrupt business model for Countrywide Financial? Sometimes ideology is just a smoke screen for the crony capitalists. In chapter 3 we turn to the cronies.

Chapter Appendix: Estimating the Ideological Map

This appendix provides a few more details and more intuition behind our estimates of legislator ideology.

Given the locations of legislators and outcomes on the ideological map, the underlying assumption of the spatial model is that each legislator votes yea or nay depending on which outcome location is closer to his or her ideal point. Think of the yea and nay as two stores and the ideal point as the residence of a shopper. The shopper should normally shop at the closer store. If the more distant store has cheaper prices or some desirable exclusive items, the shopper may make a "mistake" and go to the more distant store. Similarly, the legislator may make "mistakes" and depart from what would usually be expected, as a result of pressures from campaign contributors, constituents, courage of conviction, or just plain randomness.

But if we assume that legislators generally vote on the basis of the spatial map and that errors are infrequent, we can estimate the ideal points of the members of Congress directly from the hundreds or thousands of roll call choices made by each legislator.

To understand better how we calculate these locations, consider the following three-senator example. Suppose we observed only the following roll call voting patterns from Senators Sanders, Feinstein, and DeMint.

Roll Call	Sanders	Feinstein	DeMint
1	YEA	NAY	NAY
2	YEA	YEA	NAY
3	NAY	YEA	YEA
4	NAY	NAY	YEA
5	YEA	YEA	YEA
6	NAY	NAY	NAY

Notice that all of these votes can be explained by a simple model in which all senators are assigned an ideal point on a left-right scale and every roll call is given a cutting line that divides the senators who vote yea from those who vote nay. For example, if we assign ideal points ordered by Sanders to the left of Feinstein and Feinstein to the left of DeMint, the first vote can be perfectly explained by a cutting line between Sanders and Feinstein, and the second vote can be explained by a cutting line between Feinstein and DeMint. In fact, all six votes can be explained in this way. Note that a flipped scale with DeMint to the left of Feinstein to the left of Sanders works just as well. But, a single cutting line cannot explain votes 1–4 if the ideal points are ordered with either Feinstein left of Sanders left of DeMint or Feinstein left of DeMint left of Sanders, DeMint left of Sanders left of

Feinstein, or Sanders left of DeMint left of Feinstein. Therefore none of these orderings is consistent with a one-dimensional spatial model.

As two orderings of ideal points work equally well, which one should we choose? Given that Sanders espouses liberal (left-wing) views and DeMint is known for his conservative (right-wing) views, Sanders left of Feinstein left of DeMint seems like a logical choice.

The real world, however, is rarely so well behaved as to generate the easy patterns of the first six votes. What if we observed that DeMint and Sanders occasionally vote together against Feinstein, as in votes 7 and 8 below? Such votes cannot be explained by the ordering Sanders left of Feinstein left of DeMint.

Roll Call	Sanders	Feinstein	DeMint
7	YEA	NAY	YEA
8	NAY	YEA	NAY

If there are only a few votes like 7 and 8 (relative to votes 1–6), it's reasonable to conclude that they are generated by more or less random factors. If there are many more votes like 1–6 than there are deviant votes, all common scaling procedures generate the ordinal ranking Sanders left of Feinstein left of DeMint.

In this book, we use our DW-NOMINATE procedure for measuring ideology.[48] To match the common-language designation of liberals to the left and conservatives to the right, we adjust the DW-NOMINATE scores so that each member's *average* score lies between –1 and +1, with –1 being the most liberal position and +1 the most conservative.

In DW-NOMINATE, the frequency of the deviant votes pins down the location of the ideal points. For example, if there are few votes pitting DeMint and Sanders against Feinstein, we place DeMint and Sanders far apart, to mimic the improbability that random events lead them to vote together. Alternatively, if the DeMint-Sanders coalition were common, we would place them closer together, consistent with the idea that small random events can lead to such a pattern.

It is easy to measure the success of the one-dimensional spatial model. In our example, the "classification success" is simply the proportion of explained votes (i.e., types 1–6) compared to the total number of votes. Notice, however, that classification success will be inflated if there are lots of unanimous votes like 5 and 6, because any ranking of the senators can explain them. Therefore, the proportionate reduction in error is a useful measure of classification success.[49]

Sometimes there are so many votes like 7 and 8 that it becomes unreasonable to maintain that they are simply random. An alternative is to assume that a DeMint-Sanders coalition forms because there is some other policy dimension on which they are closer together than they are to Feinstein. We can accommodate such behavior by estimating ideal points on a second dimension. The spatial political map then becomes more like the map of the United States and less like the map of Chile. In this example, a second dimension in which DeMint and Sanders share a position distinct from Feinstein's will explain votes 7 and 8. Both dimensions combined will explain all of the votes. Obviously, in a richer example with one hundred senators rather than three, two dimensions will not explain all the votes, but the second dimension may add explanatory power. In fact, in the twenty-first century, congressional roll call voting is so highly one-dimensional that we need not consider a second dimension. In this book, we capture ideology as a liberal-conservative scale.

CHAPTER 3
Interests

Dishonest dealing and speculative enterprise are merely the occasional incidents of our real prosperity.

—President Theodore Roosevelt to George B. Cortelyou, October 25, 1907

Despite recent abuses of the public's trust, our economy remains fundamentally sound and strong, and the vast majority of business people are living by the rules. Yet, confidence is the cornerstone of our economic system, so a few bad actors can tarnish our entire free enterprise system. We must have rules and laws that restore faith in the integrity of American business. The government will fully investigate reports of corporate fraud, and hold the guilty parties accountable for misleading shareholders and employees. Executives who commit fraud will face financial penalties, and, when they are guilty of criminal wrongdoing, they will face jail time.

—President George W. Bush, weekly radio address, June 29, 2002

Never again should we let the schemes of a reckless few put the world's financial system—and our people's well-being—at risk.

—President Barack Obama, address to G20 Summit, September 25, 2009

IN THE EPIGRAPHS GIVEN HERE, Presidents Roosevelt, Bush, and Obama were doing their best to reassure financial markets when miscreants were in full public view. Roosevelt's remarks came just after the unraveling of the corner on United Copper and three weeks before the suicide of the banker Charles Barney, who was caught up in the scandal. Bush's radio address came the week before WorldCom's recently resigned CEO Bernard Ebbers was to testify before the House Financial Services Committee. ("Bad actor" Ebbers is now serving a twenty-five-year sentence in a federal prison.) Obama was speaking at the time of a widespread populist reaction to the federal bailout of financial firms and to the large bonuses received by the executives of these firms.

Of course, few would challenge these presidents' assertions about how a majority live by the rules. It is a taboo to express an opinion that almost everyone is, in fact, dishonest, or, at best, highly self-interested. This taboo is politically relevant because it legitimizes weak legal and regulatory standards and weak enforcement of those standards that do exist.

But the "few bad apples" theory invoked by the three leaders and others almost certainly understates the role of legally and ethically dubious behavior in generating the current and past financial crises. In the introduction to part I, we mentioned the steroid scandal in major league baseball. Baseball players typify the behavior of Americans. From jaywalking, to hiring illegal gardeners and nannies, to not paying social security taxes on legal domestics, to doing drugs, to cheating on taxes, to getting disability benefits when there is no disability, to speeding, to insurance fraud, and so on, most Americans engage in some law-breaking on a daily basis. We should not expect business people and financiers to behave any differently.

With specific reference to the financial crisis, former hedge fund manager Michael Burry has expressed a position quite opposite to that of the presidents: "The salient point about the modern vintage of housing-related fraud is its integral place within our nation's institutions."[1] And President John F. Kennedy once privately proclaimed, "My father always told me that all businessmen were sons of bitches."[2]

After his statement went viral, 1962 style, Kennedy did some public backtracking. In public, politicians must stick with the bad apples theory. This claim, however, invokes only half of the metaphor. The other half concerns spoiling the whole barrel. Competitive pressures in the marketplace force businesses and firms to push legal and ethical barriers simply to keep up with those firms that breach them. This was clearly the case in major league baseball as the pressure to keep up lured many more athletes into using banned substances. Bernard Madoff's ability to lure billions away from other investment funds with his Ponzi scheme may not have led other firms to directly emulate his lawbreaking, but it is likely to have led others into more risky investments so as not to lose even more investors. Similarly, competitors of Bernie Ebbers and WorldCom may have made poor investments in an attempt to emulate the false profits shown in WorldCom accounting statements.[3] The example most germane to the financial crisis is how the profits of investment banks in the first decade of the new century induced commercial banks to take on more risk to boost earnings.

Politics is also an important channel for the spread of rot. In some cases, market participants use political connections and influences to legalize and legitimate their currently illegal behavior. Our discussion of Phil Gramm in this book's introduction drew attention to one of the most important examples of this phenomenon: Enron's lobbying to exempt energy trades from government regulation.[4] The lobbying was rewarded with the infamous "Enron loophole" in the Commodity Futures Modernization Act of 2000. We also saw, in chapter 2, how Fannie Mae's 2003 annual report drew attention to that government-sponsored enterprise's connections to Angelo Mozilo of Countrywide Financial. "Friends of Angelo" loans were received by Senators Chris Dodd (D-CT) and Kent Conrad (D-ND); George W. Bush's Housing and Urban Development (HUD) secretary Alphonso Jackson; Clinton HUD secretary Donna Shalala;

diplomat Richard Holbrooke; and James Johnson, former Fannie Mae head and adviser to Walter Mondale, John Kerry, and Barack Obama.[5] (The Mozilo connection ended Johnson's formal participation in the Obama presidential campaign, but it has not kept him from a directorship at Goldman Sachs.) In 2010, Mozilo agreed to a $67.5 million settlement with the Securities and Exchange Commission (SEC) to avoid trial on fraud and insider trading charges. Most of the settlement will be paid by Bank of America, which acquired Countrywide in 2008.[6]

Firms taking questionable risks, like Countrywide, may seek political protection from government intervention. Deniz Igan, Prachi Mishra, and Thierry Tressel show that it was the most risky lenders who lobbied against tightened lending rules in the subprime crisis.[7] Thomas Romer and Barry Weingast indicate that it was the least solvent savings and loan (S&L) institutions that were the strong advocates for regulatory forbearance in the S&L crisis.[8] These were cases where firms fought against tighter regulatory standards.

Disadvantaged firms might seek government relief from the effects of questionable activities. But often the relief they seek is not for the government to clarify or enforce existing law but for it to impose weaker standards. They seek changes to the law so that they can engage in the behavior causing the harm. This dynamic led to the 1999 repeal of the Glass-Steagall Act's separation of investment and commercial banking. Many financial holding companies began exploiting loopholes in the law and its regulatory framework that allowed them to begin breaking down barriers between the two forms of banking. But rather than lobby for stronger laws and better enforcement, most of the companies who lost market share to the more integrated firms simply sought repeal so that they could compete. Similarly, the JOBS Act passed by Congress in 2012 weakened disclosure requirements for "emerging growth" companies. Appeals for lax regulation are facilitated by the "bad apples" taboo expressed in the reassuring words we cited from Presidents Roosevelt, Bush, and Obama at the beginning of this chapter. If fraud and other agency problems are rare and sporadic rather than epidemic, the financial elite can indulge in the self-serving belief that markets can self-regulate.

What explains the taboo? Politicians are much less reluctant to claim that ghettos are full of earned income tax credit fraudsters, welfare queens, drug dealers, and violent criminals. Politicians observe no taboo against singling out some categories of Americans as having a proclivity for crime; why not the financial services industry? Undoubtedly because the industry packs political power and can deliver rewards to the Phil and Wendy Gramms. We emphasize that the Gramms were far from unique. As we indicated in this book's introduction, the board of American International Group (AIG) was stocked with former officials from both Republican and Democratic administrations. In addition, White House advisers including Larry Summers, Franklin Raines, Peter Orszag, and Rahm Emanuel found their way to Wall Street or Fannie Mae at one time or another.

Our point here is that although overtly illegal behavior is important for understanding financial crises, even more focus should go to activities that qualify as legal. It's the "honest graft" of special interest politics that packs a real punch.

The Power of Special Interests

How do special interests such as those in the financial services industry influence political decision makers? Political scientists tend to focus on three different channels of influence: mobilizing constituencies, direct political expenditures in the form of campaign contributions, and the production and provision of information through lobbying. We consider each of these channels in turn.

Mobilizing Constituencies

As we discussed in the previous chapter, members of Congress do not simply channel the views of their average constituent into the legislative process. More often than not they bring their own beliefs and ideologies to bear on the decisions they make. But this is not to say that constituency preferences are not important in many circumstances. In particular, on highly salient issues toward which active constituents have strong, well-informed preferences, politicians are quite likely to heed such views.

Unlike such interest groups as the National Rifle Association (NRA) or the AARP (formerly the American Association of Retired Persons), the power of the financial sector does not arise from the raw numbers of voters it commands. Indeed, employment in the financial sector is small, but concentrated in certain regions: New York City, New Jersey, and Connecticut. As one can see from table 3.1, no congressional district has more than 14 percent of its labor force working in the financial or insurance sectors.[9] The real estate sector (see table 3.2) is smaller and less concentrated, but it is overrepresented in places like Florida, California, and Nevada, where the housing bubble was the greatest.

But despite the small size of these groups, members of Congress are very responsive to their views. First, as we saw above, employees in the financial sector are quite well-to-do. In a recent book, Larry Bartels argues that senators are considerably more responsive to the opinions of high-income than middle-income constituents, and not responsive at all to the views of low-income citizens.[10] Also (as is true for many industries) workers in the financial sector are well informed about how various laws and regulations affect their industry. They are likely to know when a legislator or regulator makes a decision adverse to those interests (and plenty of industry groups are ready to inform them if any decision escapes their attention).

The political influence of the big banks has grown in recent years as a consequence of the ending of restrictions on interstate branch banking and on brokerage activities by commercial banks. Just as defense contractors have long benefited from lobbying by subcontractors scattered throughout the country, Bank of America, Citibank, JPMorgan Chase, and Wells Fargo

TABLE 3.1

Top 25 House districts for finance and insurance employment in 2000

Incumbent (2008–9)	State	District	Party	Percentage Employment in Finance and Insurance
Carolyn Maloney	NY	14	D	13.97%
Jerrold Nadler	NY	8	D	11.95%
Michael McMahon	NY	13	R	11.92%
John Larson	CT	1	D	11.92%
Christopher Shays	CT	4	R	10.60%
Leonard Boswell	IA	3	D	10.38%
Sue Myrick	NC	9	R	10.37%
Lee Terry	NE	2	R	10.10%
Michael Castle	DE	1	R	9.99%
Ander Crenshaw	FL	4	R	9.69%
Eric Cantor	VA	7	R	9.42%
Rush Holt	NJ	12	D	9.38%
Anthony Weiner	NY	9	D	9.34%
Patrick Tiberi	OH	12	R	9.19%
Nita Lowey	NY	18	D	9.13%
Carolyn McCarthy	NY	4	D	8.95%
Peter King	NY	3	R	8.90%
Leonard Lance	NJ	7	R	8.86%
Rodney Frelinghuysen	NJ	11	R	8.85%
Erik Paulsen	MN	3	R	8.67%
Tom Tancredo	CO	6	R	8.63%
Danny Davis	IL	7	D	8.55%
John Shadegg	AZ	3	R	8.43%
Stephen Lynch	MA	9	D	8.41%
Mark Kirk	IL	10	R	8.38%
U.S. Average				5.00%

now have branches in most congressional districts. McBank has replaced the Bailey Building and Loan of *It's a Wonderful Life*.

In many ways, the political influence of the financial services industry is similar to that of other sectors of the economy. If financial services lobbying had undue influence on the Dodd-Frank Wall Street Reform and Consumer Protection Act and its subsequent implementation, the same could be said for the health care industry with regard to both Bush's prescription drug plan and Obama's health care bill. The retail drug industry

TABLE 3.2.
Top 25 districts for real estate employment in 2000

Incumbent (2008–9)	State	District	Party	Percentage Employment in Real Estate
Connie Mack	FL	14	R	4.48%
Ron Klein	FL	22	D	4.17%
John Campbell	CA	48	R	4.10%
Jose Serrano	NY	16	D	3.99%
Charles Rangel	NY	15	D	3.93%
Debbie Schultz	FL	20	D	3.89%
Henry Waxman	CA	30	D	3.85%
Ileana Ros-Lehtinen	FL	18	R	3.73%
Robert Wexler	FL	19	D	3.61%
Pete Sessions	TX	32	R	3.49%
Ric Keller	FL	8	R	3.38%
Vernon Buchanan	FL	13	R	3.33%
Mazie Hirono	HI	2	D	3.33%
Joseph Crowley	NY	7	D	3.29%
John Shadegg	AZ	3	R	3.23%
Harry Mitchell	AZ	5	D	3.22%
John Culberson	TX	7	R	3.17%
Tom Price	GA	6	R	3.15%
Carolyn Maloney	NY	14	D	3.14%
Dana Rohrabacher	CA	46	R	3.12%
Henry Brown	SC	1	R	3.06%
John Lewis	GA	5	D	3.04%
Dina Titus	NV	3	R	2.98%
Gary Ackerman	NY	5	D	2.96%
Anthony Weiner	NY	9	D	2.96%
U.S. Average				1.88%

and the hospital industry have, like retail banking, become more concentrated.

One area where the financial sector excels and is distinct is political participation. Reflecting the importance of politics to their industry, employees of the financial sector are actively engaged in politics. One aspect of this engagement is heavy participation in electoral politics. In the 2004 American National Election Study (ANES), 88 percent of those employed in finance and insurance reported voting in the presidential election compared to just 76 percent of the other respondents.[11] Employees in the financial sector are also more likely to

- Try to influence the votes of others (53 percent to 48 percent)
- Attend a campaign meeting, rally, or speech (13 percent to 7 percent)
- Work on a campaign (5 percent to 3 percent)

Not surprisingly, the political engagement of the financial services industry is even stronger in the area where money counts: campaign contributions. A full 25 percent of the ANES financial services industry respondents report making a campaign contribution in 2004, compared to just 8 percent of those who worked outside the sector. However, as we discuss below when we present the sheer magnitude of financial services campaign contributions, this seventeen-point gap radically understates the political mobilization of this sector.

Another factor that works in favor of the financial industry is that legislators are not likely to feel much cross-pressure from other constituents on matters related to finance. Such matters are technically complex and not very interesting to most voters. Voters whose stock portfolios and homes are appreciating in value may be hard to convince of a need for more financial regulation. Consider the mutual fund scandals that came to light in 2003. Mutual fund traders had a practice of executing "late trades" at the previous day's closing price. This practice essentially represents an illegal transfer from the accounts of regular mutual fund clients to the late traders.[12] Although the practice violates security laws, it appears to have been widespread before New York attorney general Eliot Spitzer and the SEC began their investigations.[13] These illegal trades were facilitated by regulations that in principle allowed after-hours trades to be executed at the closing price only if the order was made prior to closing. But lax enforcement led to rampant cheating of individual investors in favor of institutions. The complexity of the regulations surrounding these practices and the fact that individual mutual fund investors were still making money (though perhaps not as much) meant that there was little political pressure to investigate before Spitzer stepped in. Afterward the SEC proposed a "hard close" rule that prohibited executing any orders at the previous closing price after 4 p.m. But after extensive industry lobbying the rule was abandoned.

Political pressure against the financial sector builds substantially only during a crisis and in its aftermath. For example, Atif Mian, Amir Sufi, and Francesco Trebbi find that high foreclosure and delinquency rates among Republican constituents led many Republican legislators to support the Housing and Economic Recovery Act of 2008, which contained government subsidies for renegotiating mortgages.[14] But in many cases, the cross-pressure emerges not as well-informed opposition to financial market deregulation or executive compensation practices but as a populist anti–Wall Street reaction. Constituency pressure to rein in executive compensation and bonuses was obviously an important factor in the House of Representatives' vote to tax AIG retention bonuses at a punitive rate of 90 percent. In chapter 7 we show that Republican House members running for reelection in 2008 were less likely to support Secretary Paulson's initial Troubled Asset Relief Program (TARP I) than were those Republicans who had announced their retirement.

Financing Campaigns

The second weapon in the arsenal of financial interests is direct political expenditure through campaign contributions to legislators, presidential candidates, and political parties.

The importance of campaign contributions in determining policy outcomes may be exaggerated.[15] Lehman Brothers is a particularly salient example. From 2004 to 2008, Lehman employees made substantial contributions, less than those of Goldman Sachs, Citibank, and JPMorgan Chase, but ahead of Bank of America.[16] These contributions did not save Lehman from bankruptcy. It is, moreover, often the case that there is conflict within the financial services industry over policy change. Randall Kroszner and Thomas Stratmann argue that Glass-Steagall survived for sixty-six years in large part because the financial services industry, split into securities, commercial banking, and insurance sectors, could not agree on the nature of reform. Each sector, in turn, used contributions to compete for influence against the other two sectors.[17] Outside of the financial sector, the importance of interindustry competition has recently been highlighted by the conflict between entertainment and Internet organizations over the regulation of Internet piracy. But greater consolidation of different business lines into large financial holding companies has muted these intrafinance conflicts over policy.

On the other hand, even if no firm or sector wins all the time, there is little doubt that the campaign cash the financial industry contributes in each election cycle boosts its clout in Washington. When the industry "has its act together," coordinated contributions can change policy. An example is the change in bankruptcy law in 2005 brought about by the stealthily named National Consumer Bankruptcy Coalition, which coordinated contributions for major creditors.[18]

Using data provided by the Center for Responsive Politics (CRP),[19] we can examine in some detail the extent of the campaign fundraising undertaken by the financial sector. Figure 3.1 reveals that campaign contributions from the financial sector increased almost threefold between 1992 and 2008, even after adjusting for inflation. This growth exceeds that of all of the industrial sectors tracked by the CPR with the exception of the legal profession.

The current magnitudes of giving are also astonishing. Four subsectors of the industry are in the top ten of all industry contributors (securities and investments, real estate, insurance, and miscellaneous finance). Combined, the industry contributions swamp the second-place industry—the legal profession.[20]

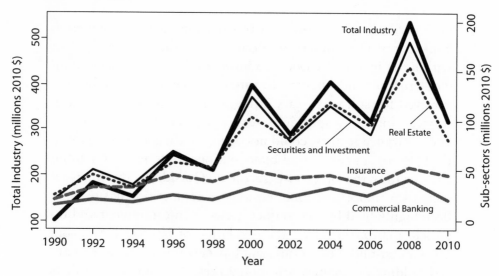

Figure 3.1. Campaign contributions from the financial sector. Campaign contributions from the financial sector have increased sharply, especially from securities, investment banking, and real estate, the sectors most involved in the subprime mortgage crisis.

Figure 3.1 also reveals that the growth in financial industry contributions has been concentrated in two sectors: securities and investments, and real estate. Securities and investments, in contrast to commercial banking, is the sector that Philippon and Reshef identify as accounting for most of the wage increases in financial services relative to other sectors of the economy.[21] It is certainly no coincidence that financial services and real estate played such a big role in the 2008 financial crisis.

Moreover, a few firms and trade associations account for the bulk of the contributions. The largest political action committee (PAC) contributor in the 2010 election cycle in the commercial banking sector was the American Bankers Association. The board of this association is basically controlled by the four big national banks, JPMorgan Chase, Bank of America, Citigroup, and Wells Fargo. The big four and the association donated $4.9 million of the total $9.0 million contributions from the commercial banking sector PACs. Goldman Sachs, Credit Suisse, and UBS had the fourth-, fifth-, and sixth-largest PACs in the securities and investments category. In total campaign contributions, which include money given directly to political parties as well as to candidates, Goldman Sachs, at $38.3 million, and Citibank, at $29.5 million, were the second- and third-largest corporate contributors from 1989 to 2012. (AT&T was the largest.)

Of course, it is not simply the magnitude of the contributions that matter but the way they are allocated. Figure 3.2 demonstrates how different financial sectors allocated their money across the two political parties since 1990. Two features stand out. The first is the importance of majority party control of Congress. The financial industry tends to shift its contributions based on which party controls Congress. Before 1994, a majority of the money went to the Democratic Party, which controlled the House and the Senate. Following the 1994 elections, contributions shifted dramatically in favor of the newly empowered Republicans. This is especially true of the contributions from insurers and commercial banks. Following the Democratic takeover in 2006, the money switched back to about where it had been in the early 1990s. It shifted back to the Republicans again after the 2010 midterm elections.

The second important point is how well the Democratic Party has done with the securities and real estate industries even during the period when it had little power in Washington. Although it may seem inconsistent with the Democratic Party's liberal ideological orientation, the financial sector has become a very important constituency for the party. Indeed, it has become the "money" wing of the party that helps compensate for the increasingly downscale "votes" wing of the party. Many factors helped seal this alliance. The first is that much of the financial sector is located on the socially liberal coasts—in New York, Boston, Los Angeles, and San Francisco.[22] It is not surprising that these areas would support liberal social and cultural causes through the Democratic Party. Perhaps not all of the money is intended to influence the Democrats on financial matters, yet clearly, the level of these contributions heightens the party's sensitivity to those interests.

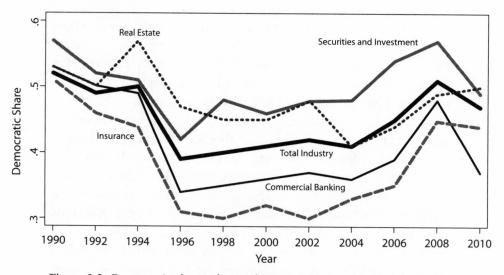

Figure 3.2. Democratic share of contributions. The Democrats have always received a substantial share of the contributions from the financial services industry. Their share is greatest when they control Congress. The figure shows contributions over each two-year election cycle. The period 1995–2006 represents years when the Republicans controlled the outgoing Congress. The Democrats controlled in 1989–94 and 2007–10.

From the party's perspective, high finance makes an ideal money wing almost as good as Hollywood. Unlike many other industries, hedge funds and banks do not directly pollute the environment and do not have especially tendentious labor relations. Thus, the industry has relatively little conflict with other Democratic constituencies such as environmentalists and labor unions.[23] Goldman Sachs is notably welcoming to gay men and lesbians.[24] Criticism of hedge funds, in particular, by other Democratic constituencies is difficult due to the light disclosure requirements for their activities. Of course, as we will see, what was an ideal alliance during the boom is not necessarily one that can survive the bust.

Perhaps more important than how the industry allocates funds across parties is how it supports individual legislators. Consider table 3.3, which outlines average financial industry contributions to various groups of House incumbents for the 2007–8 election cycle.

TABLE 3.3.
Financial industry contributions to house incumbents,
2007–8 election cycle

Group	Contribution
All members	$157,900
Democrats	$153,921
Republicans	$162,686
Financial Services Committee members	$297,883
Yes on TARP I	$187,586
No on TARP I	$131,789
Liberal Democrats	$140,374
Moderate Democrats	$169,085
Moderate Republicans	$156,780
Conservative Republicans	$169,462

The partisan differences are quite small. Only $9,000 separates the average Democrat from the average Republican. This allocation reflects the bipartisan strategies that these industries pursued.

The ideological differences are somewhat more substantial. The more conservative wing of each party (moderate Democrats and conservative Republicans) garners substantially more contributions than the more liberal factions. The emphasis on the Financial Services Committee, with its role in oversight and new legislation, is clear. The typical committee member receives almost twice as much as the average nonmember. Contributions do at least correlate with voting decisions. Contributions made during the 2007–8 election cycle appear to have paid off when the bubble popped. The members who supported the Paulson TARP bailout received substantially more contributions than those who opposed it.

Information and Lobbying

Because legislators often lack the time or expertise to master complex policy areas, they must naturally turn to others for information or advice. While members can rely on congressional and committee staffs to some degree, most of the time they depend on outside lobbyists and interest groups for information about the consequences of policy choices. This political fact of life is true across almost all policy domains, but it is especially important in financial regulation.

Finance, banking, and insurance are very complex industries. This has only become truer with the proliferation of derivatives, swaps, and other complex financial instruments. One has to be a rocket scientist (or at least on par with one mathematically) to understand much of what has gone on in the financial sector over the past generation.[25] Moreover, this expertise is lucrative. Someone who truly knows the ins and outs of the financial sector could make far more money working for a financial firm (or lobbying for it) than working as a staffer on Capitol Hill. Consequently, the "information asymmetry" between financial sector lobbyists and legislators is unusually large. The informational advantage of the financial sector should work to its advantage when its members participate in the political process and lobby.

This political information gap works much the same way that it works in private markets. Just as stock jobbers sell near worthless securities to unsophisticated buyers, financial sector lobbyists monger dubious "reforms" to legislators. The lobbyists have little incentive to push policies that contribute to the long-run economic welfare of the nation. Their focus is on short-term profits and competitive advantage. When times are good, the message that unregulated financial markets enhance the general welfare sells especially well.

The information asymmetry between the financial sector and policy makers is also a source of "negative" power for the industry. The period of the past thirty years has been one of vast innovation in the financial sector. New products routinely exploit previously unknown loopholes in securities law and regulation. A recent, relatively simple example is Goldman Sachs's creating a pool of investors to buy an interest in Facebook in 2011; the product allowed Facebook to raise capital while escaping the 499 investor limit that would force it to become a public company. (Facebook finally held its initial public offering in 2012.) After a public outcry, Goldman restricted the investment to a loophole for foreign investors who "do not count."[26] But careful regulatory oversight of the many less-transparent innovations requires intensive knowledge of the new practices and their effects. Not only is this information concentrated within the industry but the industry may have little incentive to provide it to policy makers. Indeed, a claim of "business secrets" may make it impossible for regulators to obtain it on their own. Consequently, policy makers are presented with a Morton's Fork between bad outcomes arising under laissez-faire and stifling innovation through regulation.

As an example, consider "high frequency algorithmic" trading.[27] The idea is to have powerful computers analyze, within fractions of a second, every blip and dip of markets and execute trades. The use of these algorithms may be efficiency-enhancing, but there are legitimate concerns about a destabilizing effect. What if thousands of these algorithms sold at the same dip? Might that not turn a dip into a crash? A flash crash related to high-frequency trading occurred on May 6, 2010. The incident illustrates how both the SEC and the Commodity Futures Trading Commission (CFTC) lack the capacity and information for monitoring financial transactions and innovation. The joint report of these agencies accounting for the crash was issued only on September 30 of that year.[28] Consequently, this lack of capacity has left regulation largely to the industry itself.[29]

Lobbying is extremely important for the financial sector. It spends roughly the same amount on lobbying as on campaign contributions. Since 1998, lobbying expenditures are subject to public disclosure. We cannot break out expenditures on lobbying specific legislators or political parties, but we can look at the total amounts. These are indicated for securities and investments, commercial banks, and real estate in figure 3.3.[30] Lobbying expenditures rose sharply in the first decade of the twenty-first century, particularly in the securities and investments sector.

Among commercial banks, the big four survivors of the crash, Bank of America, JPMorgan Chase, Wells Fargo, and Citibank, account for about one-third of all commercial banking lobbying

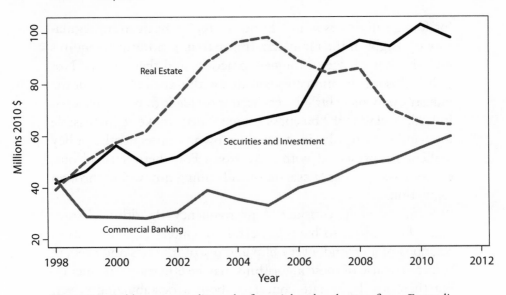

Figure 3.3. Lobbying expenditures by financial and real estate firms. Expenditures soared during the bubble and continued to grow after the pop, with the exception of real estate.

expenditures. They are also, as previously noted, on the boards of the American Bankers Association and the Consumer Bankers Association. The two associations are the biggest single lobbyists in the commercial bank category. The two trade groups, the four big banks, and Barclays represent more than half of all commercial banking lobbying expenditure. It should be no surprise that Goldman Sachs makes the highest lobbying expenditure among securities and investments firms.

As the housing bubble popped, lobbying by the real estate sector declined. The details tell a story. The largest real estate lobbying organization is the National Association of Realtors, which accounts for about one-third of all lobbying expenses in the sector, spending more than $22 million in 2011. This was not a decline, but a new record, as indicated by OpenSecrets.org. Even as home sales fell and association membership fell from 1.36 million in 2007 to 1.07 million in 2011, lobbying by the association increased.

Where, then, did the decline in real estate sector lobbying come from? A huge chunk came from Fannie and Freddie, which ended their lobbying after being nationalized in 2008. They had been the second-and third-largest lobbying organizations in the real estate sector. The National Association of Mortgage Brokers also reduced its expenditures dramatically: the group spent $2,319,485 in 2009 but only $210,000 in 2011. Mortgage brokering collapsed as the lenders turned to in-house mortgage origination with stiffer standards. Home building also collapsed. This sector, kept separately by OpenSecrets.org, showed a decline from $9.8 million in 2009 to $4.6 million in 2011. The drop would appear to be related to the large oversupply of housing after the bubble. With low expectations that Washington would favor even more building and with many builders in financial distress, the sector downsized its political activity.

Political expenditures, informational asymmetry, and constituent pressures mix into ideology as influences on the individual behavior of members of Congress and on the White House. In chapter 4 we explore how individuals interact within the political system.

CHAPTER 4
Institutions

[I]n our capital markets—in general, innovation
precedes regulation, and that's generally been good
because we grow quicker because of it.
> —Henry Paulson, quoted in Todd Purdum,
> "Henry Paulson's Longest Night"

THE FINAL PRONG OF OUR EXPLANATION is the shortcomings of
America's policy-making institutions. We have already discussed
how *interests* work to impede adequate and efficient regulation
of financial markets. Legislators and regulators are susceptible
to special-interest appeals from the financial services industry.
Moreover, the industry benefits from information asymmetries
with the government. But *interests* are far from the only roadblocks. Indeed, even if campaigns were publicly financed and all
regulators and congressional staffers held PhDs in financial engineering, the American political system would still have considerable difficulty establishing and maintaining the sort of financial
regulatory structure that would prevent the recurrence of financial crises.

Another difficulty is that policy making is approached through
ideology that is resistant to the incorporation of new information. In chapter 2, we showed how ideology can be summarized
as a position on a liberal-conservative dimension. Politics, increasingly organized in polarized liberal-conservative positions,
must create policies within *institutions* that are resistant to policy change.

The problem is that political power in the United States is so fragmented, separated, and checked that policy change requires extraordinary consensus and mobilization. It's the story those of us who grew up in America should have learned in high school. Power is separated into executive, legislative, and judicial functions. Congress and courts check the president and the executive branch. Authority is divided and shared by the states and the federal government. And so on.

Of course, limits on federal power were exactly what our founders hoped to achieve. Our constitutional blueprint has served us well for more than two hundred years, but its liabilities and weaknesses are all too apparent in rapidly changing policy domains such as financial regulation.

A second important feature of our political system and culture is our frequent national elections. The House of Representatives is elected every two years along with a third of the Senate. Every four years we hold a presidential election. Consequently, the next election is always just around the corner. No other advanced democracy has such frequent regularly scheduled legislative elections.[1] Since its first national election in 1788 the United States has never canceled an election. Elections were held even during the Civil War (1861–65).

Just as the quarterly earnings cycle is said to unduly influence the executives of public companies, the compression of the American electoral cycle causes a number of distorted incentives that complicate policy making generally, and financial regulation specifically. Biennial elections put a premium on short-run fixes over long-term solutions. They induce delay and paralysis in even-numbered years. And frequent elections exacerbate partisan divisions as policy disagreements get turned into campaign fodder.

Another important feature of the American electoral system is its heavy reliance on geography as a basis for representation. Members of the House of Representatives are elected from relatively small single-member districts. Consequently, they have strong incentives to represent the narrow interests of locally important constituents and firms. This is also true of senators, but to a lesser degree.

Although Americans probably find nothing unusual or objectionable about geographic representation, the United States is somewhat unusual in its use of it. Many other advanced democracies use some form of proportional representation in which parties are allocated seats based on the share of votes they receive nationwide. Such systems reduce localism because the electoral success of a politician is determined by how well his or her party does nationally. Consequently, the incentives to cater to local interests are greatly reduced. Proportional systems also tend to be associated with greater degrees of party discipline which reduces the opportunities of individual legislators to promote the interests of local constituencies. Other advanced democracies, even if they do not use proportional representation, exert party discipline through the power of the government to dissolve parliament and call for elections.[2] In many other countries, including those with single-member, plurality districts, national parties control candidate selection, with the "personal vote" being of less importance than in the United States. Of course, other nations have their own, severe problems in managing their financial systems, but catering to narrow local constituencies is generally not one of them.

Historically, the importance of localism to finance is shown by the prohibition on interstate banking contained in the McFadden Act of 1927. Prohibitions were a complication in the passage of the Glass-Steagall Act in 1933 (which we discuss later in this chapter), were reaffirmed in the National Banking Act of 1956, and were fully repealed only in the Riegle-Neal Act of 1994.[3] Even within states, branch banking was often sharply curtailed to protect small local banks. In Pennsylvania, no bank could operate in more than three counties. Illinois completely banned bank branches,[4] and only ten states permitted statewide branch banking.[5] The history of branch banking is a compelling demonstration of the effect of political institutions on financial structures. Most other countries, including Canada, enjoyed nationwide banking in the nineteenth century.[6]

More recently, as we noted in chapter 2, financial sector employment is concentrated in a handful of legislative districts. In the U.S. system, the representatives from these districts have strong incentives to promote the interests of the industry even if this puts them at odds with their party. In the current era the tension has been particularly acute within the Democratic Party given that financial interests are concentrated in Democratic districts. A notable example is how the otherwise reliably liberal senator Charles Schumer (D-NY) defends the "carried interest" provision in the tax code that allows hedge fund managers to pay only capital gains taxes and not (higher) income taxes on their earnings.[7]

Localism also plays an important role in the regulatory process. Legislators are keen to intervene with regulators on behalf of local economic elites. A dramatic example of this phenomenon is the so-called Keating Five scandal. Five senators were accused of improperly intervening with the Federal Home Loan Bank Board on behalf of Charles Keating, chairman of the Lincoln Savings and Loan Association. Keating built "Your Premier Luxury Resort," the Phoenician, in Scottsdale, Arizona. Not surprisingly, two of the Keating Five were Arizona senators Dennis DeConcini and John McCain. Less sensationally but more consequentially, legislative pressure for regulatory forbearance was a powerful factor in the savings and loan crisis of the 1980s.[8]

Not only is representation in the United States geographically based but change is often blocked by the sharp differences in the geographic basis of representation in the two chambers of Congress. The House of Representatives is reapportioned every decade on the basis of population. In contrast, each state, no matter how sparsely populated, has two Senate seats. This is the singular provision of the Constitution that is not subject to amendment. There is thus a permanent institutional tension between the two houses. Alaska gets as much Senate representation as California. Currently, eleven states have populations so small that they have only one or two House members; yet these states fill twenty-two of the one hundred Senate seats. A senator from nowhere can indeed command resources for a bridge to nowhere. Among senators, those from states with small populations are likely to be particularly narrowly focused.[9]

The population imbalances in Senate representation coupled with the staggered, six-year terms of the Senate, often mean that the two chambers exhibit different preferences on an issue. These bicameral differences often lead to policy delays and gridlock.[10] The consumer bankruptcy legislation discussed earlier illustrates the point. The National Consumer Bankruptcy Coalition representing credit card issuers pushed for a change in consumer bankruptcy law in the late 1990s. No bill was forthcoming in 1998 because the Senate failed to act; in 2000 a bill was produced so late that President Bill Clinton was able to pocket veto it; in 2001 a bill was killed when the House voted against a conference report that included a Senate provision that barred the use of bankruptcy by abortion clinic protesters. Only in 2005 did the two chambers, both Republican controlled, agree on a bill that was then signed by a Republican president.[11]

Pivotal Politics

To better understand the effect of checks and balances and the separation of powers on financial policy making, a simple analytical framework is helpful.

Consider what policy choices the simple one-dimensional hypothetical legislature that we discussed in chapter 2 might make. A majoritarian chamber, such as the House of Representatives, acting on its own would vote on alternatives according to majority rule. A proposal preferred by a simple majority (218 of 435 if everyone votes) to an alternative wins. If the agenda is open in the sense that any legislator can make a proposal at any time, the final outcome must be one that no majority prefers to overturn. When the legislator's ideal policies can be arrayed along a single line (as our DW-NOMINATE results from chapter 2 suggest), we can apply the *median voter theorem*—the winning policy must be the ideal point of the median legislator.[12] The median legislator, of course, is the one for whom half the ideal points are to the left and half are to the right. Any attempt to move policy away from her ideal point to the right would be opposed by this legislator and the 217 members with ideal points to her left. Similarly, any attempt to move policy to the left would be defeated by the median legislator and the 217 colleagues to her right. Any policy that is not the most preferred of the median legislator can be defeated by a simple majority. If the minimum wage is seven dollars and the median wants it to be eight, a majority composed of the median and all those legislators who desire a higher one will vote to increase it.

When a financial crisis hits, policy would be very responsive in a majoritarian, unicameral legislature. Any change in the median legislator's preferences results in a swift policy change. There are two channels for this response. First, a shock may change how policy maps onto the liberal-conservative dimension. If a financial crisis causes legislator preferences to shift in the direction of increased regulation, the legislature would immediately vote to abandon a lax regulatory regime for derivatives and implement new, tougher regulations that now correspond to the policy preferred by the median legislator. Ideology, however, limits the force of this channel. A crisis may not make a substantial change in preferences. The second channel is elections. Policy changes only when elections create a new median legislator with preferences that are very different from those of the old median. If a legislature is responsive to voters, policy will be so as well.[13]

Of course, our hypothetical majoritarian legislature serves the same purpose as the frictionless plane in physics: as a benchmark to assess the importance of deviations from ideal conditions. There are many ways in which an otherwise majoritarian legislature fails to act as described. Political parties are one potentially important friction in the legislative process.[14] An important assumption in our idealized legislature is that any counterproposal can be made at any point in the process. If policy strays from the median ideal point, a proposal can be made that brings policy back to the median. But in actuality, party leaders have a great deal of control over the agenda. They may use agenda powers to keep policy from moving too far from their own preferences or those of the majority of their party. One way of accomplishing this goal is to assert *negative agenda control*—that is, to disallow votes on issues in which the median legislator would like to coalesce with members of the minority party to move policy away from the position of the majority party and its leaders.

Negative agenda control reached its apotheosis in the current climate of polarized politics. In 2004, House Speaker Dennis Hastert announced his rule that legislation could proceed only if it was supported by a majority of the Republican Party. But Hastert was only articulating a long-standing and ongoing practice in the House.[15] The Hastert rule increases legislative paralysis, or *gridlock*. If the median legislator and the majority party leaders cannot agree on a policy change, the majority party keeps the policy off the agenda and policy remains unchanged. Policy is no longer so responsive. Changes in the status quo or in the preferences of the legislature must be substantial in order to end the stalemate. Indeed, as we will see, this was the case for financial reform. Policies can drift in one direction or another for extended periods of time before there is a legislative correction.

The DW-NOMINATE estimates of legislator ideal points provide some measure of the extent of this problem. In figure 4.1 we illustrate the gap between the liberal-conservative score for the majority party median and the score for the median House member for congresses of the recent past as well as that for some congressional terms from the much less polarized 1960s. For example, in 2005–6, when the Republicans were the majority party, the party median was a quite conservative 0.55. The House as a whole was more moderate, with a median of 0.36.

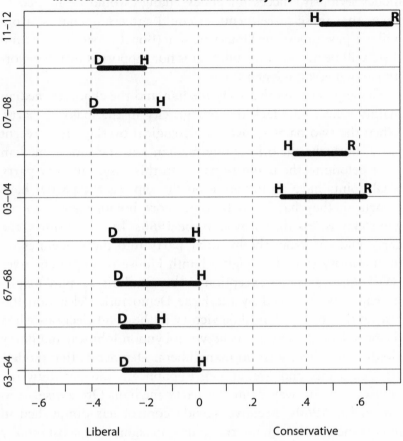

Figure 4.1. The position of chamber and majority party medians for several congressional terms, 1960s and 2000s. The length of the interval indicates the extent to which "negative agenda control" can block policy change. H shows the House median, D or R the majority party median.

The gap between the two medians is 0.19. When the gap is large, negative agenda control can be important.

Figure 4.1 raises two important points. The first is that the gaps between the medians can be substantial. For the 2009–10 term, Rick Boucher (D-VA) is the estimated House median;[16] John Yarmuth (KY) and Jim Langevin (RI) tied for the median House Democrat. So if we take the negative agenda control model seriously, successful policy change would be limited to issues that these three members could agree on. That is, a bill will not pass unless the House median (Boucher) supports it, and there will be no vote on a bill that is not supported by the majority party median member.

The gap between the party median and the chamber median mainly reflects the lack of homogeneity in the majority party. When the two parties have no ideological overlap, as in recent years, both the majority party median and the House median must belong to the majority party. In this case, minority party ideal points have no influence on the gap. As the parties have polarized, they have also become more homogeneous, so the gap today is less than it was in the 1960s. In earlier times, the gap could run from the majority party into the moderates on the minority side. The Eighty-Ninth House of Representatives (1965–66) was a rare exception to this regularity. A pure majority gap was produced by the large Democratic delegation following that party's landslide victory in the 1964 elections when the presidential contest was between Lyndon Johnson and Barry Goldwater. There were so many liberal Democrats that moderate Democrats and overlapping Republicans did not draw the House median away from the party median. Otherwise, relative to the 1960s, negative agenda control has diminished in importance. Although internal party divisions may substantially inhibit policy change in general and financial reform in particular, the effects are not as large as those caused by other features of our legislative institutions.

The Filibuster

Perhaps the largest deviation from the majoritarian ideal is the institution of cloture in the Senate. Ostensibly to protect its tradition of unfettered and unlimited debate, the Senate requires the support of three-fifths of the duly chosen and sworn senators (60 senators if all 100 members are sworn in) for a *cloture resolution* before debate can be terminated and roll call votes taken on the measure in question. Because opponents of legislation always have the option to keep talking until cloture is successfully invoked, 60 votes has become the de facto threshold for passing legislation through the Senate.[17] Rather than using majority rule, as in the House, the Senate uses supermajority rule that requires 60, instead of 51, of the 100 members to pass legislation.

To assess the importance of cloture rules for legislative responsiveness,[18] we again assume that the ideal points of senators can be arrayed from left to right. Given the cloture rules, we can characterize what a successful coalition must look like. Because 60 votes are required for passage, the senator with the 60th most liberal ideal point must support cloture. Let's call her Senator 60. Suppose the alternative for consideration was too liberal for Senator 60. Then it would also be too liberal for the 40 senators with ideal points to her right. These 40 senators and Senator 60 would vote against cloture and the bill would fail.[19] In a world of liberal-conservative voting Senator 60 is *pivotal* for policy change. If a policy is too liberal for this senator, it is too liberal for 40 more conservative senators and no change occurs. But if the policy appeals to the senator, she can push through the policy by voting with the 59 senators who are more liberal. In this sense, Senator 60 is pivotal. Just knowing the vote of this senator allows us to know if a new policy that is more liberal than the status quo will pass. Senator 41 (the 41st most liberal) is similarly pivotal. If the bill is too conservative for him, it is also too conservative for the 40 senators to his left and cloture cannot be obtained. For this reason, we refer to Senators 41 and 60 as the *filibuster pivots.*

Because the consent of both pivots is necessary for cloture— the new bill can be neither too liberal for Senator 60 nor too conservative for Senator 41— it is easy to see that no bill can be passed that would alter a status quo located between the pivots. Imagine that before the financial crisis, both Senators 41 and 60 supported no regulation of derivatives. If after the crisis, Senator 41 came to favor more regulation but Senator 60 was opposed, Senator 60 could use the cloture requirement to block any change. The distance between Senator 41 and Senator 60's ideal point is a rough gauge of the Senate's propensity to stalemate due to the cloture rule.

The Presidential Veto

The difficulties of policy change and reform do not end on Capitol Hill. Bills that survive the legislative process face the presidential veto. Certainly, presidents can from time to time use the bully pulpit to force bills through the roadblocks posed by partisan agenda control and filibusters. But for the most part, the president's *formal* legislative powers are negative.[20] The veto is a tool for blocking change rather than propagating it. A successful bill requires a presidential signature or a two-thirds vote on an override motion. Using logic exactly similar to that for the filibuster, Senator 34 becomes pivotal on the override motion for a leftist president's veto and Senator 67 becomes pivotal for a rightist veto. But because the override motion must carry both chambers, Representatives 146 and 290 are similarly empowered in the House. The more extreme of the pivotal representative and the pivotal senator on the president's side of the ideological spectrum is known as the *veto pivot*. If the veto pivot votes to sustain a presidential veto, the status quo cannot be changed. Because adding new pivotal actors always makes changing the status quo more difficult, the propensity for gridlock expands.[21]

The president has more power if Congress adjourns within ten days (excluding Sundays) of passing a law. In that case, the president can pocket veto a bill. The pocket veto is not subject to override. President Clinton pocket vetoed the bankruptcy bill, favorable to credit card issuers and unfavorable to debtors, in 2000. President Reagan, in 1981, pocket vetoed a bill amending the 1978 Bankruptcy Act.[22]

Combining the effects of the filibuster and the veto pivots, we can compute the *gridlock interval*. This interval is the policy gap between the leftmost pivot and the rightmost pivot. One or the other of these senators could block the change of any status quo in this interval by failing to vote to override the veto of the president. Therefore, the longer this interval the more likely that policy change can be blocked.[23]

Although we do not focus on the response to the crisis until part 2 of the book, it is helpful to illustrate these concepts on the 111th Senate, which was responsible for addressing the recent financial crisis. When Arlen Specter switched parties on April 28, 2009, and moved his position to the left, the gridlock interval was the policy spectrum between a veto pivot on the left and a filibuster pivot on the right. The veto pivot on the left was California Senator Dianne Feinstein, located at −.38, and the filibuster pivot was Nebraska Senator Ben Nelson at −.02. The gridlock interval therefore ranged from −.38 to −.02. After Scott Brown was elected in January of 2010, Olympia Snowe became the right pivot and the gridlock interval expanded up to her ideal point of .04.[24] After Brown was seated, the set of possible policy changes became those that Feinstein and Snowe could agree upon.

The first two years of President Barack Obama's administration followed eight years of George W. Bush, with the first six of those years having a Republican-controlled Congress. The status quo on financial policy was likely to be either in the gridlock interval or to the right of the interval. The only policies that could be changed would be those to the right of the interval. The new policies could be to the left of Ben Nelson or Scott Brown, but they would have to be moderate changes that the filibuster pivot preferred to the status quo. Dianne Feinstein's pivot position would be irrelevant. But, let's say the Republicans were to gain complete control of Congress in 2012. In this case, the veto pivot, perhaps still Feinstein, could be relevant. Obama could veto any attempts to repeal his legislative achievements and be sustained by Feinstein and the thirty-three senators to her left. The sustained veto would keep policy in the gridlock interval.

The Senate does have procedures that can be used to circumvent the supermajority requirement. The most important of these is the budgetary reconciliation process. Under these procedures, legislative debate can be limited so that measures cannot be filibustered. But there are important practical and political obstacles to using this mechanism. First, it can be used only on budgetary matters—measures that change spending or revenue. It cannot be directly applied to regulatory matters. The so-called Byrd Rule places additional, important, limits. Reconciliation can be used only on measures that change spending or revenue within the window (usually ten years) of the most recently passed budget resolution. This is why Bush's 2001 tax cuts, which were passed using reconciliation, were originally set to expire at the end of 2010. Finally, the internal politics of the majority party makes the reconciliation process controversial. By instituting majority rule, the majority party can move policy toward the median of the majority party and away from the party's moderate members. Thus, relative to the situation with supermajority cloture, reconciliation hurts party moderates.[25] Because the Democrats are more ideologically heterogeneous than the Republicans, they generally find it more difficult to use reconciliation, although they successfully employed it in the passage of the Patient Protection and Affordable Care Act (aka Obamacare) in 2010.

Figure 4.2 illustrates the location and length of the gridlock interval for a selected set of congressional terms going back to the 1960s. First, note that the gridlock intervals are much larger than the intervals due to negative agenda control.

Second, figure 4.2 shows that the gridlock interval shrank a fair bit following the 2008 elections, when the Democrats reached fifty-nine seats in the Senate. Without this shrinking, as we detail in part 2, it is unlikely that there would have been a credit card bill, the Dodd-Frank Wall Street Reform and Consumer Protection Act, a stimulus package, or a health care bill. The many concessions in the legislation passed in 2009 and 2010 reflect the fact that the interval was nonetheless fairly large by historical standards. It was larger than it was in the 1980s and slightly larger than when Clinton took over in 1993. It is about the same width as it was in the 1960s despite the rules for cloture

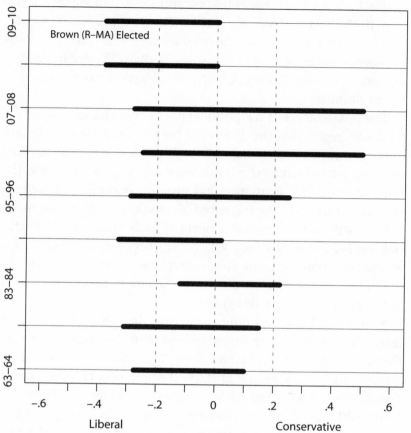

**Gridlock Interval between Veto and Filibuster Pivots
1960s to 2000s**

Figure 4.2. The gridlock interval in selected congressional terms. The interval, shown as the thick line, is the gap between the pivots. Gridlock increases as the line gets longer.

having been made less onerous. Until 1975, cloture required support of two-thirds of all senators present and voting. If all senators voted, Senators 34 and 67 were the pivots leading to larger gridlock intervals. Even then, the gridlock intervals for the 1960s were considerably smaller than those from the earlier part of the 2000s. Polarization has increased gridlock.

The change in the cloture rule in 1975 did compensate some-what for the increase in polarization. But another aspect of the filibuster both reflects the effect of polarization and amplifies gridlock. With the (important) exception of civil rights legislation, the filibuster was rarely used as a tactic for defeating legislation before the 1970s.[26] So the gridlock intervals from the 1960s are somewhat exaggerated measures of the difficulty in passing legislation during that era. Clearly the situation has worsened in recent decades.

The polarization of the political parties we discussed in chapter 2 has meant that the difference between the pivots (who are almost always members of different parties) has grown. This difference has increased relevance as the propensity to use the filibuster to defeat legislation has grown.[27] Certainly these two factors are related. The increased ideological polarization made it more difficult to sustain a norm of only using the filibuster only on big national issues. Of course, as polarization increases and policy consensus vanishes, everything becomes big stuff. As the filibuster norm broke down, the Senate became a more solidly supermajoritarian institution.

When the big-issues-only norm was in force, the majority leadership in the Senate forced filibusters to be carried out, and the Senate would be tied up for days. When Carter Glass's banking bill reached the Senate at the end of Herbert Hoover's presidency, Huey Long (D-LA) led a ten-day filibuster.[28] Now the threat of lengthy filibusters on almost everything has generated a de facto requirement for supermajority rule in which filibusters are never carried out.

Polarization of preferences makes it more likely that there will be a filibuster by senators who prefer the status quo to a proposal by the president. This hurdle has been daunting to the Obama administration, even before the 2010 midterm "shellacking." In the Great Recession, Obama found policy change far more difficult than did Franklin Delano Roosevelt in the Great Depression.[29] Polarization was falling when Roosevelt took office; he obtained a Democratic majority larger than the filibuster hurdle only in the midterm elections of 1934. But the lower level of polarization helped passage of financial regulatory legislation. Roosevelt's first two years saw the passage of

- the Emergency Banking Act
- the joint resolution nullifying gold clauses in bond contracts[30]
- the Glass-Steagall Act, which separated commercial and investment banking and which, at the insistence of Representative Henry B. Steagall, created deposit insurance
- the Securities Act of 1933
- the Securities Exchange Act of 1934, which created the Securities and Exchange Commission

The Roosevelt years re-created the financial sector in America. In contrast, we argue in chapter 7, the first three Obama years resulted in small tweaks to derivatives trading rules, commercial banking, and the way large financial bankruptcies are handled.

Strategic Disagreement

The gist of the framework we have outlined is that ideological differences can produce gridlock when there are no policy alternatives that pivotal actors prefer to the status quo. But another mechanism that transforms polarization into legislative paralysis is *strategic disagreement*, which describes a situation in which a president, party, or other political actor refuses compromise with the other side in an attempt to gain an electoral advantage by transferring the blame for the stalemate to the other side. Classical instances include attempts to bring up controversial legislation near an election in the hopes that a president will cast an unpopular veto. Congressional Democrats did this with the Family and Medical Leave Act in 1992, and Republicans did it with the Partial-Birth Abortion Ban bill before the 2000 election. Such electoral grandstanding not only lowers legislative capacity by diverting resources into an unproductive endeavor but also makes both sides less willing to engage in the compromises required by successful legislation.[31]

An example closer to our focus on financial regulation is President Clinton's veto of the Private Securities Litigation Reform Act in 1995. This bill, originally part of the Republican "Contract with America," was designed to end "frivolous" securities litigation. The bill passed both chambers with large bipartisan majorities, but the Republican-dominated conference committee made several changes that further protected defendants against claims by investors. These changes provoked Clinton's veto.[32] The veto gave Republicans an opportunity to accuse President Clinton of being captured by the trial lawyers. Moreover, the veto helped the Republicans drive a wedge between the president and his supporters in the high-tech sector who strongly backed the bill. Congressman Bill Paxson (R-NY) attacked the president on the House floor, saying, "The President's decision to veto this legislation, I believe, is a serious blow to economic opportunity, job creation and entrepreneurship in our Nation. The goal of this bipartisan legislation is to provide some protection from frivolous securities lawsuits filed against businesses, often small cutting-edge technology companies. . . . Unfortunately, this pro-growth reform legislation fell victim to some of the Nation's most powerful special interests. A win for these special interests is unfortunately a loss for the American economy."[33] Because the veto was ultimately overridden, the Republicans won on both the policy and the politics.

There are several reasons polarization exacerbates the incentives to engage in this type of "blame-game" politics. As the parties have become more extreme relative to voters, making the other side appear to be the more extreme party becomes more valuable. Grandstanding has become ubiquitous in debates about responses to the financial crisis. Republicans tried to depict Democratic proposals as leading the country down the Road to Serfdom—or worse, European-style socialism. Meanwhile,

Democrats insist that Republicans are simply water carriers for the plutocrats.

Exacerbating these incentives further is the contemporary media environment of politics. Especially since the Watergate Scandal and the Vietnam War, the media covers policy making much as it would a heavyweight boxing match, scoring the winner and loser round by round. During the period that congressional polarization has increased, the media have undergone substantial change. Television news has moved from the old network triopoly of ABC, CBS, and NBC to the entry of a host of news channels—especially Fox News on the right and MSNBC on the left. Radio has also polarized, most notably with Rush Limbaugh. More recently, the entrants, older broadcast media, and especially print media have all suffered from a loss of advertising revenue as Google and other Internet operations have surged. Sensationalism has perhaps been a matter of survival. With the media noting every punch and counterpunch, both sides are loath to make any compromises for fear of having it scored as a losing round. The result is policy stagnation.[34]

The Courts

The courts also generate hurdles for financial regulation. Although the role of judges is certainly quite different from that of legislators and presidents, ideology and even partisanship loom large in judicial decision making.[35] Consequently, judges may well strike down legislation and regulations on policy, rather than legal, grounds.

Ideological currents in the judiciary complicate attempts to regulate financial markets. The most important is the judicial corollary to free market conservatism. Conservative judges steeped in the Federalist Society and the law and economics movement have become increasingly supportive of expansive notions of property and contract rights.[36] Because financial regulation invariably involves restrictions on how financial assets may be used and what sorts of contracts can be issued and enforced, fundamentalist free market conservative views of the sanctity of property and contracts are incompatible with any serious regulation of the financial sector. Moreover, as we argue later in the book, the abrogation of certain debt contracts can be an important and efficient response to financial crises.

A second impediment is commitment of certain jurists to federalism. Many banks and insurers that operate under state charters are under the supervision of state regulators. Ideological commitments to federalism have proven to complicate efforts to bring such institutions under federal supervision. Lax state regulation contributed to the savings and loan crisis of the 1980s.[37] But, from the viewpoint of the financial sector, state's rights can go either way. When the state regulators are laxer, as in bank charters, the financial sector—or part of it—will support federalism. But if the state regulators are tough, the financial sector will push for federal regulation. Wall Street was delighted with the downfall of Eliot Spitzer, who used New York's Martin Act to pursue Wall Street practices that went unchallenged by the Bush administration.

But unlike institutions such as the veto and filibuster, the court is not exclusively an agent of gridlock. Court decisions triggered important financial deregulation. Wall Street was delighted when the Supreme Court in *Marquette National Bank of Minneapolis v. First of Omaha Service Corp.* ruled that nationally chartered banks could issue credit cards that would be exempt from the usury law of the state where the cardholder resided.[38] Citibank persuaded South Dakota to repeal its usury law, then moved its credit card operations there. Of course, Congress could in principle pass legislation that would reverse the court's decision. The court, however, is able to take advantage of gridlock in Congress.[39]

Ideology may also work differently in the courts and in Congress. Occasionally, judicial conservatives do reach conclusions that do not support the financial sector. Recently, Wall Street was surprised and annoyed when Justice Antonin Scalia turned a liberal minority on the Supreme Court into a majority in the *Cuomo v. Clearing House* case,[40] which reinforced state regulatory powers with regard to predatory lending.

The Effects of Gridlock

The most direct effect of gridlock is that it precludes legislative adjustments to policies that are ineffectual and outdated. This problem was particularly acute in the financial domain. Beginning in the 1970s, all sorts of financial products and services emerged that were never contemplated by the New Deal's regulatory framework. In 1990, less than 5 percent of mortgage debt was held in private-label mortgage-backed securities. By 2004, the share had soared to nearly 25 percent.[41] In 1996, less than $40 billion in nonprime residential mortgage–backed securities were issued; by 2005, that market had grown to more than $800 billion.[42] Similarly, commercial mortgage–backed securities and nonmortgage asset–backed securities rose at a far faster rate in this period than did traditional corporate debt. The total assets of unregulated broker-dealer banks rose from a little over 5 percent of those of regulated, traditional banks in 1990 to 30 percent in 2007.[43]

Agencies could not fit these innovations neatly under their regulatory umbrellas or were simply blocked, as when Clinton administration officials and Federal Reserve chairman Alan Greenspan overruled Commodity Futures Trading Commission head Brooksley Born. The Commodity Futures Modernization Act of 2000 ruled out the regulation of derivatives. As the new century started, the status quo for these products was close to laissez-faire. There was no midcourse correction of the casinos of the lawless Wild West of twenty-first-century financial markets. Even if some in Washington saw warning signals in the market, gridlock posed a formidable hurdle to action. Consequently, gridlock greatly benefited the financial sector, as acknowledged by this chapter's epigraph. And maintaining it was relatively straightforward: a special interest group need find only one pivot agent, the legislative, executive, or judicial branch, to block change.

The pop in which Enron, WorldCom, Adelphia, Global Crossing, and other firms went bankrupt triggered a policy response that would deal with accounting scandals and scandals in misleading reports by analysts. But another problem emerged: many employees lost heavily in the bankruptcies because their 401(k) funds were concentrated in the stock of the bankrupt firms. One reform on the table involved restricting the ability of a 401(k) plan to invest in and hold stock of the firm whose employees are covered by the plan. The Employee Retirement Income Security Act (ERISA) of 1974 contained strict rules on such holdings for traditional defined-benefit and some (but not all) defined-contribution plans. These rules came about as part of the overall fiduciary responsibility requirements of ERISA, which include a "diversification" requirement. ERISA itself came about as a result of the Studebaker bankruptcy, in which workers at the fourth-largest domestic automaker lost their defined benefit pensions when the company entered bankruptcy.[44]

So how did American companies create pension plans that had the effect of turning Enron into a rerun of Studebaker? Companies moved away from traditional defined benefit plans. ERISA contained a provision that allowed a firm with a "profit sharing" plan to invest the plan's money in the firm's own stock. The 401(k) plans were an innovative financial product developed when benefits consultant Ted Benna recognized a loophole in Section 401(k) of the Internal Revenue Code added by the 1978 Tax Reform Act. Benna's original plans were quite simple, but foreshadowing the innovations in derivatives, investment aspects of these plans became increasingly complex over time.[45] Many Americans working at Enron and other firms took a hit to their retirement plans with the accounting scandals bankruptcies (as did Lehman Brothers employees in 2008).

Politics, however, changed between 1974 and 2001. Polarization occurred. The new president, George W. Bush, was more conservative than Richard Nixon; the House was controlled by the Republican Party. Free market conservatism was triumphant. No surprise, a reform of 401(k) plans did not appear in the Sarbanes-Oxley Act, undoubtedly not as a matter of public pressure but of special interest pressure. For 401(k)s, Henry Paulson's explanation was perversely incorrect. Innovation did not just precede regulation; regulation never came. Similarly, as we explain in chapter 5, the new exotica that ruled financial markets in the bubble went unregulated. And in chapter 7, we will see that Dodd-Frank is at best weak regulation, in large part as a result of concessions to pivotal legislators such as Massachusetts senator Scott Brown.

The other consequence of polarization-induced gridlock is that policy making is channeled away from Congress toward executive and regulatory arenas. As we discuss below, these arenas were generally much more favorably inclined toward deregulation than was Congress. Consequently, deregulation occurred without congressional involvement or sanction. Such was the story behind the evisceration of Glass-Steagall preceding its eventual repeal. Executive and regulatory discretion in the 1980s permitted:

- national banks to sell mutual funds and investment trusts
- national banks to sell securities and operate discount brokerages through a subsidiary (notably, the Mellon-Dreyfus merger)
- member banks to affiliate with underwriters of commercial paper, municipal revenue bonds, and securities backed by mortgages and consumer debts, as long as the affiliate did not get more than 10 percent of its revenue from underwriting
- subsidiaries to provide brokerage and investment advice to institutional customers
- affiliates to offer retail discount brokerage service
- securities firms to offer money market checking
- all firms to engage in underwriting overseas without restrictions

The executive agencies and regulatory agencies made these changes. Because of gridlock, the changes might never have been passed by Congress. But gridlock also meant that the deregulators need not fear being overruled by Congress.

By the time Glass-Steagall was officially repealed by Congress, market participants and regulators knew full well that its terms would not be enforced. Most notably, the Citicorp-Traveler's merger was approved with the tacit understanding that required asset sales would never take place because Glass-Steagall would be repealed.[46]

Regulatory Agencies

Although the policy-making roles of legislators and presidents are important, the nuts and bolts of policy are delegated to regulators. Often these delegations are justified, in that regulators have better information than legislators.[47] But Congress has incentives to delegate that are not a simple matter of a regulator being better informed than a politician. If policies go wrong, the politicians can blame the regulator.[48] Regulatory discretion also gives politicians the ability to appear as ombudsmen who will fix things for constituents.[49] Charles Keating's five senators are a notorious example of attempted intervention by "fixers." So not only is policy delegated, it tends to be overdelegated; the ultimate job of supervising the financial sector and preventing financial crises falls to regulators. Indeed, much of the political discussion following the financial crisis centered on how to provide regulators with enough tools to prevent the next crisis. Unfortunately, the problem with the financial regulatory regime may not be a simple lack of tools.

In an ideal setting, regulators would have the resources and expertise to closely monitor developments in the regulated sector and the incentive to promulgate and implement policies that are in the public interest. The conditions for such regulatory performance are hard to meet in any domain, but the problem of regulatory capacity is particularly acute in the case of financial regulation.

The most obvious difficulty stems from the complexity of modern finance. Armies of rocket scientists are employed to develop and implement increasingly complicated financial products and trading strategies. Many of the products are not well understood by Wall Street executives, much less by outside regulators.

This problem might be mitigated somewhat if the regulatory agencies could easily draw from the same talent pool as Wall Street. But the salary differentials make competitive hiring difficult. The highest-paid financial regulators (the president of the New York Fed and the chairman of the Fed) make a fraction of a middling trader's annual bonus. Even where regulatory agencies can hire people with the background to understand the intricacies of modern finance, such individuals are usually coming through the revolving door from Wall Street. For example, the *New York Times* reported that many former top officials of the Resolution Trust Corporation created after the savings and loan crisis engaged in lucrative consulting arrangements with firms seeking Troubled Asset Relief Program funding.[50] The revolving doors undermine the autonomy of regulatory agencies from the industry they are supposed to regulate. Even if regulators are not motivated by a future Wall Street payout, they may still be inclined to share Wall Street's worldview.[51] Moreover, outside expertise from academic financial economists may also not be immune from conflicts of interest.[52]

The most direct implication of low regulatory capacity is that it undermines the informational rationale for delegation of discretionary authority to regulators, and it will be hard to sustain a regulatory regime that depends too heavily on the delegation to regulators. This concern speaks directly to the debate about whether a council of "superregulators" can monitor the financial sector for emerging systemic risks and react effectively with new capital requirements, leverage limits, or conversion of contingent bonds to equity stakes. Such a system requires that regulators have very high levels of information and expertise as well as the incentive to act in ways that may be adverse to the financial services industry. The recognition of low capacity argues against sophisticated discretionary regulatory management of the industry and in favor of blunter approaches such as banning the most systematically dangerous products and practices or capping the size of financial institutions.

Beyond the technical problems that plague low-capacity agencies, there is important political feedback to consider. Low capacity makes it harder to hold agencies accountable to congressional and presidential oversight because it is harder to distinguish between bad policies and poor implementation. This problem may cause elected leaders to be reluctant to endow agencies they cannot control with substantial discretionary power.

Reformers often strive to mitigate these problems by strengthening the informational capabilities of regulators or by beefing up accountability mechanisms (such as congressional and judicial oversight). But there are strong reasons to believe that these reforms by themselves will not significantly improve financial regulation. Better information and policy analysis can go only so far if agencies lack the resources to act effectively on that information and analysis. But the lack of expertise and information also reduces the value of increasing regulatory capacity. Why increase the ability of an agency to implement uninformed policies? Thus, expertise and capacity are complements; this creates a bureaucratic *reform trap* in which reforming capacity is eschewed because of low expertise and enhancing expertise is undermined by low capacity.[53]

A reform trap also exists with respect to improving oversight and accountability. Investing in greater oversight of agency decisions is most valuable when the links between agency policy and outcomes are the most transparent, because it is then easier to detect policies of which the Congress does not approve. Because low capacity distorts the relationship between policies and outcomes, more oversight is not very helpful. Conversely, when oversight mechanisms are poor, raising capacity is not very valuable, because the political overseers do not benefit from the increased transparency of the policy-outcome link.

The structural problems that regulatory agencies face make them prone to *capture*. That is, policy making often becomes dominated by the interests that an agency was created to regulate. As the agency increasingly comes to depend on the industry for information, expertise, and human capital, the agency becomes hard pressed to maintain its autonomy. Ultimately, its decisions become biased toward the interests of the dominant industry. Moreover, these biases are reinforced as the dominant firms in an industry adapt to the regulatory regime and become its primary defender.[54] Such cozy relationships have been all too apparent in the regulatory decisions leading up to the crisis of 2008.

Conclusion

In this chapter, we outlined the roadblocks to financial regulation and reform that are thrown up by pivotal politics and strategic disagreement in the interactions within and between the executive and legislative branches of the government. These roadblocks are exacerbated by the increase in political polarization that has been marked by increasing acceptance of free market conservatism within the executive and legislative branches. Free market ideology has also become more prevalent in the courts. Regulatory agencies lack the capacity to form a strong counterweight.

Of course, many countries with different configurations of political institutions also suffered a housing bubble followed by a financial collapse. Our focus on American institutions is not intended to suggest that institutional arrangements in other countries are necessarily better at regulating the financial sector or preventing crises. Power can be diffused and fragmented in many different ways. In this regard, the United States may be relatively healthy. Otherwise, the nation would have been less likely to become the economic superpower it is. But we do argue that in general, the institutional impediments to financial regulation are relatively more severe in the United States than elsewhere. In any event, dysfunction in the United States has far more impact than that elsewhere. Arguably, Iceland's financial sector was engaged in far more outrageous behavior than anything that has occurred on Wall Street. But Iceland could never export its problems as a worldwide recession. Many countries experienced substantial stress as the result of investments in American financial innovations based on U.S. housing markets. Others were stressed simply because of the fall in global demand for their products. The worldwide recession was the consequence of Wall Street's presence as the eight-hundred-pound gorilla. We quite deliberately restrict this book to politics and finance in the United States.

In chapter 5, we show how ideology, interests, and institutions combined to produce the bubble that popped in 2008.

CHAPTER 5
The Political Bubble
of the Crisis of 2008

Rising home values have added more than $2.5 trillion to the assets of the American family since the start of 2001. The rate of homeownership in America now stands at a record high of 68.4 percent. Yet there is room for improvement. The rate of homeownership amongst minorities is below 50 percent. And that's not right, and this country needs to do something about it.

> —President George W. Bush, remarks
> at the signing of the American Dream
> Downpayment Act of 2003

I'm delighted to be here, along with Frank Raines, my OMB Director, who used to spend some time with some of you, and Gene Sperling and others on our staff. . . . Now, we are seeing a remarkable increase in the circle of opportunity. In addition to reaching the highest level of homeownership in history, millions of Americans have been able to refinance their mortgages, which has amounted to billions and billions of dollars in tax cuts for families, putting more money in their pockets, freeing up more for investment and savings. Access to capital has spread to minorities who for years have been locked out of the economy. . . . We do see increasing homeownership rates for minorities now and I hope it will continue. Our capital markets are the strongest in the world, and clearly, they have played a major role in helping us to do well in this new economy.

> —President Bill Clinton, remarks to
> the Mortgage Bankers Association
> of America, 1998

THE *THREE I's*— IDEOLOGY, INSTITUTIONS, AND INTERESTS— combined to inflate the bubble that led to the financial crisis of 2008 and the ensuing Great Recession. The caldron was stirred for forty years, going back to the privatization of Fannie Mae in 1968. The last major ingredient was the 2000 addition of the Commodity Futures Modernization Act. We now recount how the *Three I's* resulted in errors of commission in the form of deregulation and poor regulatory structures, and errors of omission in the form of failure to regulate new products and to enforce existing law. We emphasize that the bubble grew because egalitarian ideology, the "ownership society" side of free market conservatism, converged with crony capitalism to produce a rare but dysfunctional instance of bipartisan policy consensus.

When the giant bubble emerged at the turn of the new century, the main stirrers were the *Time* magazine–designated "Committee to Save the World" of Alan Greenspan, Robert Rubin, and Larry Summers. The committee played the role of Macbeth's witches: they turned boundless prosperity and McMansions into worthless eyes of newt and toes of frog. The multi-trillion-dollar creation of wealth cherished by President Bush quickly evaporated. Homeownership rates in the United States were no higher in early 2012 than in 1996, and for blacks they were slightly lower. Hispanics fared somewhat better, but their homeownership rate nonetheless fell back to its 2001 level. In broad categories of American society, no group benefited from the policies of the Clinton and Bush years. (See figure 5.1.)

Another notion of the investor society was that Americans would prosper by investing in equities.[1] How would Americans have done by making buy-and-hold investments in the nation's largest insurance company, its largest commercial banks, its largest investment banks, or the two very large privatized government-sponsored enterprises (GSEs), Fannie Mae and Freddie Mac? These would have appeared to be safe investments. After all, their directors and executives included some of the nation's most esteemed public servants, such as Robert Rubin, Richard Holbrooke, Franklin Raines, and Martin Feldstein. Of course,

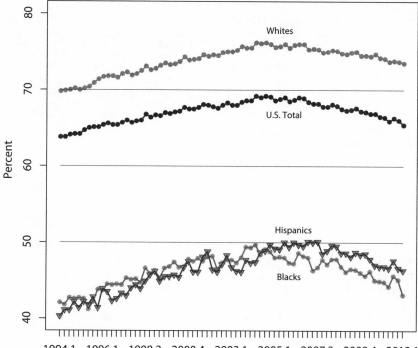

Figure 5.1. Homeownership rates by race and ethnicity, 1994–2012. Home-ownership rates have continued to decline beyond the end of the 2007–9 recession. Homeownership rates in 2012 are lower for all groups than the rates in 2002. African American homeownership rates have had a particularly steep decline and have fallen back to the level of the mid-1990s.
Source: Current Population Survey/Housing Vacancy Survey, Series H-111, Bureau of the Census.

except for some of the 1 percent, Americans cannot participate in private equity and hedge funds. So the big financial firms would appear to be the way into the financial sector for Joe the Plumber.

In table 5.1, we benchmark these investments in two ways. First, we compare returns between the end of 1999—just after Goldman Sachs, the last of the major investment banks to go public did so—and the end of 2011. Second, to give investors a longer-run perspective, we moved the start date back a decade to the end of 1989. We measured returns in two ways. First,

Table 5.1.
Returns for selected financial firms

Firm	12/31/1989–12/31/2011		12/31/1999–12/31/2011	
	% Increase Common Stock Price	% Increase, Stock Plus Dividends	% Increase Common Stock Price	% Increase, Stock Plus Dividends
Amer. International Group (AIG)	−84	−7	−98	−92
Bank of America Corp. (BAC)	−52	128	−78	−17
Citigroup Inc. (C)	19	604	−93	−64
JPMorgan Chase & Co (JPM)	234	440	−36	−10
Wells Fargo & Co (WFC)	879	1256	36	80
Wachovia Corp. (WB)	−46**	187**	−83**	−40**
WAMU (WM)	−100**	315**	−100**	−30**
Goldman Sachs Group (GS)	n.a.	n.a.	−4	7
Morgan Stanley (MS)	−44*	265*	−74	−56
S&P 500	256	n.a.	−14	n.a.

Notes: *Morgan Stanley 12/31/1993–12/31/2011; **WAMU, Wachovia until 2008.

we computed the total percentage increase in the price of common stock. This, of course, can be negative. Negative returns are bounded by −100, which corresponds to a total wipeout, as was the case for Washington Mutual (WAMU). Second, we added in dividends. We assumed no reinvestment of dividends. If, of course, the investor had reinvested the dividends in the stock, the returns would have been much worse for most of the firms. The table accounts for all stock splits, including the ten-for-one reverse split of Citigroup, necessary to keep that firm from becoming a penny stock.

If the investments were made at the end of the 1990s, they would have been a disaster, with the exception of Wells Fargo. All the other firms had negative stock returns, typically far more negative than the S&P 500 index, shown for comparison. Even with dividends, the returns are negative, with the exception of

Wells and Goldman Sachs. The latter's return of 7 percent was a paltry .75 percent on an annualized basis. So where did the money go? Goldman Sachs's partners made money in the initial public offering. The partners and other employees also had substantial income and bonuses over the period. So the "investor society" member would have provided financing to the 1 percent member inside Goldman Sachs. Morgan Stanley was worse than Goldman. Two other major investment banks, Bear Stearns and Lehman Brothers, and the two GSEs, not shown in the table, were, of course, much worse.

Over the longer period, from 1989, things look better, largely because of the better performance in the 1990s. Even over this extended period, the firms lagged the S&P 500, again with the exception of Wells Fargo. Dividends, with the exception of those of American International Group (AIG), overcame the fall in stock price to lead to positive total returns. But the returns were not huge. An annualized return of 9.28 percent is implied by the 640 percent total for Citigroup. For Bank of America, it was only 3.82 percent.

As the large financial firms grew since the 1990s, they generally performed poorly for the investor society. The firms have largely survived intact as organizations even if their equity holders have taken it on the chin. Why have they survived? Their executives and board members surely know the answer.

Thus, after the crash, long-term investors in the big financial firms were crushed. Homeownership regressed back to the level of the mid-1990s. Average Americans might have benefited in some other way if they were better able to consume goods other than housing. But this was not the case.

From 1972 to 1999, median household income (adjusted for inflation) grew steadily, with hiccups, as shown in figure 5.2. Income inequality increased dramatically in the last two decades of the twentieth century as the income of the top quintile grew much faster than the median. But income gains were generally widespread. From 1972 to 1999, median household income,

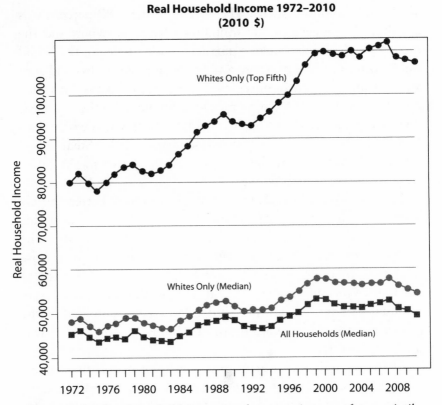

Real Household Income 1972–2010
(2010 $)

Whites Only (Top Fifth)

Whites Only (Median)

All Households (Median)

Real Household Income

40,000 50,000 60,000 70,000 80,000 90,000 100,000

1972 1976 1980 1984 1988 1992 1996 2000 2004 2008

Figure 5.2. Median household income and average income of top quintile, 1972 to 2010 (in 2010 dollars). Income never recovered to the level it reached at the end of the twentieth century under President Clinton. During the eight years of the Bush presidency (2001–8) it recovered somewhat but then fell sharply during the first two years of the Obama presidency.
Source: U.S. Census Bureau, Current Population Survey, Annual Social and Economic Supplements.

adjusted for inflation, increased from about $45,000 to $53,000. But the first decade of the new century was a lost one. By 2010, median income had not returned to the 1999 level and was below $50,000.

Just as incomes increased across the board until the new millennium, the stagnation and loss of the last decade has been broad. Even the core constituency of the Republican Party—upper-income whites[2]—suffered from the decade's experiment with unfettered financial capitalism. Incomes among top-quintile whites collapsed with the crisis and ensuing recession. Yet, as indicated by the results of the 2010 congressional elections, the losses did little to undermine the commitment of those voters to the Republican Party and free market conservatism.

The lethal concoction that destroyed the investor society and the broader standard of living had five components—all rooted in our *Three I's*. The first was deregulation that permitted innovative new financial instruments, such as exotic mortgage products, collateralized debt obligation tranches, and credit default swaps to emerge without meaningful regulation. The second was deregulation that permitted financial firms to engage in a riskier range of activities. The third was a reduction in the monitoring capacity of regulators, either through deliberate neglect, as reflected in the tenures of Alan Greenspan at the Federal Reserve and Harvey Pitt and Christopher Cox at the Securities and Exchange Commission (SEC), or as a result of the failure of staffing and budgets to expand at the same rate as the markets they were supposed to regulate. The fourth was the shifts in competition policy that allowed the creation of financial institutions that were too big (and too politically powerful) to fail. The fifth component was the privatization of government financing of mortgages through Fannie and Freddie, which created two additional too-big-to-fail institutions.

We can tell much of our story about the lethal concoction that devastated the economy from 2007 to 2009 by relating the history of a single bank account. In 1993, one of us moved to Princeton, New Jersey. Out of convenience he opened a checking account at the bank with a branch closest to his office, New Jersey National. Given the insurance of deposits and the lack of banks with national ATM networks, there was no need to shop carefully. In 1994, the Riegle-Neal Act initiated a wave of bank mergers. Subsequently, New Jersey National, locally based in Trenton, was acquired by CoreStates, based in Philadelphia. CoreStates was later acquired by First Union, which in turn was gobbled up by Wachovia in 2001. The account at tiny New

Jersey National became an account at the fourth largest commercial bank in the country.

Wachovia also acquired firms from outside of commercial banking, such as Prudential Securities. But its biggest trouble started in its mortgage business. Wachovia's acquisition of Golden West Financial exposed it to tremendous risks in the mortgage market, as Golden West was the innovator of the so-called pick-a-payment mortgage with a negative amortization option (through which the borrower could pay less than the interest owed, and the principal would increase).

Wachovia sought profits in many ways other than acquisitions. It facilitated check cashing in identity theft cases and money laundering by international drug cartels. It rigged bids for municipal bonds.[3] It engaged in illegal practices with telemarketers.[4] Of course, the top executives at Wachovia claimed that they bore no responsibility for these activities. The malfeasance was just the work of a few "rotten apples" or "reckless few" among thousands of hardworking and honest employees. The firm was slapped on the wrist with fines or settlements, and the federal government accommodated. But by growing as it did, moreover, Wachovia became too big to fail. As is typical of the ever-spinning revolving door, Paulson's undersecretary at the Treasury, Goldman Sachs alumnus Bob Steele, presided over the last six months of Wachovia's existence. Unlike the smaller bank Washington Mutual, whose equity holders lost everything, Wachovia's shareholders received $7 a share when Wachovia was acquired by Wells Fargo in 2008. The acquisition price was just a sop, as Wachovia had been selling for more than $37 at the beginning of the year and more than $56 a share in early 2007. Quite a haircut, but not WAMU's beheading.

The acquisition of Wachovia by Wells Fargo echoes the circumstances of the acquisition of National City by PNC that was discussed in the introduction. Part of what made Wachovia an attractive target for Wells Fargo was that the Internal Revenue Service, with Paulson's blessing, made an on-the-spot change in the taxation of inherited losses.[5] The account at tiny New Jersey National is now a Wells Fargo account.

Wachovia's fall and subsequent rescue might have been avoided either if firms like Golden West had not been allowed to issue the dubious adjustable-rate interest-only mortgages or if the acquisition of Golden West had been blocked by regulators. Perhaps if regulators had prevented the acquisition of First Union, Wachovia might have been small enough to fail. If there had been better monitoring of Wachovia, there might have been less identity theft and money laundering. At least, the firm should have paid a higher price for lacking the necessary internal controls. Wrist slaps only abet the culture that makes such incidents far too common. Ultimately Wachovia failed as the bubble popped and politics, not the market, determined that Wachovia was to be allocated to Wells Fargo and not to another suitor, Citigroup.

There was nothing special about Wachovia. The same chronology could be repeated for dozens of other financial firms. Just as Wachovia was crippled by Golden West, Bank of America was badly wounded by its acquisitions of Countrywide Financial and Merrill Lynch. When an industry becomes populated with Wachovias and Bank of Americas, the case for relying solely on market discipline and self-regulation unravels.

How did politics fuel Wachovia and other firms in the bubble?

Debate over the origins of the bubble and the financial crisis has quickly become, consistent with our findings in *Polarized America: The Dance of Ideology and Unequal Riches*, ideologically driven as much as based on fact. The findings of the Financial Crisis Inquiry Commission, created by Congress and the president to "examine the causes of the current financial and economic crisis," typify the ideological debate. The Democratic-appointed majority blamed the failure of *private sector* markets in mortgage origination, securitization, and swaps—that is, firms like Wachovia. The minority report by Republican appointees downplayed the role that deregulation played in the crisis, stressing instead global fiscal imbalances that lowered the cost of credit. In a separate dissent, Republican minority commission member Peter Wallison blamed the government-sponsored enterprises (GSEs) Fannie and Freddie, as well as liberal policies such as the Community Reinvestment Act.

Our own view is that there is certainly more than enough blame to go around, but that Wall Street should be nailed to the highest pole. However, to understand the bubble one does need to consider all the changes in government policy that affected the housing market. So we begin there.

The Housing Market's Off-Budget Subsidy

Roughly speaking, the government can support housing for its citizens in two ways. First, it can do so directly by building and then selling or leasing its own housing units. Second, it can do so by subsidizing the private sector. One way to subsidize housing would be direct transfers to individuals as we do for welfare, food stamps, social security, and unemployment insurance. These expenditures would be on budget. Congress would have to appropriate the funds. Another way would be to make off-budget subsidies both to individual home buyers and to firms involved in the construction, mortgage lending, and rental markets. From time to time, the U.S. government has used both mechanisms. But by and large policy has moved away from public housing toward private subsidies. Private subsidies have, in turn, largely been of the off-budget variety, given public aversion both to redistribution and to taxation. No doubt some of this shift reflects the major shortcomings of government-run housing projects. But the shift toward a subsidy-based system with an emphasis on ownership has important political underpinnings. Not only was the policy shift responsive to the economic *interests* of the housing sector but it was sustained by the marriage of egalitarian *ideology* and the "ownership society" offshoot of free market conservatism.[6]

The housing industry, which includes not only those directly involved in housing finance but also real estate agents and developers, has long been politically powerful. It has succeeded in obtaining huge direct and indirect support from the government. The largest housing subsidy is the income tax deductibility of home mortgage interest payments and property taxes. Demonstrating its political clout, the housing industry was able to preserve the home mortgage interest deduction in the Tax Reform Act of 1986 when the deductibility of all other consumer interest was eliminated.[7] Not surprisingly, this continued subsidy spawned new financial products such as home equity loans and lines of credit. The debt acquired from home equity loans was responsible for many homeowners "going underwater" (i.e., having mortgage debt that exceeded their home equity) when the bubble burst.

An important source of the housing industry's political power is that there is little transparency about the nature and magnitude of off-budget subsidies.[8] The power of the housing lobby is not limited to the federal level. For example, some state governments, notably those of Texas and Florida, further subsidize housing by exempting home equity from creditors in personal bankruptcies. In states that exempt large amounts of equity, the real estate lobby has fought hard against a national bankruptcy standard. Just as the mortgage interest tax subsidy does, the home equity bankruptcy exemption distorts the housing market by making homeownership relatively more attractive than other equity investments and renting.[9] The industry was also well served by the taxpayer revolt that occurred in many American states, starting with Proposition 13 in California in 1978, closely followed by Proposition 2½ in "Taxachusetts." These revolts resulted in limitations on property taxes. The subsequent shift from property taxes to sales taxes provided yet another subsidy for homeownership.

Other government policies also increased the demand for housing in the lead-up to the crisis. Monetary policies targeting low interest rates, per the Fed's response to the 2001–2 recession, reduced the cost of mortgages. The reduction in income and loan-to-value standards for qualifying for a mortgage increased the number and size of mortgages. But the most debated policy link to the crisis concerns the role played by the so-called government-sponsored enterprises Fannie Mae and Freddie Mac. These entities, which we discuss in more detail below, subsidized the housing market by purchasing certain qualifying mortgages from lenders. Lenders in turn used the proceeds of these sales to issue more mortgages, which lowered borrowing costs and stimulated housing demand. The subsidy embedded in Fannie and Freddie was enhanced by the ultimately correct perception that the government guaranteed their debt. This guarantee reduced their borrowing costs below those of other corporate borrowers.[10] So the mortgage industry, as symbolized by Countrywide Financial's CEO Angelo Mozilo's full-page color photograph in the 2003 Fannie Mae annual report, provided crucial political support for the GSEs.

In short, a variety of government policies favor housing. *Interests* fight for these policies.

Government housing policy also reflects *ideology*. One strand stems from the egalitarian ideologies typically associated with the political left. Egalitarians view adequate housing as an entitlement, like nutrition, schooling, and medical care. Of course, housing could be provided directly through publicly owned rental housing or on-budget rent subsidies. That was the initial federal response to housing problems. The first federal housing programs originated in the Great Depression when tax rates were relatively high, political polarization was low, and the belief in government effectiveness was very high. In the last thirty years, however, real federal on-budget housing expenditures have remained relatively constant in inflation-adjusted dollars despite large increases in the American population.[11] The lack of growth of the on-budget housing subsidies reflects both the decline in support for tax rates that would generate the required revenue and the association of many public housing projects with violence and drug use, as illustrated by the notorious Cabrini-Green project in Chicago.[12]

A second ideological strand, this one from the right, also fostered the shift in federal policy toward the support of homeownership.

Many conservatives believe that homeowners are better citizens than renters because they have a higher stake in their communities.[13] So advocates of an "ownership society" such as the late Jack Kemp (Bob Dole's vice presidential running mate in 1996 and a former secretary of Housing and Urban Development) argued that government should aggressively support homeownership and the privatization of public housing projects.

There is no logical reason for government housing subsidies to take the form they did. In principle, a switch from public rental housing to owner-occupied housing could have been accomplished transparently and on budget. For example, every citizen could be given a once-in-a-lifetime $50,000 down payment grant that, coupled with strict loan-to-value standards, would largely eliminate incentives for strategic default. But the aversion to direct redistribution left federal policy directed at off-budget policies that primarily supported homeownership through a loosely regulated mortgage market. As we will see, the decision to promote homeownership off budget helped foster the creation of the Byzantine sorts of financial products that opened the road to the crisis.

The Government-Sponsored Enterprises

The move to off-budget housing subsidies began in 1968 when Fannie Mae was fully privatized. The motivation was not a strong belief that a privately run Fannie would be more efficient. Rather it was an accounting trick perpetrated by the administration of president Lyndon Johnson. The privatization of Fannie removed its debt from the books of the federal government.[14]

Initially, Fannie was limited to the repurchase of government-insured Federal Housing Administration (FHA) mortgages. But by 1970 the government permitted Fannie to buy mortgages directly from private issuers. At the same time, Congress created Freddie Mac to compete with Fannie Mae.

The goal of better access to mortgage credit for minorities led to the Community Reinvestment Act (CRA) of 1977, passed under President Jimmy Carter. The act required institutions insured by the Federal Deposit Insurance Corporation (FDIC) to stop *redlining*, a banking practice that discriminated against loan applications from minority neighborhoods. But the CRA did not require either the GSEs or other financial institutions to make high-risk loans to minorities.

In the 1990s Congress began pushing the GSEs into financing low-income housing. The Housing and Community Development Act of 1992 passed under George H. W. Bush and was expanded during the Clinton administration. This act required the Housing and Urban Development secretary to establish goals for each of the GSEs for the purchase of mortgages for low- and moderate-income families. Title VIII of that act (known as the Federal Housing Enterprises Financial Safety and Soundness Act) encouraged a greater number of loans where only 5 percent down payments were required.[15] Again, we emphasize that this expansion was completely off the federal budget. Over time, the loan portfolios of Fannie and Freddie became increasingly risky. Numerous warnings were disregarded in part because the GSEs hid the risks by manipulating their accounting. The combination of implicit government guarantees and too-rosy accounting numbers drew large numbers of private investors to the GSEs. Fannie Mae's stock rose to more than $86 a share in 2000, before its accounting deceptions became public. Although the stock never fully recovered, its price was as high as $67 in 2007. But now that Fannie is in government receivership, its remaining private-sector stock trades over the counter for less than a quarter.

Many observers argue that Fannie and Freddie, for all their problems, took on less risk than did many non-GSE firms that were into mortgage origination and securitization.[16] But the privatization of Fannie and Freddie abetted the crisis in several ways. First, they were open to holdings by other financial companies. Citigroup held 6.3 percent of Fannie's common stock in 2006 and 2007.[17] SEC filings do not disclose whether this investment represented client holdings or a direct investment, but any direct investment would not have provided liquidity to Citigroup as both firms went down.

Second, even if Fannie bought only relatively good mortgages from Angelo Mozilo's Countrywide and others, the purchases provided resources for these firms to originate more loans that could then be foisted off on the private mortgage-backed securities (MBS) market.

Third, resources were also freed up for the private MBS market as the GSEs increasingly bought back their own MBS issues. The profits of the two GSEs originally came from the guarantee fees they charged on the MBSs that were privately held. But, as time progressed, the profits were largely generated by the spread between the interest on the repurchased MBSs and the low borrowing costs enjoyed from the government guarantee. As Dwight Jaffee pointed out in 2003, the strategy exposed Fannie and Freddie to interest rate risk.[18] The gamble contributed to the two firms' collapse and subsequent nationalization. Future taxpayer costs are to be determined.

Fourth, Fannie's lower borrowing costs, abetted by its implicit government guarantee, gave it a competitive advantage over private MBS issuers when it came to purchasing less risky mortgages. This competitive advantage did not extend to the riskier subprime mortgages that the GSEs were not allowed to buy, which in turn may have encouraged the private label securitizers to focus on that part of the market.[19]

In the good times, Fannie and Freddie were also preserved and protected by *institutions*, most likely fostered by future interests embedded by crony capitalism. Not surprisingly, Democrats were opposed to reform. But Newt Gingrich (R-GA), the Speaker of the House, and Michael Oxley (R-OH), the chair of House Financial Services, used their *institutional* power to block reform in Republican-controlled Congresses. Speaker Gingrich kiboshed a mid-1990s attempt to levy fees on the GSEs to pay for the costs of the savings and loan (S&L) bailout. As a result those costs were passed on to general taxpayers.[20] In 2002, House

Financial Services Subcommittee on Capital Markets chair Richard Baker (R-LA) introduced a reform bill. This legislation got nowhere, after it failed to gain Oxley's support.[21] In 2005, the House and Senate made attempts at reform, but no legislation reached the president's desk. In retirement, Oxley became a lobbyist for NASDAQ and the private sector's "self-regulator," the Financial Industry Regulatory Authority. Gingrich's 2012 Republican presidential nomination bid was damaged by the revelation that his Gingrich Group had previously received a $1.6 million fee from Freddie Mac.

Interests within the GSEs were also active in maintaining gridlock. Fannie, during the 1991–2004 reigns of James Johnson and Franklin Raines, was a money machine for career Democrats. Replacing Raines with Daniel Mudd did not result in a clean house. Mudd, two other Fannie executives, and three Freddie executives were charged with securities fraud by the SEC in December 2011.[22] Although the GSEs were most entrenched within the Democratic Party, they always sought bipartisan support by cultivating ties to important Republican policy makers.

Support of Fannie and Freddie extended beyond elected policy makers to the academic policy community. Three career Democrats, Nobel Prize Laureate Joseph Stiglitz and Peter and Jon Orszag, wrote a 2002 Fannie Mae report in which they claimed there was less than a 1 in 500,000 chance that Fannie could fail. The report was published twice, once with a foreword by FDIC chief Sheila Bair and again with a foreword by Fannie senior vice president Paula Christiansen. The two forewords were identical, word for word.[23] Fannie also blessed itself with a study by Glenn Hubbard, chair of the Council of Economic Advisors under George W. Bush and now dean of the Columbia Business School, and adviser to presidential candidate Mitt Romney.[24]

These reports need not have been disingenuous. Indeed, they were based on state-of-the art economic analysis. (On the other hand, the paper from Stiglitz and the Orszags was quickly criticized by UC–Berkeley Haas Business School professor Dwight Jaffee.[25]) Rather, our concern with these kinds of studies is that they ignore the political context. The blue-ribbon endorsements emboldened the GSEs to pursue their course more aggressively as they were inoculated further from political interference. The groupthink forewords only added to these political risks.

The semiprivate status of Fannie and Freddie has long been a source of political risk. When Fannie was privatized, free market conservatism and deregulation had not taken root—Barry Goldwater's brand of free market conservatism was soundly rejected at the polls in 1964. The privatization was just part of taking the housing subsidy off the books. But once the GSEs were created, gridlock rendered reforming them very difficult. Although the pop of the bubble forced the GSEs back into the public sector, their ultimate status is unclear as the Dodd-Frank Wall Street Reform and Consumer Protection Act left the issue untouched. Effective reforms will be unlikely in the current polarized environment.

Deregulation and Innovation in the Private Sector

Despite the complicity of housing policies, the bubble would not have happened without the substantial deregulation of financial markets that took place over the past several decades. The main deregulatory actions centered on relaxing constraints on home mortgage products—most notably the lifting of interest rate caps and allowing adjustable rate mortgages; permitting mergers and acquisitions that concentrated the banking industry; and the complete deregulation of derivatives markets including mortgage-backed securities and swaps. At the same time, regulatory monitoring was diminished and new products were not proactively vetted.

There is an ideological aspect to this movement toward financial deregulation. Consider the electronics market, which is unregulated and works well. Consumers appear to make decisions without great harm. If competition results in the failure of certain firms (Digital Equipment, Gateway, RCA, etc.), there is no lasting loss to the economy. The idea that competition benefits

consumers, central to free market conservatism, was applied—
starting in the Carter years—to deregulate many markets, notably in transportation and telecommunications. Moreover, even if
deregulation led to only a few large firms, the efficiency benefits
might exceed the costs of monopoly power. Deregulation of the
railroad industry, accomplished by the Staggers Rail Act of 1980,
is seen as a great success, even if the United States today has only
two major railroads in the east and two in the west. Conservative ideology, already in place before the presidency of Ronald
Reagan, held that deregulated markets were good and that industry concentration was not bad per se.[26]

Now contrast the electronics industry with health care. We
might allow consumers to make their own decisions: prescrip-
tions would not be necessary, and drug manufacturers would
not be monitored. The Food and Drug Administration would be
abolished and anything could be sold. Megafirms, say Hospital
of America or Citihealth, could operate facilities that any quack
could rent to carry out surgery. Schools would not require that
children be vaccinated. Extreme libertarians might support such
an unfettered market like this but most Americans would not.
First, information about quality is difficult to obtain, so most of
us would like a reliable, disinterested party to inform us about
the safety of a drug or the competence of a surgeon. Second,
bad individual decisions, if they resulted in epidemics, generate
"systemic risks."

Deregulation of energy markets is instructive. The Energy
Policy Act of 1992 (EPACT) effectively repealed the Public Utility Holding Company Act (PUHCA) of 1935, the electric-power
equivalent of the Glass-Steagall Act. Its repeal generated large political risk. Under the PUHCA, most utilities were vertically integrated, generating, transmitting, and distributing electric power.
EPACT permitted the industry to be restructured; whereby these
three activities could be separated and run by independent firms.

The California "restructuring," supported by Republican governor Pete Wilson and Democrats in the legislature, proved to be
unworkable. Local utilities, such as the Pacific Gas and Electric

Corporation (PG&E), were forced to sell off their generating capacity. But politics increased risk by not allowing the distributing firms to make long-term contracts for power. They could only buy power from wholesale generators on the instant, "spot" market. The distributors were also forced to hold rates low. The now infamous Enron Corporation moved into wholesale generation. In the absence of effective monitoring of the deregulated market, Enron deliberately manipulated the spot market for electricity by selectively shutting down power plants for "maintenance."[27] Blackouts ensued (but the vertically integrated "socialist" public power operations of Los Angeles and Sacramento were spared). PG&E filed for bankruptcy. Polarized blame-game politics, as outlined in chapter 4, came to the fore. Conservatives blamed Democratic governor Gray Davis, who only inherited the restructured market. Liberals blamed Enron. After the California fiasco, states put restructuring on hold. Restructured states rarely rolled back their deregulation plans. Those who had not restructured did not go forward. The outcome attests to the power of the status quo with American political institutions.

Financial markets appear to us to be closer to health care and electric power than to electronics. In a home purchase the consumer is making a decision of far greater economic import than is involved in the purchase of a smartphone. In making a decision about knee surgery or a home mortgage, the consumer has far less opportunity to learn than when she makes frequent purchases of paper towels. Choosing the wrong product offered by a greedy lender parallels receiving unnecessary surgery from a quack. Failure in financial markets can lead to systemic risk. Just like the power grid, the entire economy can black out.

When Congress, the White House, and the independent regulatory agencies turned to the deregulation of financial markets, it appears that they had electronics more than health care in mind. Moreover, as an ideology, free market conservatism does not fully admit the differences in these markets. And when these ideas were pushed by powerful interests, deregulated financial markets were the inevitable outcome.

One of the first regulatory changes that facilitated the bubble was, like the privatization of Fannie, motivated by a desire to shift a big problem off the federal budget. In this case, the problem was the crisis in the savings and loan industry. The thrifts, as S&L banks were known, were highly regulated. When the industry developed, S&Ls were largely nonprofits that were restricted to making fixed-rate residential mortgages and accepting deposits. The interest rates for both of these transactions were tightly regulated. But by the late 1970s, most thrifts were for-profit firms faced with increased competition for deposits, primarily from money market mutual funds. At the same time, the profitability of the thrifts was jeopardized when the Federal Reserve under Paul Volcker pursued tight money policies to end the inflation of the 1970s. When interest rates spiked, the S&Ls were forced to pay high rates on their deposits while receiving low rates on their existing loan portfolios.

The federal government did not respond with prudential reform of the industry. That reform would have involved the industry's deposit insurer, the Federal Savings and Loan Insurance Corporation (FSLIC), shutting down insolvent thrifts and paying off the depositors. But when the industry became insolvent, the FSLIC lacked the sufficient funds. Appropriating the funds would have been a politically unpopular addition to the federal budget deficit. So Congress and the president decided it was better to deregulate the industry and allow the thrifts to "gamble for resurrection."

The Depository Institutions Deregulation and Monetary Control Act of 1980 was the first important step toward deregulation. This legislation sailed through the House of Representatives, with only thirty-nine members voting against final passage and fourteen voting against the conference report. The opponents were ideologically scattered. Similarly, only nine senators opposed passage.

The 1980 Act did reflect the tensions between local constituencies, described in chapter 4, and Wall Street. On the one hand, the Senate incorporated an amendment that promoted moral hazard for some federally insured institutions. The amendment striped the Fed of authority to impose reserve requirements on banks, largely small and local, that were not members of the Federal Reserve system. On the other hand, the 1980 act deregulated interest rates and overrode all related state regulations.

Deregulated interest rates allow risky lenders to attract deposits by paying more than their competitors. But because these deposits were insured, depositors were shielded from the risks. The insurance created the opportunity for the insolvent "zombie thrifts" to use their new deposits to make even riskier investments. Absent proper supervision, the interest rate deregulation increased the moral hazard of federal deposit insurance. At the same time, deregulated lenders had incentives to make loans at high interest rates to risky borrowers. Consequently, home mortgage providers had more in common with payday lenders than they did with the conservative institutions of the era of interest rate regulation.

The reregulation of interest rates is not a popular idea, but rate ceilings and usury laws may serve two important economic purposes. First, these regulations promote credit rationing when low-income, high-risk borrowers simply do not participate in the home mortgage market. Of course, this rationing may hurt the poor, but there are far better policy responses to poverty than promoting credit and debt. Second, as economists Edward Glaeser and Jose Scheinkman have pointed out, interest rate ceilings and usury laws represent a form of social insurance for the poor. If the demand of the poor for loans increases in an unregulated market, interest rates increase as the poor compete against each other for loans. Usury laws limit this competition and put a brake on high interest rates.[28] The motivation for deregulating interest rates under President Carter was more of a matter of helping an industry than of carefully thinking through the implications for consumer welfare. The legislation likely increased risk in the S&L industry. As in the S&L crisis, risky investment of federally insured deposits was central to the crisis of 2008. The 1980 legislation was a first step down the road to the subprime crisis.

As the S&L crisis grew, the thrifts (and other lenders) received new opportunities in the Garn–St. Germain Act of 1982. Perhaps the biggest one with respect to the bubble of 2008 was the new power for financial institutions to make adjustable-rate mortgages (ARMs). In principle, ARMs are win-wins. An indexed mortgage removes the risk that the lender will end up paying more on deposits that it receives from long-term loans—the so called interest-rate mismatch. A borrower willing to accept the risk of rising interest rates receives a lower expected interest rate over the duration of the mortgage.

But because there has been little regulation and supervision of adjustable-rate mortgage (ARM) contracts, lenders have devised a dizzying array of complex mortgage products. Much of the razzle-dazzle in ARM contracts seems designed more to confuse unsophisticated borrowers than to perfect a risk-sharing arrangement. For example, many ARMs locked in low "teaser" rates for two or three years before adjusting to a much higher rate. These teasers might be attractive for professionals who are "sure" that their salary will increase over time; they also make sense for strategic buyers intent on flipping houses in a rising market—at least until the market crashes. But they make little sense for unsophisticated borrowers unable to deal with the long-term consequences of such a loan contract. The same could be said for the so-called pick-a-payment loans innovated by Golden West. Moreover, by the 1990s, it became apparent that some lenders were simply defrauding borrowers by incorrectly applying the adjustments.

Teaser loans were certainly not the only toxin in mortgages in the bubble caldron. Loans were made without income or asset verification. Loans were also made with insufficient down payments so that loan-to-value ratios were too high to prevent strategic default when housing prices declined.[29] But the teaser aspect of low or no interest payments initially suckered some people into buying homes. Without the more exotic ARMs, much of the damage of the subprime crisis could have been avoided.

Although the increasing complexity of mortgage contracts may be the change of the 1980s that had the greatest impact on the bubble, other changes contributed to the regulatory climate of the bubble:

1. In order to pretend that the S&Ls were solvent and keep the whole mess off budget, accounting standards for the industry were loosened.
2. So that they could "gamble for resurrection" the S&Ls were allowed to make investments outside of their traditional business of home mortgages. By the end of the 1980s, it was "anything goes."
3. Private sector participation in mortgage-backed securities was encouraged. State regulation of these securities was preempted.[30]
4. When the government finally dealt with the S&L crisis by passing the Financial Institutions Reform, Recovery, and Enforcement Act (FIRREA) of 1989, it created a regulator that turned out to be extraordinarily weak, the Office of Thrift Supervision (OTS). Washington Mutual, IndyMac, and AIG were able to dodge regulation by the Federal Reserve by choosing the OTS as their regulator.

The deregulatory, nonpunitive climate of the S&L crisis and its aftermath continued with the governmental response to the accounting scandals of the early years of the new century. Although Enron's accounting firm Arthur Andersen was bankrupted and forced out of business, the other four major accounting firms, far from blameless in those scandals, became too big to fail. The legislative response, the Sarbanes-Oxley Act, was weak. Sarbanes-Oxley was not motivated by problems in the financial sector, as the biggest scandals involved Enron, World-Com, and other nonfinancial firms. Still, legislators might have imposed tighter standards for corporations, including those in financial services. Enron's problems were related to hiding losses in off-balance-sheet "special purpose entities." Similarly, in the bubble, banks invented off-balance-sheet vehicles that created leverage without violating the Basel I capital requirements. Wall Street innovated; Washington acquiesced.

In addition to deregulation, financial innovation was central to the crisis. The problems in the home mortgage market would not have produced a crisis bubble without important changes in how these loans were securitized. The innovations involved the development of three new products: privately issued mortgage-backed securities, the tranching of the securities, and the swaps market that insured the securities. But perhaps the most important innovation involved the extent to which these investments were leveraged. In other countries such as Germany and the Netherlands, securitization of mortgages comes in the form of covered bonds. Unlike the securitization that took place in the United States, the issuers of covered bonds are required to post sufficient capital to cover losses on the underlying mortgages. Moreover, in case of default, investors have a general claim on the issuing bank and can seize the underlying mortgages.[31]

Before we discuss these innovations in detail, it is important to stress that they owe as much to the interaction of *ideology, interests,* and *institutions* as they do to the cleverness of the Wall Street quants. In chapter 3 we discussed how campaign contributions from the financial services industry, particularly the sectors concerned with the new products, increased dramatically in the decade of the bubble. We noted that the Democrats have become dependent on the money wing of the party. We also showed that the purveyors of risky financial products were particularly active in lobbying. When Bill Clinton, Bob Rubin, and Larry Summers prevented Brooksley Born from regulating derivatives, they were reflecting some mixture of faith in the self-regulatory framework of free market conservatism and support of their allies on Wall Street. All three did well financially after the Clinton administration—the latter two directly on Wall Street.

The derivatives that led to the bubble were in part fed by predatory mortgage lending. Some states—even a mostly red state, North Carolina—moved to regulate mortgage lending. But by 2005, forces were moving in opposite directions within Congress. Republican Bob Ney and Democrat Paul Kanjorski introduced a bill to preempt all state predatory lending laws, and Democrat Brad Miller made a proposal that would essentially impose North Carolina's tough standard nationally. Gridlock blocked the passage of both bills. The Miller Bill was one of sixteen congressional efforts between 2000 and 2006 to curb predatory lending; none made it into law. Lobbying, especially by risky lenders, ensured that the institutional hurdles were formidable.[32]

In an age when Wall Street could safely assume that Washington would be incapable of further regulation, new financial products proliferated. Indeed, with weak reactions to each warning signal—LTCM, Enron, WorldCom, Amaranth, the Orange County bankruptcy—Wall Street saw a green light for financial "development."

Lewis Ranieri is credited with the invention of the private mortgage-backed security, first issued by Salomon Brothers and Bank of America in 1977. At the time of the innovation, the product was a legal investment in only fifteen states.[33] With successful lobbying the innovation went viral at the beginning of the new century.

When investors buy a private mortgage-backed security, they want some assurance of the quality of the underlying investments. But there are at least three channels for misrepresentation in a deregulated market. First, if the originators of the mortgages have no obligation to "keep skin in the game" by maintaining an interest in the mortgages they underwrite, they have incentives to misrepresent the quality of loans and to present fraudulent loan documents. Second, if the creators of the mortgage securities sell the bonds, they have weak incentives to conduct due diligence on the documents prepared by the originators.[34] Third, credit ratings agencies that that are hired to bless the bonds have incentives to keep clients happy and understate the riskiness of the investment.

The problems with a privately issued MBS were compounded when the process of tranching emerged. In 1997, the credit derivatives team at JPMorgan came up with two innovations. First, corporate bonds could be pooled into a security; the security in turn could be cut up into pieces known as tranches. The lowest tranche took the highest risk on defaults of bonds in the portfolio and was last in line for cash flow. That tranche has rights to cash flows but no claim on assets. Collateralized debt obligations (CDOs) based on subprime tranches suffered the greatest problems with inaccurate ratings.[35] The highest tranche was most protected from a decline in the value of the mortgage security. Thus, the top tranche was viewed as essentially riskless. But to make the investment truly riskless, AIG agreed to issue credit default swaps (CDSs) that insured these investments for a pittance. By 1999, the innovation extended into consumer debt, most notably into mortgage debt. But JPMorgan saw mortgages as riskier than corporate bonds, so the firm barely got into the business of the slicing and dicing of mortgages.[36] But others were more than willing to pick up the ball and keep running.

How does Washington handle product innovation in financial markets? Almost not at all, as long as no current laws are violated. And if current laws are inconvenient, lobbying typically gets a fix. This process fits well with free market conservatism. All products are welcome in the marketplace. If people are nuts enough to buy tickets to see Charlie Sheen or products endorsed by "reckless few" members like Roger Clemens and Martha Stewart, *de gustibus non est disputandum*; the products have little potential to inflict harm. New drugs, however, cannot simply be marketed where consumers have the "freedom to choose." For drugs there is a complicated approval process that requires testing and strict procedures. And if pseudoephedrine hydrochloride gets remanufactured into crystal meth, sale requirements are toughened. Although many might carp at the specifics of how new product introduction in health care is regulated, few would want to get rid of the process entirely. Product failures can have irreversible consequences. Thalidomide, which led to deformed babies, is not an Apple Newton that had no bite. Unfortunately, free market conservatism treats financial products like consumer electronics rather than like drugs.

Worse, whatever regulation existed with regard to derivatives was largely eliminated by the Commodity Futures Modernization Act (CFMA) of 2000. And worst, the CFMA favored derivative owners over debt holders in bankruptcy. Speculative investment bankers had higher priority than bondholders. After Bill Clinton put his signature on this bill and on the Gramm-Leach-Bliley Act, the frenzy of the Bush years followed. A recent Dallas Federal Reserve working paper shows that the markets in nonprime residential mortgage-backed securities and in credit default swaps soared after passage of the CFMA.[37]

While Washington was deregulating the derivatives that were fundamental to the bubble, Congress also passed some minor measures that facilitated mortgage origination. The American Home-ownership and Economic Opportunity Act of 2000—directed at easing financing of mortgages, including reverse mortgages, and at increasing financial assistance for homeownership by the poor, elderly, and disabled—was passed by voice vote in the House and unanimous consent in the Senate. The American Dream Down-payment Act of 2003 was passed by unanimous consent in the Senate and without objection in the House.[38] It was enthusiastically signed into law by President Bush as a measure that would build the "ownership society" by providing "$200 million per year in down payment assistance to at least 40,000 low-income families."[39] In an era of polarized politics, egalitarians and free market conservatives could come together at least over housing.

The budgetary implications of these overhyped pieces of legislation were minimal. The Congressional Budget Office estimated the net budgetary costs of the 2000 act at under $100 million.[40] Although the 2003 legislation authorized $200 million annually in down payment assistance, the most Congress ever appropriated was $87 million in 2004. By 2008, the appropriation was down to $10 million.[41] What Washington was prepared to spend on homes for the poor was a pittance compared to what Goldman Sachs and John Paulson were to make by the former's promoting and the latter's shorting the Abacus CDO based on residential MBSs. Both "American" acts relaxed standards for lenders and they provided a bit more hot air for bubble products.

The development of new products was largely facilitated by the introduction of computer technology and the Internet to financial markets. When Long Term Capital Management (LTCM) collapsed in 1998, the New York Fed found it necessary to intervene because of potential systemic risk. The business model pursued by LTCM required mathematical models and trading strategies that would have been infeasible without high-speed computing. The "flash crash" of May 2010 was caused by high-frequency trading strategies that high-speed computing made possible. Yet government permitted such strategies to be used without vetting them, and as SEC chair Mary Schapiro has acknowledged, the government did not even have the ability to get a quick grasp on what happened.

The Internet and high-speed computing also contribute to the globalization of finance. A substantial chunk of the bailout money for AIG ultimately landed in foreign banks, including Deutsche Bank, Credit Suisse, Barclays, and UBS. That is, the systemic risk initiated by subprime mortgage products extended to the global economy and not just the United States. The implications of globalization for U.S. markets have generally led to political arguments that regulation must be relaxed or business activity will relocate abroad. Arguments that the United States would one day bail out foreign banks were hard to find.

Concentration and Regulatory Retrenchment

Systemic risk is also heightened when a few large financial firms dominate markets. Regulators paid little attention when the nation's largest insurance company, AIG, came to dominate the credit default swap market. Commercial banks became larger and larger by acquiring risky assets, Countrywide in the case of Bank of America and Golden West in the case of Wachovia. Consolidation was facilitated both by free market conservative opposition to government intervention and by its antitax sentiment limiting the government's ability to shut down failing banks. In 2005, *Global Finance* listed eight American banks among the fifty largest in the world: Citigroup, JPMorgan Chase, Bank of America, Merrill Lynch, Goldman Sachs, Wachovia, Wells Fargo, and Lehman Brothers. By 2009, three of the eight no longer existed. Wachovia was the fourth largest commercial bank in the United States in 2005. The sixth largest, Washington Mutual, is also gone.

Concentration made it more likely that the failure of one or more of the mega-institutions would cripple the economy. This problem was accentuated by the historical evolution of the mortgage market from one in which a large preponderance of mortgages was held by dispersed, small institutions to one in which mortgages went through the MBS pipeline. Mortgage originators everywhere participated in the national and international markets created by securitization. Based on historical correlations, the mathematical models used to price these securities assumed that geographic variation in real estate prices would be low. But the models failed to consider how the market was fundamentally altered by the securitization assembly lines.

Part of the assembly line was the rating of the securities. The ratings were the product of only three firms: Moody's, Standard & Poor's, and Fitch. If these agencies all produced biased reports, the bad information would be highly correlated across MBSs, so when one went sour it would be highly likely that others would follow. Moreover, even though securitization was predicated on the notion of diversifying risk across mortgages, the end result was to create millions of CDOs that were not only correlated but nearly statistically equivalent. So any firm that invested in large numbers of mortgage-backed securities was concentrating, rather than diversifying, its risk.

As the bubble inflated, Washington allowed increased concentration in financial services and failed to control new financial products and new financial market structures. Part of the failure

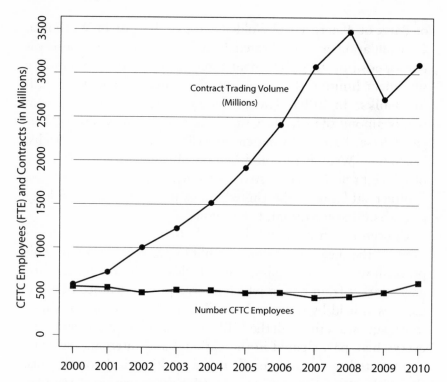

Figure 5.3. Growth of volume of futures and options contracts and CFTC full-time equivalent employees. Trading volume in futures and options contract trading expanded rapidly. The CFTC had practically no increase in staff. The figure plots the number of full-time equivalent (FTE) CFTC employees and the number (in millions) of futures and options contracts.
Source: Commodity Futures Trading Commission (2011).

was a sheer lack of regulatory resources. As the new markets grew explosively, regulatory resources failed to keep pace. The pattern appears in the budgets and staffing of the FDIC, the Fed, the SEC, and the CFTC.

The problem is illustrated by figure 5.3, which we have reproduced from the CFTC's 2012 budget statement. The CFTC noted that during the bubble, "The agency had shrunk from a staffing level of 567 FTE in 1999 to 437 FTE in FY 2007—a 23 percent decline in staff while during the same period the futures and options markets increased five-fold."[42] This decline reflects both the self-regulatory and antitax beliefs of free market conservatism. The SEC and the CFTC together had about 4,400 employees in 2010, while the FDIC had 7,000. In contrast, the Food and Drug Administration and the Centers for Disease Control and Prevention have more than 25,000 employees. Yet "toxic assets," the tag applied to the new financial products, proved exceedingly dangerous to the nation's health. The nation saw the full bore of toxicity only when the bubble popped.

Time line of deregulation of financial markets

1978	Supreme Court deregulates consumer interest rates on credit cards; Maine allows entry of out-of-state banks. Similar laws passed in all states except Hawaii by 1992.
1980	Depository Institutions Deregulation and Monetary Control Act. Eliminates regulation of interest rates.
1982	Garn-St. Germain Act. Allows for adjustable rate mortgages and interstate acquisitions of troubled banks.
1983	Federal Reserve. Bank holding companies allowed to acquire discount securities brokers.
1984	Secondary Mortgage Market Enhancement Act. Facilitates private issuance of mortgage-backed securities. Preemption of state regulation.
1987, 1989, 1996	Fed expands securities underwriting capacity of banks.
1989	FIRREA passed to resolve savings and loan crisis, weak regulatory structure implemented.
1994	Riegle-Neal Interstate Banking and Branching Efficiency Act of 1994, interstate acquisitions and branching permitted.
1999	Gramm-Leach-Bliley, Financial Services Modernization Act. Repeals Glass-Steagall separation of investment and commercial banking.
2000	Commodity Futures Modernization Act. Deregulates derivatives markets. American Homeownership and Economic Opportunity Act.
2003	American Dream Downpayment Act.
2004	SEC allows investment banks to expand leverage.
2005	Congressional impasse on predatory lending. Republicans seek to eliminate state regulation, Democrats seek stronger regulation.

Sources: Santomero (2001); Strahan (2002); Atlas (2007).

Time line of minority and low-income housing legislation

1977	Community Reinvestment Act. Bans redlining. Used to increase low-income loans of banks seeking merger approval.
1990	Cranston-Gonzalez National Affordable Housing Act (the HOME Investment Partnerships Act).
1992	Housing and Community Development Act—Section VIII: Federal Housing Enterprises Financial Safety and Soundness Act, lowered down-payment requirements.
1996	Housing Opportunity Program Extension Act of 1996.
2000	American Homeownership and Economic Opportunity Act.
2003	American Dream Downpayment Act.

Source: U.S. Department of Housing and Urban Development, "Affordable Housing," http://www.hud.gov/offices/cpd/affordablehousing/; authors' notes.

PART II

• •

POPS

Why Washington Delays in Solving Financial Crises

Introduction

As we saw in part I, government rarely acts to keep a bubble from getting out of hand. But surely when the bubble ultimately pops, governments do better? If only they did.

Many observers, including us, have been dismayed at how little and how poorly the financial system has been reorganized in the aftermath of the crash of 2008. Ideology, interests, and institutions all moved in the wrong direction.

As we show in chapter 7, the ideological positions of members of Congress elected before 2008 went virtually unchanged. The midterm elections of 2010 brought about not only a Republican majority but a movement of that party to the right after an influx of Tea Party members. As we show in chapter 8, the ideological response, in the form of populism, was weak. While Occupy Wall Street largely fizzled on the left, whereas the Tea Party on the right was quickly provided with direction and resources by elite fundamentalist free market conservatives, such as former Texas congressman Richard Armey and the Club for Growth.

A new set of dangerous interests was created in the pop by the government bailout and government-directed mergers and acquisitions. In the introduction we touched on PNC's acquisition of National City Corporation with funds from the Troubled Asset Relief Program. In chapter 5, we showed how an account at a small bank in New Jersey eventually wound up at Wells Fargo after the latter acquired the failing Wachovia. More generally, the financial sector has become more concentrated, as further indicated by JPMorgan Chase's acquisition of Bear Stearns and Washington Mutual, and by Bank of America's acquisition of Countrywide Financial and Merrill Lynch. Many of Lehman Brothers' viable operations were acquired by Barclays. The upshot is a less competitive industry that is now bigger than too big to fail.

After the Supreme Court's decision in *Citizens United v. Federal Elections Commission*,[1] the financial sector has new opportunities to use its resources to influence political campaigns.[2] And because the concentration has eliminated all the old cleavages among commercial banks, investment banks, and insurance companies, the industry has better aligned political preferences and can lobby with one voice.[3]

Institutions sharply limited legislative response to the pop. In chapter 7 we show in some detail how pivotal politics played out, in the form of a Senate filibuster threat, to limit the content of both President Barack Obama's stimulus package and the Dodd-Frank Wall Street Reform and Consumer Protection Act on financial regulation. Dodd-Frank, in our opinion, was far too complex and left far too much to the discretion of regulators. The costs of this regulatory discretion have been exemplified by the unseemly lobbying, most notably by MF Global's CEO Jon Corzine of his former Goldman colleague, Commodity Futures Trading Commission head Gary Gensler, and by JPMorgan Chase CEO Jamie Dimon's efforts to limit the regulation of derivatives and swaps. Institutions have also played out in Republican attempts to limit or repeal parts of Dodd-Frank. A filibuster threat torpedoed any possible nomination of Elizabeth Warren to head the new Consumer Financial Protection Bureau and forced Obama to circumvent the Senate by appointing Richard Cordray as bureau head during a Senate recess.[4] Lack of consensus has left the future of Fannie Mae and Freddie Mac up in the air.

That the *Three I's*—ideology, institutions, and interests— combined to render Washington an ineffective responder to the pop is not surprising. This time is no different. In chapter 6, we show how the *Three I's* have shaped historical responses to pops, and argue that the *Three I's* help explain some regularities about how American government deals with financial crises. Then in chapter 7 we demonstrate how the *Three I's* reproduced these regularities in response to the events of 2008 and beyond. Chapter 8 explores why the populist responses to the crisis were insufficient to push politicians through the hurdles created by the *Three I's*. Chapter 9 concludes.

CHAPTER 6
Historical Lessons of the Responses to Pops

[L]iquidate labor, liquidate stocks, liquidate farmers, liquidate real estate . . . [a panic] will purge the rottenness out of the system. High costs of living and high living will come down. People will work harder, live a more moral life. Values will be adjusted, and enterprising people will pick up from less competent people.

—Andrew Mellon, quoted in Herbert Hoover, *Memoirs*

AMERICAN HISTORY SUGGESTS four common characteristics of government responses to pops:

1. Legislative responses to financial crises and economic downturns have generally been limited and delayed.
2. The response often awaits a transition in political power. This partisan delay reflects the idea that the cause of the crisis is generally rooted in the ideology of the incumbent party.
3. Future change in political power often reverses the initial legislative response. The reversal contributes to the next crisis. This point is central to the inevitability of future financial crises.
4. Short-term reelection concerns undermine the search for longer-term solutions.

All these characteristics are direct byproducts of the *Three I's*. Institutions, ideological rigidity, and interest-group opposition produce delays and limits. Ideological rigidity plus polarized parties means that transitions are required for reform and that future transitions often lead to retrenchment. Short time horizons are induced by our penchant for frequent elections.

The regularities suggest two important hypotheses. First, delay appears to be inherent in democracy, or at least in American democracy. The same incentives for gridlock that we argue undermine government intervention in bubbles do not simply disappear when the financial system comes crashing down. If anything these incentives get worse, as blame-game politics become paramount.

Second, the importance of political transitions, as from Herbert Hoover to Franklin Delano Roosevelt or from George W. Bush to Barack Obama, suggests that ideology is an important impediment to a response. If politicians were pragmatic problem solvers, policy should easily adjust according to the best available evidence about the causes of the financial crisis. But, as ideological commitments make common interpretations of that evidence unlikely, adjustments are impeded. Either the new policies violate core beliefs or switching course would be interpreted by voters as an admission of the liabilities of the incumbent party's ideological positions.

We regard the four regularities as fairly universal in the American experience, but we also note that the magnitudes of these negative consequences are directly related to the extent of party polarization. During periods of low polarization such as the one from the 1930s to the 1970s (recall figure 2.2), the tendency toward delayed and inadequate responses is muted. Once a transition occurs, the response is substantial and relatively permanent. But during an era of high polarization such as the late nineteenth century and today, those problems are magnified.

Unwinding Pops: A Political History

Before presenting the historical evidence of the regularities identified above, we begin with a brief overview of credit markets in the United States and the available policy instruments for handling pops in the markets. Both the markets and the policy instruments in earlier episodes were quite different from those in the subprime bubble.

Early Credit Markets and Politics

In the eighteenth and nineteenth centuries, the federal government engaged in very little macroeconomic policy making. The population was primarily agrarian. Agrarian interests were represented by the Democrat-Republicans and their successors, the Democrats, who held the presidency for all but eight years between the inauguration of Thomas Jefferson in 1801 and that of Abraham Lincoln in 1861. The primary policy goal of the agrarians, as exemplified by Jefferson and Andrew Jackson, was to limit the reach of the federal government.[1] Most important, Jackson prevented the development of a national banking system and a central bank. Today, of course, interests have flipped; the interventionists are the Democrats.

From George Washington's first inaugural in 1789 until 1900, the United States endured many severe economic downturns, known as panics. Leaving aside those associated with the Civil War and its aftermath, panics occurred in 1792, 1797, 1819, 1837, 1857, 1873, and 1893.

Credit markets in the eighteenth and nineteenth centuries were markedly different from the shadow banking system that crashed in 2008. No firms were too big to fail. In the second half of the nineteenth century, the development of railroads introduced an exception. If a railroad collapsed, its clients would be without practical transportation alternatives. The economic impact would be severe. In the absence of the modern Chapter 11 bankruptcy provisions for corporate reorganization, a defaulting railroad was in danger of a run by creditors. Individual secured creditors could seize piecemeal portions of the railroad's locomotives, rolling stock, and track. Preserving the railroad in its entirety was in "the public interest." True, railroad reorganizations were privately handled, largely presided over by J. P. Morgan and his competitor Jacob Schiff at Kuhn, Loeb.[2] Morgan and Schiff, however, needed a way to force recalcitrant creditors to accept a reorganization plan. Federal courts were used to push through reorganization.[3] So in effect, Morgan needed government intervention in private contracts to allow him to favor some private investors at the expense of others. Of course, private rent seeking undermined the public interest as stakeholders in the railroad bickered over the reorganization. So if Morgan broke eggs, his omelets may have served the greater good.

Most early credit markets, unlike railroads, were centered on relatively small, short-term transactions that often did not involve financial intermediaries. Parallel to 2008, real estate speculation had some part in the crises, particularly in 1797, 1819, and 1837. Credit contracts in real estate were short-term and did not involve intermediaries. The contracts were either between private parties or between a private borrower and the federal government. No big financial institutions concentrated the market by buying up mortgages from originate-and-sell shysters.

Similarly, business and consumer credit appeared as trade credit. Trade credit took the form of short-term loans from importers or manufacturers to wholesalers, wholesalers to retailers, and retailers to consumers. Consumers had no credit card debt to a financial intermediary but would owe money directly to their grocery and hardware stores. When there were widespread defaults on short-term debt, the whole economy could lock up, just as the run on the overnight repo market in 2008 threatened to bring down the whole economy.

Even though there were no too-big-to-fail firms in the trade credit and mortgage markets, a macroeconomic crisis would lead governments, federal and state, to implement policies that ignored moral hazard. After three of these crises, Congress enacted a bankruptcy law that allowed debtors as individuals to wipe out debt.[4]

Bankruptcy law was not the only policy instrument employed when the early bubbles popped. In 1819, real estate debtors were concentrated among those who had bought federal land on credit. The Democrat-Republicans, with James Monroe as president, had no taste for exercising the bankruptcy powers the Constitution gave to the federal government. They did seek, however, to relieve their voter base of debt. Congress did something that has been proposed (albeit with little success) for private creditors today. It jiggered the debt contract either to give debtors extended payment terms or to allow for immediate repayment at a 37.5 percent discount.[5] That is, Congress voted that the federal government take a haircut. The measure generated sharp divisions in Congress. Representatives of states with few land debtors (mostly on the Atlantic Seaboard) and with individuals holding federal obligations opposed these measures and were able to limit them. Specifically, by banning future government sales of land on credit, Congress ended the federal role in real estate finance until the Great Depression (the Homestead Act of 1862 simply made land available for free).

In the absence of federal policy to address the problem of private debt in the Panic of 1819, state governments intervened. Specifically, many states, predominantly on the frontier, enacted stay laws—that is, debt moratoriums—and other measures to grant relief to debtors. These measures were ruled unconstitutional (but only after the panic was well past) by the Supreme Court.[6] When the Panic of 1893 hit, neither the states nor the federal government were capable of rapid intervention.

In summary, major policy responses to pops in the eighteenth and nineteenth centuries included the passage of national bankruptcy laws; state measures of debtor relief, including moratoriums; and federal restructuring of real estate debt. Pops resulting from a potential collapse of the transportation system were averted by judicial innovation in railroad reorganization.

Some of these policies reappeared during the Great Depression. Twenty-five states passed moratoriums on farm mortgages.[7] At the federal level, the Farm Credit Administration refinanced one-fifth of all farm mortgages. By 1939, federal land banks held 40 percent of all farm mortgage debt. The federal government acquired and directly refinanced one million residential mortgages.[8] These restructured mortgages took place in a nation with only thirty million households and a homeownership rate below 50 percent. A very different type of debt relief also appeared in the Depression. Before the Depression, almost all industrial bonds contained gold clauses that allowed the creditor to demand payment in gold rather than in dollars. Such clauses would have dramatically increased corporate indebtedness when FDR devalued the dollar. When Congress acceded to his request to cancel the gold clauses in debt contracts, it greatly reduced, on the order of 31 percent, the real value of corporate debt.[9]

None of these policy instruments used before World War II have been used since. Demands for farm mortgage moratoriums fell on deaf ears during the 1981 recession, at the time the largest downturn since World War II. (The Agricultural Credit Act of 1987 was a very belated attempt at relief.) During the 2008 presidential campaign, Barack Obama advocated a three-month moratorium on mortgage foreclosures. He did not, however, push for legislation after he took office. Senate Democrats were unsuccessful in passing legislation to allow bankruptcy courts to prevent foreclosures. Consequently, the restructuring of home mortgages was largely left to the private sector. As we show in chapter 7, relatively few mortgages have been restructured. In the pop of 2008, Washington rushed to bail out the commercial and investment banks and American International Group (AIG), but did little to relieve small debtors.

Opponents of mortgage relief draw on moral hazard arguments made by free market conservatives. They contend that if mortgage holders are let off the hook now for houses they could never afford, they are less likely to feel an obligation to pay debts they incur in the future. But the earlier government interventions in the economy did not cause the economic collapse of the United States. Political intervention in debt contracts after speculative bubbles in real estate and equities did not, obviously, permanently impair credit markets. The canceled debt provided a fresh start to the debtors and to the economy as a whole.

The reset button was pressed for the entire economy by the 1841 bankruptcy law. The number of filings was equal to 1 percent of the adult male white population. Because bankruptcy was unavailable to the 69 percent of the labor force in agriculture and rarely pursued by wage earners, that 1 percent represents an important segment of the business community. Similarly, with 21 percent of the labor force still in farming in 1930, farm mortgage relief hit a large segment of the population. Fundamentalist adherents of "do nothing because of moral hazard" can find little evidence in the American experience that would support their belief. Home mortgage relief, as we indicated earlier, was also significant. Moreover, when the federal government bought up home mortgages in the Depression, the bailout did not go primarily to Wall Street. Only about 5 percent of home mortgages in the 1930s were held by commercial banks, and commercial banking was far less concentrated than today. Federal intervention in the housing market in the 1930s saved rather than killed the mortgage market. Similarly, the corporate bond market, rather than failing, actually strengthened after the gold clauses were canceled.[10] Investors may dislike haircuts, but they abhor the threat of a collapsed economy. There are no atheists in foxholes, and there should be no ideologues in financial crises.

Mortgage haircuts, canceled clauses in corporate bond contracts, and temporary bankruptcy laws that erased debt across the economy were used only in financial crises before and during the Great Depression. Another policy intervention, however—government purchase of banking securities—was used well before it was adopted by Henry Paulson and Ben Bernanke. In the very first panic after ratification of the Constitution, the first Treasury secretary, Alexander Hamilton, made similar purchases, most notably in securities of the Bank of New York.

The history of government intervention in pops might be surprising to true red twenty-first-century free market conservatives such as Senator Jim Bunning of Kentucky. Bunning thought he "woke up in France" after the Federal Reserve intervened in the purchase of Bear Stearns by JPMorgan Chase and in the federal takeover of Fannie Mae and Freddie Mac.[11] But earlier Kentucky politicians had no problem in intervening in the free market. The Kentucky legislature passed a stay law that made it difficult to collect debts following the Panic of 1819.

In contrast, when Congress contracted credit in the response to a popped bubble, economic development was often hindered. After the Panic of 1819, the federal government stopped selling land on credit and sold it only for cash. In the ensuing years, federal land sales slowed considerably; the 1818 level was never again reached in the South and was passed in the West only in 1835. Movement to the frontier also slowed considerably. After the admission of Maine and Missouri in 1820, no new states entered the Union until Michigan and Arkansas in 1837. With the exception of the 1821 restriction on *future* federal land sales on credit, the response to macroeconomic crisis in the eighteenth and nineteenth centuries was typically friendly to debtors. Debtor friendliness in a crisis did not prevent the United States from becoming the largest economy in the world by 1892 and remaining so into the twenty-first century.

Response to Pops: Delayed and Limited

Delays

At the federal level, the responses to crisis were generally delayed, per our first regularity. The bankruptcy laws were enacted several years after an economic collapse. The Panic of 1797 began in 1796; a bankruptcy law was passed only in 1800. The bankruptcy law of 1841 followed the Panic of 1837 by four years; that of 1898 followed the Panic of 1893 by five years. The delays continued into the twentieth century. The Panic of 1907 was followed by the Aldrich-Vreeland Act in 1908. But this response was quite limited, as monetary policy coordination was left in private hands. Significant reform in the form of a central bank waited until 1913 and the passage of the Federal Reserve Act.

The response to the Great Depression is the starkest case of delay. The stock market crashed in October 1929, just seven months after the inauguration of Herbert Hoover. Hoover's Treasury secretary, Pittsburgh banker Andrew Mellon, did little more than hope that the Depression would weed out inefficient firms. The major legislative responses awaited Roosevelt, including the Banking Act of 1933 (the official name of the Glass-Steagall Act), which separated commercial and investment banking and created deposit insurance, the creation of the Securities Exchange Commission, the Public Utility Holding Company Act (PUHCA), and the Investment Act of 1940. Two closely related factors helped the Roosevelt presidency to make these changes. First, the Depression was exceptionally severe. By the time Roosevelt took office in 1933 a prolonged decline of the economy and a run on the traditional banking system had created a sense of urgency similar to that surrounding the passage of the Troubled Asset Relief Program (TARP) in 2008 and the stimulus package in 2009. Second, Roosevelt enjoyed huge partisan majorities. In the four Congresses following Roosevelt's first inaugural (1933–41), the Republicans never held more than 169 of the 435 House seats.[12] In the last three of these Congresses, they never held more than 25 of 96 Senate seats.[13]

The first of these Congresses, the Seventy-Third, was that of the 100 days. In addition to financial legislation, the Seventy-Third Congress also enacted many "stimulus" programs, ranging from the Tennessee Valley Authority to the Civilian Conservation Corps. Roosevelt got this legislation through Congress despite the absence of the filibuster-proof majorities that he was able to command beginning in 1935. In 1933, Roosevelt faced 36 Republican senators in a 96-seat Senate, a two-thirds filibuster threshold, and no possibility of using the reconciliation process—a tougher hurdle than Barack Obama's facing 40 GOP members, a three-fifths hurdle, and reconciliation available to pass some legislation with bare majorities.[14] How was FDR able to accomplish so much compared to Obama?

A first explanation might be that the financial sector was much more politically influential in 2009 than in 1933. After all, the reforms in 1933 came in the fourth year of a financial slump. The prolonged crisis diminished the clout of the financial industry whereas the recession that started in 2007 had ended and U.S. banks were earning record profits by the time the ink dried on the Dodd-Frank Act. In addition, the clout of the industry in the Depression was diminished when its public image was harmed by evidence of malfeasance produced by the Pecora Commission.[15] But other indicators suggest that the financial industry was still a political force. The financial wages data (see figure 2.3) suggest that the premium to finance did not peak until 1936. So the industry's *relative* economic position seems not to have deteriorated before the New Deal reforms were enacted. Moreover, the influence of finance on the Democratic Party in 1933 seems to be roughly similar to 2009. The Obama administration has been criticized for close ties to Wall Street, and FDR relied heavily on financiers such as Bernard Baruch, Joseph Kennedy, and Herbert Lehman. (Yes, Lehman was a partner at Lehman Brothers.) Campaign finance records from the predisclosure era are sketchy, but there is evidence that Roosevelt and the Democratic Party raised large sums from the financial sector in the 1932 election.[16]

The Supreme Court, a quite conservative body at the time, provides another, more promising clue. Creditors were affected not only by Roosevelt's voiding of the gold clauses but also by the farm mortgage moratoriums passed by twenty-five states.[17] State farm mortgage moratoriums appear to violate the contracts clause of the Constitution; indeed, the court in the nineteenth century held moratoriums to be unconstitutional. Yet the court—albeit hostile to Roosevelt on the National Industrial Recovery Act and other measures—went along, deciding that a macroeconomic emergency trumped a strict construction of the founders' intent.[18] Undoubtedly, the emergency of the Depression made Republicans, who paid dearly for the follies of Hoover and Mellon, accommodative.

The sense of emergency was complemented by the absence of political polarization in the Senate. The difference between the Democrat and Republican mean ideological scores, our measure of polarization, had been declining since the start of the twentieth century and reached its historical low in the sixteen years of FDR and Harry Truman. The collapse of polarization reflected not only Northern and Southern Democrats becoming less liberal (and less populist) but also Republicans, all Northern, becoming less conservative. These were long-run trends, abetted by the emergence of the progressive wing of the Republican Party. They were not a direct consequence of the Depression.

To the extent that there were disputes about financial reform, they tended to revolve around cleavages within the financial sector. Consider Glass-Steagall. When Congress passed this bill, the most controversial provision was not the separation of commercial and investment banking but issues like the branching of national banks, the establishment of deposit insurance, and the eligibility of banks to participate in deposit insurance. A bank bill first reached the Senate in the lame duck session that followed the 1932 elections. The bill allowed national banks to open branches in states that allowed branching of state banks; this provision led populist Democrat Huey Long to direct a filibuster of the bill for ten days in early 1933.[19] After the new Congress was seated in March of 1933, conservative Republican Arthur Vandenberg successfully amended the reintroduced bill to speed up the creation of the deposit insurance fund. The Vandenberg amendment provoked a veto threat from FDR; his Republican Treasury secretary William Woodin opposed deposit insurance.[20] Long threatened to oppose the final bill until state banks were allowed to participate in the deposit insurance program. Unlike the divisions over Dodd-Frank, the conflicts were not structured so heavily around party and ideology. This lack of structure facilitated the compromises necessary to move the legislation forward. FDR was able to do business with practical, compromising politicians. In contrast, as we documented in part I, Obama is faced with a pack of ideologues.

A half century after the Great Depression, delayed policy responses characterized the savings and loan crisis of the 1980s (discussed in chapter 5).[21] Recall that as a consequence of the abrupt increase in interest rates initiated by the Federal Reserve under Paul Volcker and the ensuing severe recession of 1981–82, the mismatch between the rates at which the thrifts could borrow in the short term and what they earned on their long-term loans critically undermined their financial situation. To the further detriment of the thrifts, real estate values collapsed, especially in the oil patch and the farm belt. Thus, savings and loans (S&Ls) not only lost money on their good mortgages but also ran into a blizzard of defaults. By 1982 more than two-thirds of the thrifts were unprofitable. Based on the regulatory capital standards of the time, the aggregate S&L industry liabilities exceeded aggregate assets—the industry as a whole was insolvent. The industry's regulator, the Federal Home Loan Bank Board (FHLBB) was well aware of the situation. The problem, however, was that the deposit insurer, the Federal Savings and Loan Insurance Corporation (FSLIC), had insufficient funds to shut down the insolvent S&Ls and pay off depositors.

Rather than recapitalize the FSLIC and face politically unpopular thrift closures, the political response was to relax regulatory standards and to expand the set of assets that thrifts were allowed to own. That the FSLIC was not granted additional funding authority ensured a policy of regulatory forbearance against failing thrifts.

The profitability of some S&Ls temporarily improved. But the extra risk taking encouraged by regulatory forbearance soon took its toll. By 1987, the magnitude of the industry's insolvency problem had increased dramatically. Yet the Thrift Industry Recovery Act of 1987 enshrined continued regulatory forbearance by extending the use of lenient accounting rules and weakened capital standards. At the same time, Congress reaffirmed the "full faith and credit" government backing of FSLIC-insured deposits, without providing the agency the additional financing authority to move aggressively against the owners of bankrupt

S&Ls.[22] Equity holders and management in the insolvent firms bore virtually no downward risk. In a classic case of moral hazard, as long as these thrifts were allowed to operate, they would benefit from any success of risky gambles that restored profitability but be insulated from losses.[23] The "zombie thrifts" made increasingly risky bets as they gambled for resurrection.

By early 1989, shutting down failed S&Ls and recapitalizing the deposit insurance fund could no longer be delayed. Congress passed the Financial Institutions Reform, Recovery, and Enforcement Act of 1989 (FIRREA), which President George H. W. Bush signed that August. Insured deposits were paid off. The assets of the failed thrifts were disposed of by a new entity, the Resolution Trust Corporation (RTC), and part of the financing of the bailout came from debt issued by the RTC.[24] Twenty percent of the net income of Federal Home Loan Banks today goes to paying the interest on that debt.[25] The costs of delay in the 1980s have extended well into the twenty-first century.

Limits

Our first regularity also indicated that responses were often limited in that they stopped short of fundamental reorganization of parts of the economic system. The Great Depression provides a partial exception. Glass-Steagall separated commercial and investment banking and introduced deposit insurance. The PUHCA broke up the investor-owned electric power industry in the United States into a large number of relatively small firms that were generally barred from mergers and acquisitions. But the response to most other crises falls well short of these standards.

Consider the accounting scandals from the early years of the new century that resulted only in the very mild reforms of the Sarbanes-Oxley Act. A dramatic reform on the order of Glass-Steagall or the PUHCA after Enron/WorldCom might have restructured the accounting industry. Instead the status quo was enshrined, and the industry, as chapter 5 pointed out, became more concentrated.

Another missed reform opportunity in the accounting scandals concerned 401(k) plans. As discussed in chapter 4, Congress might have restructured 401(k)s to sharply limit the stock held in the corporation itself. No changes were made.

Not surprisingly, the accounting firms of the investment banks did not blow the whistle during the subprime crisis. Ironically, one of the big four, Ernst & Young, worked for the government as a contract auditor for TARP.[26] In 2010, it was charged with doctoring Lehman Brothers' balance sheet.[27] And Lehman froze its pension plan as it went down.

We contend that reforms like Sarbanes-Oxley are the norm and those like Glass-Steagall are exceptions. Limitations in legislative changes were certainly found in early bankruptcy law. Farmers were protected from involuntary bankruptcy.[28] The 1800 Bankruptcy Act contained a sunset provision.[29] The 1898 act reserved the power to set exemptions and priorities to the states and left litigation over fraudulent conveyance (transfer of assets designed to put them outside the reach of a creditor) in the hands of state courts.[30] Although fraudulent conveyance laws were eventually federalized, priority (who is first in line) and exemption (what assets cannot be seized by creditors) policies are anachronisms. States such as Florida and Texas, where home equity is totally shielded from creditors, respond to their local real estate industry, which has, along with their congressional delegations, successfully fought to maintain these state exemptions. States where creditors controlled politics in 1900 continue to restrict the exemption of home equity. In those states, if you do not pay your credit card bill, your home is not your castle. Both the absence of a national exemption policy and the diversity of state policies largely reflect economic and political conditions in the late nineteenth century. This observation is mighty testimony to the combined power of local economic interests and institutional gridlock to create status quo bias in economic policy.

Local interests also managed to limit the development of national regulations for banking during the creation of the Federal Reserve after the Panic of 1907 and of the mortgage market after the onset of the Great Depression. Unlike the Social Security Administration, which operates effectively as a single national organization, the Fed was set up as twelve regional banks. Power was transferred to Washington only with the creation of the Board of Governors in the National Banking Act of 1935. The FHLBB established under Hoover also comprised twelve regional banks; only six of the twelve cities are common both to the Fed and the FHLBB, an indication that pork barrel jockeying influences location decisions. (Carter Glass, then a House member from Virginia, managed the Federal Reserve Act in the House in 1913. Today there is a Federal Reserve Bank, but no Federal Home Loan Bank, in Richmond.)

Empowering the regional Feds rather than a national central bank was a dose of pork barrel and another dose of populist (1913-style) mistrust of Washington and Wall Street. But the New York Fed was no populist creation. It served the purpose of giving Wall Street direct influence.

The role of the New York Fed reflects political tensions that arose in the wake of the Panic of 1907. The go-to person in the Senate after the Panic was Nelson Aldrich (R-RI), the father-in-law of John D. Rockefeller Jr. Rockefeller was the largest shareholder in the largest bank in the world, Chase National (the predecessor of Chase Manhattan Bank and subsequently JPMorgan Chase). His uncle, William Rockefeller, held a large interest in James Stillman's National City Bank (the predecessor of Citibank). Not surprisingly, Aldrich sought to further limit monetary policy by leaving it in the hands of private bankers. Aldrich's proposal, fleshed out at the 1910 Jekyll Island meeting of the nabobs of Wall Street, never became law.[31] The Fed was set up as a government institution in 1913.

The Fed was established in a period when political polarization was extremely high, at a level that went unmatched until recent years. Not surprisingly, the Democrats' plan for a central bank as a public sector institution drew opposition from conservative Republicans. When the House approved the conference report on December 12, 1913, all but two Democrats

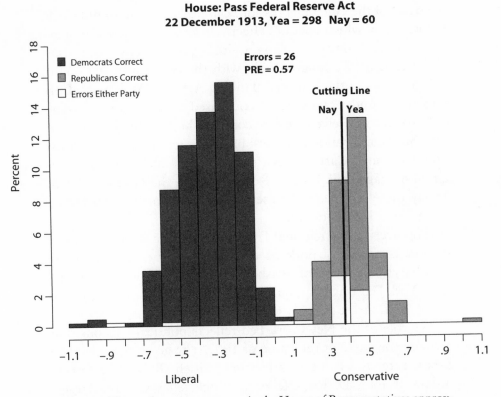

House: Pass Federal Reserve Act
22 December 1913, Yea = 298 Nay = 60

Figure 6.1. The conference report vote in the House of Representatives approving the Federal Reserve Act. The vote divides conservative Republicans, who opposed the act, from moderate Republicans and Democrats, who voted in favor. Note that Republicans on the yea side of the cutting line who voted as predicted voted yea. The white portions of the histogram bars are the prediction errors—nay voters on the yea side of the cutting line, and yea voters on the nay side.

voted in favor, and a majority of Republicans opposed. The vote, as shown in figure 6.1, was strongly along liberal-conservative lines. Conservative Republicans were against it, whereas moderate Republicans voted with the Democrats. The Senate approved the conference report on December 23 in close to a straight party-line vote with all Democrats but only three Republicans in favor. Representative Ron Paul, the self-appointed harasser of the Fed today, would have happily joined the minority in 1913.

The split on reform after the Panic of 1907 foreshadows the polarized ideological splits that would occur a century later.

With the Banking Act of 1935 and the establishment of the Board of Governors in Washington, the Fed became firmly established as an independent regulatory agency of the national government. Although central banking authority has shifted to Washington, the New York Fed retained a special status as the only regional bank with a guaranteed slot on the Open Market Committee. Aldrich's plan still reflects how the boards of the regional Feds are organized today. They continue to have directors from financial institutions with conflicts of interests commensurate with Aldrich's a century ago.

Aldrich might be particularly pleased with the New York Fed board. Lehman Brothers CEO Dick Fuld was a Fed board member until just before the firm's demise.[32] Current New York members include Jamie Dimon, whose JPMorgan Chase obtained government assistance in acquiring Bear Stearns. Former board members include Sandy Weill of Citigroup and Stephen Friedman and John Whitehead of Goldman Sachs. In board seats reserved for representatives of nonprofit organizations, Columbia University, New York University, Princeton University, and the Metropolitan Museum of Art have all been represented by administrators and other worthies; these institutions are dependent on donations from the financial firms and their executives.

Today, regulation remains hampered by the limited response to the Panic of 1907 and the failure to establish a central bank that is more independent of Wall Street and regional banking interests. Moreover, Congress passed entirely on the regulation of securities markets after the Panic of 1907. One of the root causes of the Panic of 1907 was securities speculation. Charles Barney of Knickerbocker Trust had attempted to corner shares in the United Copper Company. Beginning in the 1890s, trust companies, which were created to serve as trustees for large individual investors, corporations, and estates, began to act like banks and accept commercial deposits. Because they faced more relaxed reserve requirements, trust companies paid higher returns on deposits than did banks. Moreover, unlike national banks at that time, trust companies could directly hold securities.[33] Something like Glass-Steagall would have prevented effects of such security speculation from spilling over into commercial banking. A Securities and Exchange Commission (SEC) might have monitored transactions. None of this seemed necessary until the far more severe crisis that began with the stock market crash of 1929.

Although major changes were brought about by Glass-Steagall and the PUHCA, other responses to the Depression were limited. The SEC, unlike the Fed, does not have a source of funding that is independent of Congress. The SEC never secured authority over futures markets because the agricultural committees, rather than the banking committees, in Congress historically had jurisdiction over trading in agricultural commodities. Pork bellies stayed in the pork barrel. The SEC does not have the power to pursue criminal charges without going through the Justice Department. The SEC was made a participant in the bankruptcy proceedings of publically owned corporations by the Chandler Act of 1938, but corporations quickly found chapters of the law and work-arounds that excluded the SEC. The Bankruptcy Reform Act of 1978 removed all SEC powers.[34] The SEC deferred to the securities industry and its advocates in Congress by allowing the New York Stock Exchange to fix prices on brokerage commissions until 1975.[35] If Bernard Madoff's clients believed that the SEC would protect them, they were very unsophisticated investors.

The next financial crisis after the Depression, the meltdown of the S&Ls, saw even more limited changes. FIRREA folded up the FHLBB and put in a new regulator, the Office of Thrift Supervision (OTS), which represented a soft reform. By the beginning of the twenty-first century it was a regulatory venue of choice for mortgage institutions seeking to escape the stricter regulatory arm of the Fed. A concession to the industry in 1989, OTS in more recent years accommodated the likes of Washington Mutual, IndyMac, AIG, and many others. That is, the changes represented by FIRREA were worse than limited; they contributed to the next financial crisis.

What was true of FIRREA was even truer of the earlier policy changes of the forbearance period of the 1980s—deregulating interest rates, allowing adjustable rate mortgages, and permitting S&Ls to trade commercial real estate, junk bonds, and other more exotic investments. Deregulated interest rates encouraged subprime products with higher interest rates for riskier consumers. Adjustable rate mortgages became ever more complex. The crony capitalism of the 1980s, shrouded in the virtues of free market conservatism, led directly to the blowup of 2008. Inadequate responses to previous crises can make a future crisis much worse.

After the S&L crisis, the failure of Long Term Capital Management (LTCM) in 1998 created a mini-crisis. In a nutshell, the LTCM cocktail contained most of the economic and political ingredients that were to form the lethal Kool-Aid of 2008. On the economic side, LTCM made highly leveraged bets involving derivatives. The firm employed some of the best and the brightest quants, including Nobel Prize Laureates Myron Scholes and Robert Merton. Five of the partners, including Scholes and Merton, had been professors at Harvard or Stanford Universities. But big brains sometimes make big mistakes. LTCM's trades were conducted through Bear Stearns, and investors were recruited by Merrill Lynch; both firms went under in 2008. The LTCM crisis reveals behavior that was at best ethically dubious. LTCM's CEO, John Meriwether, was chased from Salomon Brothers when that firm was found to have violated government rules about bidding on Treasury securities. Yet Wall Street and private investors quickly gave him a fresh start and backed him and LTCM. The firm wound up blowing $4.6 billion. Partner Scholes was upbraided by a federal judge in New Haven for tax strategies pursued by LTCM.

On the political side, former assistant Treasury secretary and Fed vice chair David Mullins became an LTCM partner, pushing the revolving door before the end of his term to join LTCM.

Before LTCM's collapse, Mullins was often mentioned as a possible successor to Fed chairman Alan Greenspan.[36]

What was the response to the pop of LTCM? Although the New York Fed brought together major Wall Street firms to organize and finance an orderly liquidation, the legislative and regulatory response in this case was less than limited. Nothing happened. In contrast to the subprime crisis, in which many large investment and commercial banks made bad bets, LTCM was just a single firm that failed.

It should have been a warning about potential systemic risk arising from the use of derivatives. But no new regulations of consequence ensued. Specifically, one of the reasons the New York Fed was so eager to organize a bailout is that derivative contracts are exempt from the automatic stay provisions of bankruptcy.[37] When this exemption was put into law, Republican senator and future presidential candidate Bob Dole touted the exemption as a means of preventing systemic risk, but experience proved to the contrary, as acknowledged by Fed chairman Greenspan and New York Fed president William McDonough.[38] Bankruptcy would not have prevented a mad rush of counterparties trying to seize collateral. The automatic stay exemption could have exacerbated, not diminished, the problem of systemic risk.[39] But no legislative attempt to remedy this problem followed the failure of LTCM. Possible changes could have eliminated the automatic stay exemption or increased regulation of derivative markets, including moving over-the-counter derivative trades onto exchanges. The International Swaps and Derivatives Association lobbied heavily against any change.[40] Even after collateral runs took down Lehman and others in the 2008 crisis, the financial reform of Dodd-Frank did not alter the automatic stay exemption for derivative contracts.[41]

So business as usual prevailed. Five months after LTCM failed, a *Time* cover designated Greenspan, Rubin, and Summers the "Committee to Save the World." Free market conservatism, with a little help from the New York Fed, stayed the course. Meriwether, like P. T. Barnum, knew that suckers are born every day. So he and four of the nonacademic partners went on to set up a new, much smaller hedge fund. This fund, JWM Partners, tanked in the financial crisis and was shuttered in 2009.

The pop of the dot-com equity bubble in 2001 is our final example of delay. At times a response can occur only when events are so bad as to force the hands of free market advocates. The equity bubble was associated both with misleading ratings and analyst recommendations, and with accommodating accounting and audits. These events presented a warning of the effect of bogus information on financial markets. After the Enron scandal broke, Maryland Democrat Paul Sarbanes, the chair of the Senate Banking Committee in 2001–2, sought to increase regulation. The House Financial Services Committee, however, was headed by free market conservative advocate Michael Oxley. Oxley blocked any change until the WorldCom bankruptcy created additional public pressure for action. WorldCom was the largest bankruptcy in American history and held the record until the failure of Lehman Brothers.[42] WorldCom forced Oxley's reluctant hand to move, if only an inch or two.

TRANSITIONS

Limitations and delay in legislation regulating securities, derivatives, and credit markets have their roots in politics. This brings us to our second regularity, that a transition in power is often needed to act to resolve a crisis. This is likely to reflect the fact that incumbents' ideological commitments block action. Politicians rarely adjust to new information about structural problems in the financial sector; gridlock is broken only when the voters throw some of the incumbents out of office.

Nowhere were political preferences more important than with respect to bankruptcy law. The first four bankruptcy acts were passed when the business party—the Federalists in 1800, the Whigs in 1841, and the Republicans in 1867 and 1898—controlled both houses of Congress and the presidency. Unified control was necessary because the agrarian Democrats were opposed to federal intervention per se. In the antebellum era, the Democratic opposition reflected the Jeffersonian ideology of small government, Jefferson's interest in seeing British creditors unable to collect his personal debts through federal courts, and an unwillingness to set any precedent for federal intervention that might lead to intervention on slavery.

The opposition of the Jeffersonian Democrat-Republicans and their successors the Jackson Democrats prevented the passage of bankruptcy laws following the Panics of 1819 and 1857. The passage of the 1841 and 1898 acts occurred not at the outset of the 1837 and 1893 Panics but only after transitions of party control. In 1840, the Whigs gained unified control of the federal government. Republicans were able to pass the 1898 act only after they gained unified control following McKinley's victory in the 1896 election.

The Panic of 1893 hit with the Democrats in control of the executive and legislative branches of the federal government. The Panic contributed to the Republicans securing large gains in the midterm elections of 1894, obtaining a large majority in the House but only a thin plurality in the Senate.[43] Moreover, Cleveland remained in the White House. The Bailey Bill of 1894 was a serious attempt at bankruptcy legislation, but it failed to become law. Moreover, it was limited in that it contained a sunset provision. It mimicked all previous laws that functioned as purely temporary measures to write off the bad debts incurred in a macroeconomic crisis. The Democrats, always wary of bankruptcy as a permanent institution, tried unsuccessfully to attach a sunset provision to the 1898 law.

The 1898 law, advocated by trade creditors, passed mainly with the votes of ideological conservatives.[44] A second dimension, no longer present in American politics, also intervened. Moderate "Wall Street" Democrats from the Middle Atlantic region supported the bill; agrarian Republicans were against it. Interest group politics also was manifest. Representatives from constituencies in forty-three cities that were banking centers, as identified by Dun and Bradstreet, were more likely to support the bankruptcy bill.[45] The ideological lines on bankruptcy reproduced the same divisions found on economic policy throughout the late nineteenth century. When the Interstate Commerce Act was passed in 1887 to regulate the railroads, a liberal and agrarian bloc in Congress opposed a conservative and urban one. The South at the time represented the left wing of the Democratic Party. The Interstate Commerce Act was managed in the House by Judge John Reagan of Texas, the former postmaster general of the Confederacy.[46] As political power transited from one bloc to another, economic policy changed.

Why then did no later transition back to the Democrats undo the 1898 law, as happened in 1803? Why has bankruptcy become a permanent fixture? The eminent bankruptcy scholar David Skeel has argued that sixteen years of Republican government allowed the creation of a bankruptcy bar whose interests supported a permanent law. By the time the Democrats returned to power with Woodrow Wilson as president in 1913, the law had become an institution. As polarization declined, institutionalization meant that bankruptcy policy became a noncontroversial issue. A major revision to the 1898 act, the Chandler Act of 1938, and a complete replacement of the 1898 act by the Bankruptcy Reform Act of 1978 both became law without recorded roll call votes on passage in either the House or the Senate.

The importance of political transitions to bankruptcy law reappeared in a more polarized era with the innovation of credit cards. In the 1990s, credit card issuers flooded mailboxes with card offers and erected enticing booths on college campuses and in airports. When consumers found they could use Chapter 7 of the bankruptcy code to walk away from credit card debt, financial institutions became adamant about "reform," just as they are adamant today about not allowing NINJA (no income, no job, no asset) mortgagees to shelter their homes from foreclosure. Although two successive Republican-controlled Houses passed "reform" during President Bill Clinton's second term, neither became law. Legislation also failed when the Democrats controlled the Senate in the first two years of the George W.

Bush presidency. The bill finally passed, with unified Republican control, in 2005.

The delay forced by the need for a transition in enacting the early bankruptcy laws was costly. Bankruptcy law has two main purposes. One is composition, which prevents creditors from engaging individually in a run on the debtor. The other is the fresh start, which allows the debtor to resume entrepreneurial activity. Failure at one time should not, as is recognized in venture capital markets, entail a permanent ban from borrowing, let alone imprisonment. Not having a permanent legal mechanism for bankruptcy meant foregoing these benefits. The benefits might, for the macroeconomy, be especially useful at the beginning of a crisis. Having to wait several years is costly.

The costs are exacerbated when delay and lack of permanence further imply that cases must be resolved by officials who are both inexperienced and deluged with the defaults that have accumulated in a crisis. Government is limited in capacity and expertise and is open to corruption, all the more in a financial crisis. The historian Edward Balleisen studied the application of the 1841 Bankruptcy Act; he found a judicial system that was overwhelmed by filings. People who had filed for bankruptcy provided legal counsel to those about to file; fraudulent conveyance was rife, as were payoffs to printers and court officials.[47]

The 1841 bankruptcy experience testifies to the moral hazard implicit in anticipated government intervention. Abuse was particularly prominent under the 1841 law. Yet the United States appears to have prospered even if its bankruptcy laws were not only inefficient but also regarded as particularly debtor-friendly when compared to those of European nations. And if government intervention makes sense, we should tackle it earlier rather than later.

Political transition was necessary for policy change in the twentieth century, too. The Panic of 1907 was largely redressed by the personal efforts of J. P. Morgan. Government was peripheral. As mentioned earlier, the major response to the Panic, the Federal Reserve Act, was passed only in 1913, after power passed to the Democrats.

The Great Depression is, of course, the quintessential illustration of our claim that responses to pops await transitions in political power. The delayed policy response was much less limited than prior responses, and was truly a New Deal. The response reflected a severe crisis, a strongly unified government, and the absence of polarization. Earlier in the chapter we summarized the New Deal changes. The Hoover administration did make some efforts to deal with the crisis, establishing the Reconstruction Finance Corporation and the FHLBB. Neither of these measures went far enough to stem the crisis, and neither dealt with the collapsing banking system. Roosevelt was forced to declare a bank holiday when he took office.

Under Hoover, Treasury secretary Mellon was a deficit hawk. He advocated that the federal response should be like what state governments would later be forced to do in the Great Recession of 2007–9: cut spending to offset decreased tax revenues. The effect was the absence of any fiscal stimulus. Budget balance, a constitutional commitment for American states, became an ideological commitment for the Hoover administration. The ideology extended beyond the administration. Budget balance was part of Roosevelt's platform in the 1932 election campaign. Deficit aversion also is said to have caused Roosevelt to damage the recovery in 1937.

The ideology of budget balance in the 1930s illustrates a more general point. The core ideology of one party can often pull the other party in the same direction and limit the impact of a transition. This may be particularly true when polarization is relatively low, as was the case in the 1930s. Even as polarization grows, such pulls, attentive to mass beliefs rather than evidence, could result. The antideficit message of Ross Perot in the 1992 presidential campaign may have led Bill Clinton to push tax increases that gave Congress to the Republicans in the 1994 midterm elections.[48] Tax increases run smack into fundamentalist free market conservative ideology—tax increases, no matter what, are bad. For fundamentalists, low taxes appear to trump budget balance, and deficits can grow. Similarly, the deregulatory aspect of free market conservatism can sweep over both parties, abetting the savings and loan crisis, the accounting scandals at the turn of the twenty-first century, and the implosion of 2008.

Although transitions appear to lead to the most significant policy shifts in response to crises, when things get bad enough some response is necessary even in the absence of transition. A real response to the savings and loan crisis could be delayed throughout the divided government that prevailed for the entire Reagan presidency. A divided government in Washington could no longer put off a response once George H. W. Bush assumed the presidency. The muted response of FIRREA failed to strengthen the regulatory environment. Similarly, the Sarbanes-Oxley Bill can be viewed as a minimal concession to public opinion as a result of the accounting scandals. The legislation might have looked different if the Democrats had had unified control when the scandals broke. Such a scenario would have required not only a presidential victory on the part of Al Gore in 2000 but the Democrats taking control of the House in the same elections and Barney Frank taking control of the House Financial Services Committee.

Our main point, however, does not concern relatively minor adjustments to policy that occur in the absence of transition. What should be stressed is that major changes follow financial crises only after transitions in power, as evidenced by the adoption of bankruptcy laws in the nineteenth century and, in the twentieth, by the Federal Reserve Act and the several innovations of the New Deal.

REVERSALS

Our third regularity was that policies instituted when there is a transition in power are often reversed after subsequent shifts. Few of these reversals take place immediately, but there is one example of a very rapid reversal. The 1841 bankruptcy bill was passed in August of that year. This delayed response to the Panic of 1837 was later repealed by the very Congress that had enacted the legislation. Repeal attempts in 1842 may have been motivated by electoral concerns, but repeal passed only in a lame duck session, in February 1843. Earlier support for the law may have been undermined by corruption and inefficiency in court processing of bankruptcy claims. Bad experiences with the bill did not keep the most conservative members of Congress, New England and Middle Atlantic Whigs, from voting *against* repeal. Repeal resulted when more agrarian—Southern and Midwestern—Whigs switched sides. For these members, as the economic crisis wound down, states' rights considerations may have been stronger than the arguments for a permanent federal law. Both passage and repeal were straightforward left-right votes, but events moved the cutting line to the right, increasing the votes of the left faction.

To our knowledge, the 1841 Bankruptcy Act is the only instance of any legislation being repealed by the enacting Congress.[49] Changes in power are generally required. The 1800 bankruptcy bill, enacted by the Federalists in 1800 was quickly repealed by the Jeffersonians in 1803. More common is an interplay of the *Three I's* that leads to a long process of undoing, in which a shift in power in Congress, the presidency, and the courts; a shift in beliefs; and administrative and judicial intervention all combine to alter the landscape of financial regulation. We summarized, in chapter 5, how shifts beginning in the late 1970s altered the regulatory landscape in a way that laid the conditions for the crisis of 2008. Here we draw attention to the shifting control of federal institutions that occurred.

In table 6.1, we have divided the eighty years since Franklin Delano Roosevelt became president into four twenty-year blocks of time. For each block we have indicated the number of years with a Democratic president, a Democratic-controlled House, a Democratic-controlled Senate, and the number of years a majority of the sitting Supreme Court justices were appointees of Democratic presidents. We also note the number of years that the Democrats had a filibuster-proof majority in the Senate.

TABLE 6.1.
Democratic control of federal government, 1933–2012

	1933–1952	1953–1972	1973–1992	1993–2012
Years Democratic Presidency	20	8	4	12
Years Democratic House Majority	18	18	20	6
Years Democratic Senate Majority	18	18	14	9
Years Filibuster Proof Majority Democrats	10	2	2	0
Maj. of Supreme Court Dem. Appointments	14	19	0	0*

Note: *The Democrats did have a filibuster-proof majority for a portion of the 111th Congress.

In the first period, the Democrats were firmly in control. By 1939, Roosevelt had been able to appoint a majority on the Supreme Court. For half of the period, starting in 1935, he enjoyed filibuster-proof majorities. In the Eightieth Congress (1947–48), control of both houses did revert briefly to the Republicans but otherwise the Democrats were dominant. The same was largely true of the next twenty-year period, from 1953 to 1972. Republican appointees formed a Supreme Court majority only in 1972 after Nixon made two appointments. The Democrats, however, had largely lost the ability to block filibusters. It would have been increasingly easy for conservatives to block any financial regulation that moved away from free market conservatism. Republican power to block continued thereafter, even though the number of votes needed for cloture was cut from sixty-seven to sixty in 1975. In the last period, which takes us from Clinton to Obama, the Democrats did have more success in presidential elections. This success should not mask the continued hold of Republicans on the Supreme Court. An equally important observation is the continuation of declining Democratic fortunes in congressional elections. Although there may be some use in crabbing about the unpopularity of health care reform, the Tea Party, and continued unemployment in the 2010 midterm elections, the resurgence of House Republicans is unsurprising in the longer perspective provided by the table.

The Republicans, moreover, enjoyed these electoral successes while moving in a conservative direction more strongly than the Democrats moved in a liberal direction. This movement by the Republicans became the driving force in increasing polarization. Their move to the right further tilted the scales against any government intervention in financial markets. If voter preferences had remained constant from the 1960s onward, the Republican move to the right should have been an electoral disaster, continuing the Barry Goldwater debacle of 1964. Au contraire. In chapter 9 we return to this topic and discuss the political shift to free market conservatism. For the moment, we note that the trend away from the Democrats fully matches the numerous acts that undid the financial regulatory landscape of the 1930s and the many failures to take regulatory action as new financial products were developed.

ELECTORAL CONCERNS

Our final regularity is that the response to pops is delayed and influenced by short-run electoral concerns. The executives of financial sector firms are often criticized for responding to incentives that generate a short-term focus and excessively risky investments. Politicians also have a short-term focus. Just as an executive may care only about his firm's stock price a year out, politicians may care only about winning the next election.

Short-term reelection concerns were clearly evident in how the response to the savings and loan crisis was delayed until after the 1988 elections. Dealing with the crisis required a large recapitalization of the FSLIC. The insurance premiums collected by the FSLIC from the S&Ls would not suffice were it to shut down the failed S&Ls and pay off their insured depositors. To make up for this shortfall, Congress needed to make a substantial appropriation. Unlike most other government inefficiencies, such as defense procurement and bridges to nowhere, which are parts of the normal annual budget cycle, recapitalization would have required a large, exceptional expenditure. Incumbents of both parties were concerned that dealing with the crisis would look like a bailout and be unpopular with the voters in November 1988. Any recapitalization could be seen as the failure of the banking deregulation and regulatory forbearance that had been supported by both parties. Even though the gravity of the S&L industry's situation was widely recognized by experts both inside and outside the Beltway, discussion of the crisis by the candidates was essentially absent from the campaign. In a period of divided government, with a Republican president and a Democratic Congress, incumbent protection was valuable all around. The response to the S&L crisis foreshadowed the flight from responsibility of many members of Congress following the demise of Lehman Brothers and the government takeover of AIG.

Electoral concerns, as in the S&L crisis, can arise directly when the response to a pop is likely to be sufficiently salient that it evokes a response in the mass public. But an indirect channel can be of even greater importance: campaign contributions. In chapter 4 we presented evidence that campaign contributions by the financial sector have risen in importance. They are also bipartisan. Members of Congress are likely to be aware that when the pop is over they will still need financial sector dollars for their campaigns. As a result, they may do only what is needed to resolve the current crisis without putting any teeth into legislation that would make a future crisis less likely to occur. We saw such an outcome when FIRREA was passed to resolve the S&L crisis. Money was appropriated to write off that crisis but a very lax regulatory structure was left in place. The new regulatory approach was, as we indicated earlier, a limitation that permitted regulatory venue shopping and contributed to the subprime mortgage crisis.

Worse, short-termism among those in the executive branch and Congress reflects not only electoral imperatives but opportunities upon exiting government service. Republicans Phil and Wendy Gramm went from Washington to UBS and Enron, respectively. Robert Rubin just made a stop at the Treasury Department on his way from Goldman Sachs to Citicorp. Rahm Emanuel and Larry Summers both did stints on Wall Street after the Clinton administration. Peter Orszag went to Citigroup from the Obama White House. Both the opportunity to raise campaign funds and the opportunity to enjoy some of the Wall Street rents are, at the least, likely to cloud judgments about the appropriate response to not only a financial bubble but also a financial pop.

Conclusion

In this chapter we have indicated how politics delays and limits the response to a pop. Changes in political power and the short-term incentives of political actors combine to condition the timing and the extent of the response. In the ensuing chapters, we return to these themes as we detail their impact on the pop of 2008.

CHAPTER 7
The Pop of 2008

Introduction

We have seen that, historically, responses to pops have been limited and delayed. This pattern continued in the recent crisis. Housing prices began to slide in 2006 and market bubbles began popping in 2007 but serious government intervention through legislation was delayed until American International Group (AIG) collapsed the day after Lehman Brothers fell in September 2008. In April of that year Treasury officials Neel Kashkari and Phillip Swagel had developed a plan to recapitalize the banks in the event of a meltdown.[1] Before AIG collapsed, giving the force of legislation to such a plan was unthinkable. Congress was populated not only by free market conservatives but also by liberals opposed to any sort of Wall Street bailout, especially one proposed by a Republican administration. After AIG's collapse, the plan became imperative. It was taken off the shelf and turned into the Troubled Asset Relief Program (TARP). Regulatory reform of the financial system was delayed until after a partisan transition in power.

Even after the transition, the administration of President Barack Obama gave several indications that any change in financial regulation would be limited. The administration likely was cautious so as to reassure financial markets. Despite the passage of TARP in September 2008, markets were edgy well into the first months of the new administration. The Dow Jones Industrial Average, still over 9000 at the beginning of 2009, plunged as low as 6600 in early March. Whether to assure markets, to appease the "Money Wing," or because of ideological sympathies, the Obama administration restored the ancien régime,

Figure 7.1. The ancien régime. Former Clinton economic advisor Gene Sperling and Robert Rubin—dynasty members Peter Orszag, Tim Geithner, and Larry Summers at the White House, February 9, 2009. *Source*: Official White House photo by Pete Souza.

former officials who had presided over deregulation and previous bailouts in the administration of Bill Clinton in the 1990s. Former Treasury secretary Lawrence Summers was brought into the White House; Timothy Geithner became Treasury secretary. Geithner had been Summers's undersecretary, and then, as New York Federal Reserve president, he participated in organizing the Bear Stearns takeover, the AIG bailout, and other responses of the administration of George W. Bush to the near collapse of the financial system in 2008. Summers and Geithner were protégés of Clinton's first Treasury secretary and Citigroup vice chair Robert Rubin, as was Peter Orszag, who became head of the Office of Management and Budget.[2] Obama's team deserves credit for stabilizing the markets. Stress tests were imposed on nineteen large banks. The tests, conducted with rigor, indicated better than expected health. The results most likely made an important contribution to recovery in the financial markets. At the same time, the presence of the team undoubtedly signaled that no major structural change was planned.

President Obama's political ties to figures in the financial sector did not suggest that the administration would discipline individuals and firms whose behavior had been inappropriate. During the 2008 campaign, Obama appointed James Johnson, a former Fannie Mae CEO and currently a member of the board at Goldman Sachs, as head of his vice presidential selection team. After the election, in the summer of 2009, Obama allowed himself to be photographed playing golf on Martha's Vineyard with UBS North America CEO Robert Wolf, a major fundraiser. UBS had received billions in funds through the AIG rescue after paying a $780 million fine for providing hidden bank accounts to thousands of Americans. Obama also appointed Steven Rattner, a partner in the investment firm Quadrangle Group, to preside over the auto industry bailout. Rattner was later forced out of Quadrangle as a result of a scandal involving the New York State Common Retirement Fund. Rattner also agreed to pay a civil fine and to be barred from the securities industry for two years.

We stress Obama's ties to the financial sector and his chosen advisers not to question the competence or expert knowledge or contacts of these people. We suggest only that Obama failed to promote the high ethical standards and fundamental reform of financial markets that he promised during his presidential campaign. His calculation was that replacing the "reckless few" with some semireckless savvy would reassure Wall Street.

The Obama administration also signaled policy preferences inconsistent with substantial reform. In March 2009, Obama continued the Bush administration's support of the big banks in *Cuomo v. Clearing House.*[3] This position placed the administration in opposition to the four liberal justices on the Court, consumer organizations, and the former Democratic attorney general of New York, Eliot Spitzer, and his successor, Andrew Cuomo. The administration initially sided with Wall Street by opposing

Figure 7.2. Economic reform. Elizabeth Warren, Barack Obama, and Timothy Geithner at the White House. This appears to be the only White House website photo of Ms. Warren. *Source*: Official White House photo by Pete Souza.

the Volcker Rule until pressure from congressional Democrats made that position untenable. Finally, the administration kept its distance from reform advocate Elizabeth Warren, whom Congress had charged with oversight of TARP. Again under pressure from congressional Democrats, the administration did give Warren the lead in setting up the Consumer Financial Protection Bureau that was established by the Wall Street Reform and Consumer Protection Act, better known as the Dodd-Frank Bill after its primary authors, Connecticut Senator Christopher Dodd and Massachusetts Representative Barney Frank.

Dodd-Frank was the main piece of regulatory legislation responding to the pop. President Obama signed the bill into law on July 21, 2010, well over two years after the Federal Reserve was forced to finance the sale of Bear Stearns to JPMorgan Chase, and nearly two years after Fannie Mae and Freddie Mac were placed in government conservatorship. Even though the legislation was thousands of pages long, Dodd-Frank left much to rule making by federal agencies, introducing even further delays. Many of these rules are yet to be promulgated (as of this writing at the end of 2012).

Rules on credit risk retention are an example of the delay. Only on March 28, 2011, did agencies announce initial regulations for how much "skin in the game" mortgage originators and securitizers would be required to retain.[4] The regulations will not become final until after a period for public comment— where, of course, the "public" means financial industry lobbyists. A final rule is not expected until 2013; it would be effective only one year later. This pattern of delay appears endemic. A report from the law firm Davis Polk indicates that as of June 1, 2012, regulators had missed statutory deadlines on 67 percent of the required rules under Dodd-Frank.[5]

The final disposition of Fannie and Freddie will be even more delayed. The fate of the government-sponsored enterprises (GSEs) was not dealt with by Dodd-Frank and remains undecided at the end of 2012.

The delay in financial reform reflects, as has historically been the case, partisan politics. Dodd-Frank was passed after two sets of elections, in 2006 and 2008, moved the United States from unified Republican control of the executive and legislature to unified Democratic control. Dodd-Frank undoubtedly is quite different from what would have resulted if the Republicans had retained power. The best evidence for this counterfactual scenario is the eagerness of House Republicans to undo parts of Dodd-Frank after regaining control in the 2010 midterm elections. As a corollary, Wall Street has largely shifted its support away from Barack Obama and toward Mitt Romney for the 2012 presidential election. Pressure to undo the reform is present even though Dodd-Frank was limited.

Reforms were limited by giving regulators extensive rule-making authority. Regulators will be under considerable pressure from the industry (and the Republican House of Representatives) to accommodate Wall Street interests. Consider again the example of "skin in the game" rules for mortgage originators and securitizers. In the March 2011 proposed rule, financial institutions would not be required to retain a share of all mortgages and would be permitted considerable flexibility in how they meet the requirement for other mortgages. Another example of lax implementation of Dodd-Frank is Treasury Secretary Geithner's decision to remove foreign exchange swaps from clearing and exchange requirements that Dodd-Frank imposed on other derivatives contracts.[6] An ideal reform would have limited the scope of regulator discretion in order to stem the inevitable drift toward outcomes preferred by Wall Street. But such a bill was unobtainable because the Democrats lacked a filibuster-proof majority in the 111th Senate. Moreover, several Democrats, such as Senator Ben Nelson of Nebraska, could hardly be classified as "progressives." On critical amendments, ten or more moderate Democrats often peeled off from the progressives and voted with the Republicans.

Two other limits to the government's response to the financial crisis are as important as the limitations of Dodd-Frank. First, as just mentioned, the future of the giant GSEs Fannie and Freddie remains up in the air. Second, little has been done to stem the tide of mortgage foreclosures.

Congress passed a mortgage modification bill, the American Housing Rescue and Foreclosure Prevention Act (AHRFPA) in 2008. Because AHRFPA relied on private sector participation and did little to change private incentives, it was ineffective. Then in February 2009, the president announced the Home Affordable Modification Program (HAMP). This effort, as outlined by former TARP inspector general Neil Barofsky, has also been ineffective.[7] By the end of 2011, in a nation in which two-thirds of 117 million households own homes, only 600,000 mortgages had been renegotiated through a government-sponsored program.

The low number of renegotiated mortgages is hardly surprising; HAMP relied on the same private financial intermediaries that sought profits through subprime mortgages and their derivatives.[8] In refinancing, these lenders may have the benefit of lowering the probability of default, but hampering the refinancing allows the holder of the mortgage to continue to receive payments at higher interest rates than would be paid in a restructured mortgage. The government accommodated lenders by signing watered-down consent agreements with mortgage servicers on foreclosures and loan modifications.[9] As of April 2011 6.7 million homes had been foreclosed, and another 3.3 million foreclosures were expected through 2012.[10] Another version of the program, the Home Affordable Refinance Program (HARP 2.0), finally appears to have led to increased restructuring in the first quarter of 2012.[11] But by the summer of 2012, foreclosures began to rise again after legal uncertainties were resolved by a legal settlement between banks and state attorneys general over mortgage abuses.[12] Foreclosures are a primary factor in the drop in homeownership shown in figure 5.1.

Ideology Remained Unchanged in the Pop

Despite the shortcomings of Dodd-Frank and other policy initiatives undertaken by the Obama White House and the Democratic-controlled Congress, the shift to unified government was an important factor in the response to the pop. As we document below, this power shift was far more important than any shift in ideology at the level of individual politicians. Things changed because of electoral victories, not because of a change in the beliefs of legislators. Few, if any members of Congress, expressed a change in conviction about free market conservatism similar to that of Richard Posner, chief judge of the Seventh Court of Appeals and faculty member at the University of Chicago Law School,[13] or even as much as Alan Greenspan, who testified to Congress that he had been misled by his ideology (see chapter 2).

To document the ideological stability in Congress, we compute two new sets of ideology scores to capture a shift induced by the financial crisis.[14] The two scores are fully independent measures of ideology. The first set is based on all roll call votes in the 110th Congress before September 15, 2008, the date of Lehman Brothers' bankruptcy. The second set is based on the remaining roll calls in the 110th Congress and all roll calls in the 111th, which passed Dodd-Frank in 2010.[15] Figure 7.3 displays the results as scatter plots. Each legislator is described by a token, with *D* for Democrats and *R* for Republicans.[16] The horizontal axis in the figure captures ideology before the date of Lehman Brothers' bankruptcy; the vertical, after that bankruptcy.

In the House there is no indication of important change. The tokens pretty much sit on a line. If the pre-Lehman and post-Lehman scores were unrelated, the correlation would be 0. If they sat perfectly on a line, the correlation would be 1.0. The actual correlation is 0.99. Even within each party, the correlations are greater than 0.92. In other words, Republicans did not change their liberal-conservative positions relative to one another. Neither did Democrats.

The Senate story is the same, except for a lower correlation for Democrats. This looser relationship is due in large part to the aberrant behavior of Russ Feingold, whose estimated position moved from that of a very liberal to that of a moderate member of the Democratic delegation. Feingold's move partly reflects his vote against the Dodd-Frank Bill. Without Feingold, the correlation increased from 0.74 to 0.79. Some of the discrepancy arose because the Senate scores are based on far fewer votes (641 before Lehman and 712 after) than those for the House (1,765 and 1,747, respectively).

That we did not find a major reordering of positions pre- and post-Lehman suggests that the financial crisis and high unemployment did not dramatically change the degree to which free market conservatism is internalized in Congress. This is especially true of the Republicans. Of course, it is technically possible that financial regulation's mapping onto ideology changed. Perhaps all the legislators moved to the left—away from pure free market conservatism. This is very unlikely, though, given the 2011 efforts of House Republicans to undo major portions of Dodd-Frank.

The stability shown in figure 7.3, moreover, masks important political changes, as it is based only on legislators who served in both the 110th and 111th Congresses. When the Democrats gained in the 2008 elections, free market conservatives did not

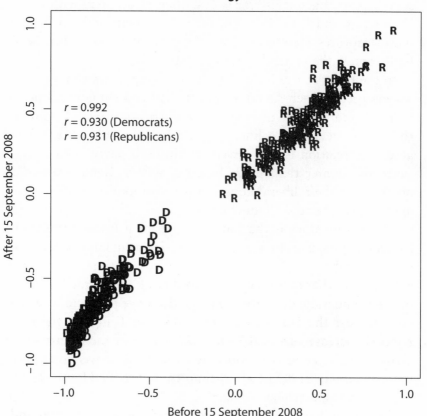

Figure 7.3. Ideology scores before and after the collapse of Lehman Brothers. Each token represents a member of Congress. Each token plots the member's pre- and post-Lehman ideological score. The points fall nearly on a line, indicating that the financial crisis did not change the ideological alignment in either chamber.

exit to be replaced by liberals of the Ted Kennedy and Russ Feingold stripe. On the contrary, the Democrats gained by recruiting moderate candidates to run in constituencies that were more "purple" than "blue."

In contrast, when the Republicans gained in the 2010 elections, the party moved in a sharply conservative direction. For example, Pat Toomey, a staunch proponent of free market conservatism

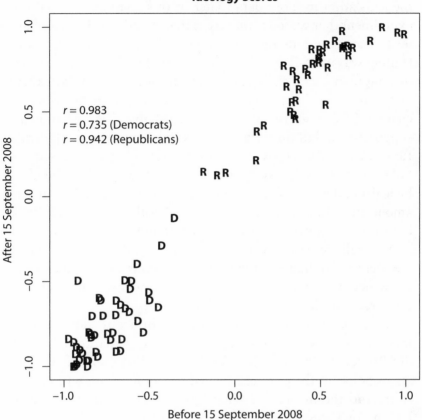

Senate: Before Lehman vs. after Lehman Ideology Scores

$r = 0.983$
$r = 0.735$ (Democrats)
$r = 0.942$ (Republicans)

After 15 September 2008

Before 15 September 2008

Figure 7.3. (*cont.*)

and a former president of the Club for Growth, replaced Pennsylvania senator Arlen Specter, a moderate whose support was important to the passage of both the stimulus package and Dodd-Frank. Perversely, free market conservatism has been strengthened by the financial crisis and the ensuing recession. Ideology, as figure 7.3 shows, exhibited no reordering at the individual level.

Our conclusion that beliefs did not change is buttressed by studying two votes on a proposal by Brad Miller (D-NC) to regulate predatory lending. The first vote took place in 2007 (pre-Lehman), the second in 2009 (post-Lehman). We discuss the legislation in more detail later in this chapter. The natural experiment that we focus on here is that the Miller Bill (see chapter 5) was essentially the same in both years. Because predatory lending was identified as a major source of subprime mortgages, one might expect a strong shift in favor of the bill. In fact, there was almost no shift; the cutting points (a concept described in chapter 2) are statistically indistinguishable.[17] All Democrats supported the bill on both votes, as did a number of moderate Republicans. Extremely conservative Republicans opposed the bill both times. What switching occurred took place in the ideological middle of House Republicans. There were 23 switchers among the 132 Republicans who voted both in 2007 and 2009, but there was a net increase of only 5 Republican votes in favor. The overall increase in votes for the Miller Bill occurred because the Democrats had a large increase in seats as a result of the 2008 elections. The pop of 2008 did not persuade Republicans that predatory lending needed regulation.

Congress as a whole failed to move in a direction strongly favoring increased government regulation of markets. Neither did President Obama. Therefore, in our discussion of the policy response to the pop, we are justified in focusing on electoral shifts and the institutional structure of American government and in downplaying the role of any ideological shift.

Legislation after the Pop

The legislative reaction to the pop consisted primarily of the Troubled Asset Relief Program (TARP), passed in October 2008; the Economic Recovery Act (the "stimulus package"), passed in February 2009; and the Dodd-Frank Act, passed in July 2010. These three pieces of legislation illustrate the problems of delay, limits, transition, and electoral incentives. In our discussion we make use of the theoretical approach we presented in chapters 2 through 4. That framework focused on one-dimensional liberal-conservative politics in which agenda setters need to obtain the support of actors such as the filibuster and veto pivots.

Candidate Barack Obama campaigned on a model of the legislative process that is quite different from the pivotal politics model. As a candidate, Obama asserted that "Americans of every political stripe were hungry for . . . a new kind of politics," one in which reasonable public policy compromises could be worked out with the opposition.[18] But polarization precludes that sort of new bipartisan politics. Obama might have been better served by accepting from the get-go that he would never get more than sixty votes in the Senate.[19] Broad-based compromises never happened. The pivots ruled.

For both the stimulus package and Dodd-Frank, the pivotal politics model provides a nearly complete accounting of the outcome. The roll call votes on passage nearly perfectly divide liberals and conservatives. In each case the successful Democratic proposal is one that just barely satisfied the filibuster pivot in the Senate. For the stimulus package, the filibuster pivot was Olympia Snowe of Maine. She demanded and received important concessions that trimmed $200 billion from the bill. The death of Edward Kennedy resulted in Scott Brown of Massachusetts becoming the filibuster pivot on Dodd-Frank. Brown also received an important concession—the elimination of a $19 billion tax on banks. The pivotal politics story does poorly in explaining votes on Henry Paulson's TARP, however. Voting on TARP reflected electoral concerns in the shadow of a failed presidency, blame-game politics, and the proposal going against core elements of Republican ideology, because TARP represented not only government intervention but also government expenditure. We begin by applying the pivotal politics model to the stimulus package and Dodd-Frank and then return to claim that TARP is truly an exception that proves the rule.

Economic Stimulus and Financial Regulation in the 111th Congress

The 111th Congress closely followed the pivotal politics script. The legislative coalitions that passed the administration's three major pieces of legislation—the stimulus package, health care reform, and financial reform—were all of minimal winning size. That is, they controlled just enough votes to avoid a filibuster in the Senate. Not only were these coalitions of minimal size, they were essentially the same. Nearly the same sixty votes were used to pass the two pieces of legislation related to the financial crisis and the Senate version of the health care bill that was passed before the election of Scott Brown. Not surprisingly, the splits pitted liberals against conservatives. A small deviation from this pattern occurred when Russ Feingold, a very liberal member of the Senate, voted against the Dodd-Frank Bill on the principle that it did not go far enough. But by and large the playbook for the first two years of the Obama presidency was to persuade sixty Senate liberals and moderates to take on forty conservatives. The House of Representatives also divided into liberal and conservative blocs. In that chamber, which has no filibuster, the Democrats held large majorities. A few members could vote out of line without endangering passage of the legislation.

The Mapping of Complex Legislation: An Aside

Before we show how roll call voting on these major bills conformed to the pivotal politics model, we pause to ask how it would be possible to take issues as complex as economic stimulus and financial regulation and shoehorn them into a simple battle along a single liberal-conservative dimension.

Legislation is far from a simple yes-no decision like "credit card late payment fees are limited to a maximum of ten dollars per month," which might be thought to provoke a liberal-conservative split. Quite the opposite: rhetoric, framing, and manipulation—that is, plain old wheeling and dealing—are important for holding a coalition together. As a result, acts of Congress now are hundreds or thousands of pages long, each sentence representing a bit of persuasion for someone. Not only do we, as citizens, not want to know what is in these rotten

sausages, we don't have the time to know. Coalition maintenance tends to benefit from a lack of transparency.

These lengthy bills clearly involve many dimensions. At first
glance, the coalitions that support them might be thought to be
unstable. Opponents could tweak a proposal that would buy
off a legislator. For example, on the stimulus package, Olympia
Snowe demanded and received a large cut in funds that were to
be used to preserve jobs for state and local public employees.
Could members more liberal than Snowe be led into opposition by a proposal to cut highway construction funding as well?
Unlikely. Could they be led into opposition by a proposal to
increase the highway construction portion? Not credible. The
many components of a bill may in fact stabilize it into a liberal-
conservative alignment. Snowe could be brought on board more
easily by allowing her to cut a portion of the bill she strongly
disliked rather than restricting her to making an across-the-
board cut.

The complexity of the bills, moreover, may not arise from
additions to the pork barrel. These provisions may be directed
at broadening the bill to incorporate the core ideology of the
agenda-setting party, thereby helping to define the bill as a
liberal-conservative choice. The financial crisis led to the Dodd-
Frank Bill. On the financial side, the central issue was certainly
how to solve the problem of systemic risk.

Systemic risk is hardly a liberal-conservative issue. Each regulatory piece involves complex regulatory trade-offs. For example,
mandates about down payments and loan-to-value may limit
risk by making default less likely. The same mandates, however,
would exclude lower-income people from the mortgage market.
As another example, large financial institutions may well want
to know that in the future they can gamble with impunity, but in
the larger society neither liberals nor conservatives are gunning
for another TARP.

On the one hand, there is a danger of overregulation. How
does one deal with systemic risk when building, as was necessary with Dodd-Frank, a coalition of liberals? Building this

coalition was very difficult given the complexity of the trade-offs. On the other hand, the core ideological belief of the liberals—egalitarianism—calls for redistribution, especially targeted to ascriptive identities of race, ethnicity, and gender. So it is not surprising that the legislation created a Consumer Financial Protection Bureau with a dedicated budget outside congressional control. It is also not surprising that this is the portion of the bill most contested by the new Republican House majority.

Furthermore, the bill, at the urging of Maxine Waters (D-CA), an African American congresswoman, included the new Offices of Minority and Women Inclusion in regulatory agencies. It also includes provisions aimed at ending human rights violations connected to armed conflict and trade in minerals from the Republic of the Congo. All these provisions likely increased liberal support for the bill as a whole and may well have decreased conservative support.

In summary, lengthy bills may readily induce splits on the liberal-conservative dimension, and making a bill longer may in fact reinforce how well the bill maps onto the dimension.

The Politics of Stimulus: Getting Along with Pivots

Following a noticeable slowdown in the economy at the end of 2007, the Bush administration proposed an economic stimulus package in January 2008. The centerpieces of this proposal were one-time income tax rebate checks and business tax breaks. Although discretionary fiscal policy had long fallen out of favor among conservatives, the focus on tax cutting minimized the break with ideological orthodoxy.

Democrats also supported an expansionary fiscal program, but they did not support the Bush plan's sole reliance on tax relief. Democratic legislators argued strongly that the package should also include increased spending especially on unemployment insurance, aid to states, and public works. Leading Democratic presidential candidate Hillary Clinton put forward a plan for $70 billion in spending for housing, heating subsidies, state aid, and $40 billion in tax rebates if conditions worsened. Another point of ideological conflict was the refusal of the administration and Republicans to support rebate checks for workers who did not pay federal income tax, essentially arguing that rebates for non–income tax payers constituted a form of welfare.

In formulating their response to the president's plan, Democratic leaders faced two problems. First, the 2006 elections that had provided them with their legislative majority also added a large number of fiscal conservatives to their caucus who were more likely to oppose expansions of social spending to stimulate the economy. Second, the leadership was concerned with the party's fiscal image. The Democratic Party had used the spiraling deficits of the Bush years to put itself forward as a party of fiscal responsibility. This new reputation solidified the support not just of independent voters but of the party's "money" wing. Consequently, Democratic leaders were wary of getting so far in front of the president that they might once again be branded as big spenders. A further complication was that any stimulus plan would involve the Democratic Congress waiving the "pay as you go" budget rules that they reinstituted when they regained control of Congress.[20]

So despite important partisan and ideological differences over the structure of a stimulus plan, the House of Representatives quickly passed a $164 billion package that more or less hewed to the Bush administration's priorities. But the Democratic leadership of the Senate pushed for a much more extensive plan that cost $204 billon, which included extensions of unemployment insurance, subsidies for home heating, and subsidies for the coal mining industry.[21] Although the larger measure earned the support of eight Republican senators (including several in tough reelection situations), Democratic leaders failed to obtain cloture and the measure failed.[22] The Senate tacked payments to Social Security recipients and disabled veterans onto the House bill and passed the measure 81–16. The House then adopted the Senate version with a vote of 380–34.[23] President Bush signed the final $168 billion package.

Although an unusual level of bipartisanship (especially for the House) led to very quick passage of the first stimulus bill, the necessary political expedients minimized its effectiveness. The insistence on rebate checks rather than adjusted tax withholding meant that it took several months for the money to hit the economy.[24] Moreover, because the rebates came in the form of income tax credits rather than offsets to payroll taxes, many low-income Americans (those most likely to spend the refunds) did not receive assistance. The lack of aid to states and support for unemployment extensions also allowed the financial situation of states and the unemployed to deteriorate. Moreover, the polarized debate over making the Bush tax cuts permanent precluded discussions of any durable changes in tax law that might have had stronger economic effects.[25]

The bill heralded the end of bipartisan cooperation on fiscal stimulus. As the 2008 elections approached, Democrats increasingly called for a second round of stimulus, which Republicans were just as adamant in resisting. The shape of the next fiscal program would be delayed, to be determined by the presidential and congressional elections that fall. The partisan debate followed the traditional ideological pattern: John McCain and the Republicans argued that any future stimulus ought to focus on personal and business income tax cuts (by making the Bush-era tax cuts permanent) while Barack Obama and the Democrats argued for more spending targeted toward those of low income, the unemployed, and struggling homeowners. The Democrats also stressed the need to boost infrastructure spending by funding "shovel-ready projects."

After Obama won the election in November 2008, many thought that he might encourage a lame duck congressional session to pass stimulus measures. But it was determined that any such measures might be limited by opposition from President Bush. Consequently, stimulus legislation was further delayed until the new Congress convened in January, with the expectation that passage would not occur until after the inauguration.[26]

While candidate Obama campaigned on behalf of a $175 billion stimulus plan, spiraling job losses and cuts in production suggested that a much more expensive package would be necessary. By the end of November, Democratic leaders were pushing for a package closer to $300 billion. By December, the target number had reached $600 billion. Some economists, both Democrat and Republican, argued that the package should be twice that large.

Several factors complicated the formulation of the 2009 stimulus package, formally designated the American Recovery and Investment Act. The first is that the urgency of the situation and the exigencies of a presidential transition (much of the economic team was not yet in place) meant that the administration would have to defer to Congress on many of the details in the package. This opened the door to funding many congressional pet projects that were hard to justify on purely macroeconomic grounds.[27]

In some sense, the loading up of pork was unavoidable. Most economists were pushing for a very large number, and the money had to be spent on something. This outcome, however, helped foster an image of the new administration as fiscally undisciplined. That Republicans were able to exploit this image undermined any hopes of the Obama administration for a bipartisan pact. Cross-party cooperation was considered important both because Obama had promised to foster a postpartisan environment in Washington and because it would have better insulated him against charges of pursuing a left-wing agenda.

By January, the size of the proposed package had reached $775 billion. It grew to $825 billion by the end of the month. But it remained much smaller than what even some Republican economists were advocating. (This advocacy had little effect on Republican politicians, however.) Moreover, fissures within the Democratic Party emerged over the size of the tax cut provisions relative to social spending and investment in infrastructure.[28] For their part, the Republicans began to attack the program as too large and too light on tax cuts. Concerns about deficits and debt began to be expressed openly by both Republicans and moderate Democrats.

The two houses of Congress approved the conference report on the stimulus package on February 13, 2009. We begin with the House vote, shown in figure 7.4. Because the House operates

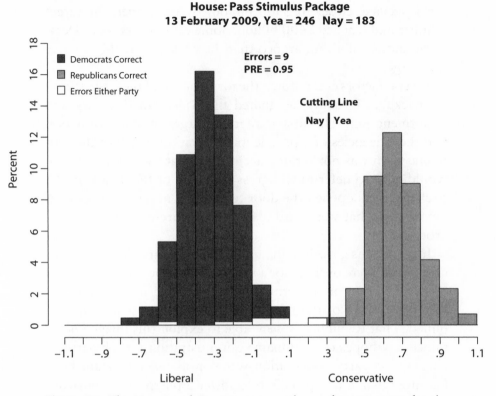

Figure 7.4. The House and Senate votes on the conference report for the Stimulus Package. In the Senate vote, the single prediction error represents Voinovich (R-OH).

by majority rule without a filibuster, 255 Democrats, in a chamber of 435 members, had a relatively easy time passing legislation in the lower house. The conference report was approved by a lopsided vote of 246 to 183.[29]

The vote went strict along party lines with the exception of seven Democrats who voted against the stimulus package.[30] None of the seven—Bobby Bright (AL), Peter DeFazio (OR), Parker Griffith (AL), Walt Minnick (ID), Collin Peterson (MN), Heath Shuler (NC), and Gene Taylor (MS)—held a safe seat. Four were defeated for reelection in 2010; the other three obtained 55 percent of the vote or less. With one exception, DeFazio, all seven had ideological positions close to the vote's cutting line. In other words, they were estimated to be nearly indifferent on the

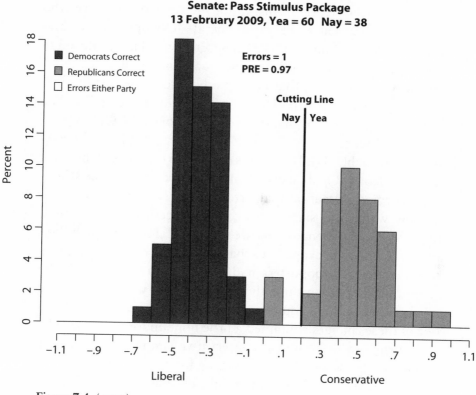

Senate: Pass Stimulus Package
13 February 2009, Yea = 60 Nay = 38

Figure 7.4. (*cont.*)

issue. One may have already been tilting conservative. In September 2009, Parker Griffith of Alabama continued a pattern, started by Strom Thurmond, of Southern Democrats switching to the Republican Party. When Griffith switched parties his DW-NOMINATE score jumped all the way from moderate center to conservative (the numerical change was from −0.01 to +0.54). Griffith was far from pivotal. Party discipline was not necessary to bring him or other defectors into line.

The Senate vote on the stimulus package conference report, shown in figure 7.4, is a different story. To get to sixty votes, the administration needed all fifty-six voting Democrats as well as Bernie Sanders, the Independent. (Ted Kennedy was too ill to vote, and Minnesota's Al Franken had not yet been seated following a contested election.) The administration also needed three votes from Republicans. It got the votes of the three who are by our estimates the most liberal—Olympia Snowe and Susan Collins of Maine and Arlen Specter (who later switched to the Democratic Party) of Pennsylvania.[31] The result was a minimal winning coalition that fit perfectly onto a one-dimensional liberal-conservative map. The vote is shown in figure 7.4. The only prediction error is that of George Voinovich (R-OH), whose ideological score was to the right of Specter's but is statistically indistinguishable. The Democrats did obtain the votes of the three most moderate Republicans. Voinovich's vote against the stimulus package represents a small error for our statistical model.[32]

How were these sixty votes cobbled together? Media attention focused on Senator Snowe's demand for a $200 billion reduction in the package in exchange for her vote. One suspects that many other supporters had their demands met, with the result that more than three thousand changes were made to the bill between initial House passage and final enactment. Each one of these changes contained a little bonbon for someone. The vote turns out to be liberal-conservative simply because fewer bonbons were needed for liberals than for conservatives.

Upon signing the $787 billion bill, President Obama did not rule out a second stimulus package.[33] But public support for the package was never very strong. At the time of passage, a bare majority supported it.[34] But strong majorities felt that tax cuts rather than spending increases were the most effective part of the package.[35]

When joblessness failed to decline, not only did the Recovery Act decline in popularity but voters increasingly split on partisan lines. Most important, independent voters who had been crucial to Obama's election began to accept the Republican narrative that the stimulus package had harmed the economy. Table 7.1 provides partisan breakdowns for two questions asked in July 2009:

So far, do you think the government's stimulus package has made the economy better, made the economy worse, or has it had no impact on the economy so far?

TABLE 7.1.
Voter attitudes about the impact of the Obama stimulus plan on the economy as of July 2009

Partisan Identification	Better	Worse	No Impact
All Voters—So Far	24.7	12.5	57.3
All Voters—Long Run	44.3	21.9	28.1
Republican—So Far	15.1	26.2	51.6
Democrat—So Far	35.6	3.7	55.5
Independent—So Far	22.0	12.4	61.0
Republican—Long Run	22.7	37.4	33.7
Democrat—Long Run	59.7	10.2	25.6
Independent—Long Run	44.1	22.2	6.6

In the long run, do you think the government's stimulus package will make the economy better, will make the economy worse, or will it have no impact on the economy in the long run?

The polls also found that 65 percent of the public opposed a new stimulus package, and strong majorities prioritized deficit reduction.[36] When public opinion turned against additional stimulus, it became more difficult to sell a new package to moderate Democrats. Those facing tough reelection contest in 2010 were especially reluctant to support more spending.[37] Consequently, the administration rejected calls from the left for a second round of fiscal expansion.

Some individual elements of the stimulus package were modestly popular with voters—especially the extension of unemployment benefits. So the administration strategy shifted from a focus on macroeconomic stimulus to targeted social and infrastructure spending as well as tax breaks designed to subsidize job creation.[38] But even these more modest approaches were contentious. Republicans filibustered a bill to extend unemployment benefits for several weeks. The bill passed only when newly elected moderate Republican Scott Brown switched his vote in favor.

Assessing the extent to which ideology and polarization inhibited the U.S. fiscal response is somewhat complicated. The United States did have one of the largest discretionary stimulus bills among developed economies.[39] This does not mean that the highly polarized U.S. political environment had no impact on the passage of the stimulus bill.

First, because the financial crisis that precipitated the worldwide recession was focused on the United States, one would expect the need for a compensatory fiscal response to be higher, *ceteris paribus*. Second, although political constraints were important in the United States, economic and financial ones were less so. The status of the dollar as the international reserve currency and the flight to the security of U.S. treasuries during the crisis made deficit spending much cheaper in the United States. The Europeans were more concerned with the impact of spending on the value of their common currency, a concern that continued into 2012 with the government and bank debt crises of Ireland, Greece, Spain, Portugal, and Italy. Third, the $787 billion price tag vastly overstates the stimulative effect of the bill. Much of the package was used to offset declines in state and local spending.[40]

Many provisions in the package would have passed as standalone legislation. For example, 10 percent of the package was an adjustment to the alternative minimum tax, like those Congress has repeatedly made over the past decade. As even President Obama now admits, the infrastructure spending was very delayed in getting into the economy.[41] Finally, the size of the U.S. package needed to be larger because it was delayed for several months due to the presidential election and transition. By comparison, most of the other stimulus packages in the Organisation for Economic Co-operation and Development countries were passed in November 2008.

Ultimately, the size, delay, and composition of the stimulus bill limited its impact. Stanford University economist Robert Hall, affiliated with the generally conservative Hoover Institution think tank, estimates that the stimulus package reduced the shortfall in gross domestic product during the recession by 2 percent, from 10.2 percent to 8.2 percent.[42]

In summary, the U.S. fiscal response to the crisis was affected in important ways by the ideological and constituency structure of the party system. Although modest bipartisanship was possible at the beginning of the recession, the window for cooperation closed quickly as the crisis deepened and the 2010 election neared. A quick and coherent response was undermined both by the divergent ideological commitments across the parties and divisions within the Democratic Party.

Financial Market Reform

Between passage of the stimulus bill and the Dodd-Frank Bill, Congress passed and the president signed a bill imposing new regulations on the financial services industry. The Credit Card Accountability Responsibility and Disclosure Act of 2009 became law in May 2009. This legislation was low-hanging fruit, proconsumer regulation that had been on the Democrats' agenda for years.[43] Abusive practices, such as repeated penalties for small overdrafts on debit cards, had received widespread attention. The bill passed easily in the House, with only seventy votes against it, all but one coming from Republicans, generally the most conservative members. The bill was then modified and approved in a near unanimous 90–5 vote in the Senate.

One Senate modification, Section 512, put the bill in potential danger when the House took a vote on accepting the Senate bill. Section 512 allowed private individuals to carry weapons on public lands such as national parks. If the Senate bill were voted on as a whole in the House, it might have been killed, with liberals voting against guns and conservatives voting against economic regulation. The House leadership deftly split the Senate bill into two votes. The first, on everything but Section 512, passed with only sixty-four votes against, again all but one coming from Republicans. Then Section 512 was adopted. On this roll call, Democrats cast the vast majority of the negative votes, 145 of 147. Consequently the bill passed, to the delight of both the consumer lobby and the gun lobby. The votes indicated that a liberal-conservative split was likely on the larger issues of financial reform to be addressed in the Dodd-Frank Bill.

The major push on financial reform began in June 2009 when the Obama administration released an eighty-nine-page outline of its reform priorities. The plan focused on four principal areas: the creation of the Financial Stability Oversight Council, which would help coordinate regulatory agencies and provide macro-prudential oversight, a modest revamping of the structure of banking regulation, enhancement of the government's ability to take over and unwind failed financial firms, and the creation of a new regulatory structure for consumer and investor protection. The proposal was immediately attacked from the left and right ends of the ideological spectrum.

The criticism from the left focused on what was missing from the bill. In particular, the administration had not proposed enough to regulate executive compensation practices that many felt were responsible for excessive risk taking. Moreover, the administration's proposal was seen as having a light touch in reg-ulating derivative and securitization markets. The proposal also did little to reform credit rating agencies whose AAA certifica-tions of subprime securitizations helped trigger the crisis.

Conservatives focused on two other aspects. First, there was general opposition to more regulation, especially in the area of consumer and investor protection. Second, conservatives feared that the creation of a resolution pool for unwinding failed finan-cial firms would perpetuate moral hazard and lead to more government bailouts. This fear was previously manifested in conservative opposition to TARP. One area where the Left and the Right converged was in the criticism of the expanded role of the Federal Reserve, which the Left blamed for ignoring the crisis and the Right blamed for being too quick with bailouts. The convergence, as we show in chapter 8, appeared in the thirty negative votes against Ben Bernanke's reappointment to a sec-ond term as Fed chairman in January 2010.

In the fall of 2009, House and Senate committees began work on legislation. Despite concerns that progressives in the House would try to pull the bill to the left, the bill that emerged from the House Financial Services Committee hewed closely to the administration's blueprint. When the bill came to the floor, the two most substantial amendments came from Bart Stupak (D-MI), to tighten rules for central clearing of derivative contracts and for securitization.[44] These amendments were supported overwhelmingly by the left wing of the Democratic Party and allowed those members to go on the record as supporting much more stringent regulation of Wall Street. Ultimately, House Bill 4173 passed on December 11, 2009, by a margin of 223–203. All Republicans voted against the bill, as did 27 Democrats. As would be expected, the Democratic defectors were heavily concentrated in the moderate wing of the party (as measured by DW-NOMINATE scores). Some liberal members did oppose the bill, claiming it did not go far enough.

The main Senate proposal was unveiled in November 2009. Senate Banking Chairman Chris Dodd proposed sweeping changes in the power of the Federal Reserve to regulate banks. The changes would have given the Fed little role in consumer protection and systemic risk regulation. Consequently, the Dodd proposal was seen as considerably more ambitious than the administration proposal or the House bill. Dodd and his staff probably felt that the bill would appeal to the populist, anti-Fed Republicans.[45]

But Republican opposition to Dodd's original plan was substantial. Following Brown's victory in the special Senate election in Massachusetts, it became clear that some Republican support would be necessary to secure the sixty votes needed for cloture. Consequently, Senator Dodd spent several weeks trying to negotiate with some of the panel's Republican members in hopes of securing some level of bipartisanship. After negotiations with ranking minority member Richard Shelby (R-AL) collapsed, Dodd engaged Republican senator Robert Corker of Tennessee. The primary sticking point in these negotiations was the structure of the proposed Consumer Financial Protection Agency (CFPA).[46] The CFPA's backers insisted that for the agency to be effective it must be totally independent, with full rule-making and enforcement power. Republican opponents wanted any new powers vested in an existing agency, preferably the Federal Reserve. But these negotiations collapsed.

Senator Dodd unveiled his final plan on March 15, 2009. In many ways, the plan moved much closer to the House bill and scaled back many of its earlier provisions. It adopted some Republican demands in the hopes of ultimately attracting GOP support but it did include the so-called Volcker Rule banning proprietary trading by deposit-taking banks.[47] Although such a prescription had been pushed by former Fed chair Paul Volcker, it was not endorsed by the administration until early in 2010. This endorsement was at least in part a response to criticism from the left that the administration's proposals were toothless.

The Senate version moved in a considerably proregulation direction when a measure backed by Arkansas Democrat Blanche Lincoln was added to the bill. Lincoln's provision called for the largest commercial banks to spin off their lucrative derivatives trading operations.[48] Initially, the proposal engendered opposition not only among Republicans but also within the administration and among Democrats from New York.

The resulting financial reform bill fit into pivotal politics along the same lines as the economic recovery package, not only in falling along liberal-conservative lines but also in squeaking through with just enough votes on the conference report to beat a Senate filibuster. The House agreed to the conference report on June 30, 2010, by a vote of 237–192. Again, with a large House majority, the Senate was the pivotal chamber. There were, in comparison to the stimulus package, more partisan defections in the House, with 19 Democrats voting against the bill.

The number of prediction errors was twenty-one, including three Republicans who voted in favor (see figure 7.5). Two of these were among the most moderate Republicans, Walter Jones of North Carolina and Joseph Cao of Louisiana.[49] The third yea vote came from Michael Castle of Delaware, the second ranking Republican on the House Financial Services committee. Castle was closer to the center of the party.[50] His attempt to move on to the Senate was derailed in the Republican 2010 primary by Tea Party candidate Christine O'Donnell. Cao was a freshman representative who had defeated the corruption-tainted William Jefferson in New Orleans. By 2010 Cao's district returned to its usual status by electing an African American Democrat, so Cao did not return to the House in 2011.

Of the three House Republicans who deviated from free market conservatism and supported Dodd-Frank, two are no longer in Congress. These small changes in representation are part of the larger process of increasing polarization, a process that will also increase the vulnerability of Dodd-Frank if the Republicans ever reassert unified control of the White House and Congress. Castle's defeat at the hands of the Tea Party was far from Obama's fantasy about politicians of all stripes engaging in compromise.

The Senate vote on the conference report for the Dodd-Frank financial reform bill paralleled action on the stimulus package. Again the Democrats needed three Republican votes, even though Al Franken had by now been sworn in and Arlen Specter had switched parties. One difficulty the Democrats faced was that Robert Byrd had died, leaving a West Virginia seat vacant.

The Senate vote had four exceptions to a perfect liberal-conservative split. The interesting exception was Russ Feingold of Wisconsin. Feingold's "error" is shown as the leftmost white block in figure 7.5. Feingold, previously one of the most liberal Democrats, decided to stand on principle and refused to vote for cloture. So a third Republican vote, in the person of Scott Brown, was needed.

As it turns out, there were real consequences to Feingold promoting Brown into the pivot position. One of the provisions to come out of the House-Senate conference was a levy on large

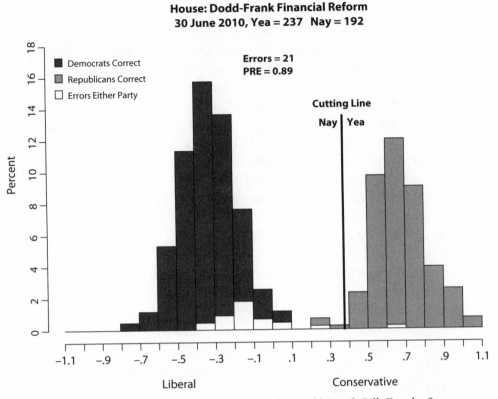

House: Dodd-Frank Financial Reform
30 June 2010, Yea = 237 Nay = 192

Figure 7.5. The conference report votes on the Dodd-Frank Bill. For the Senate, the prediction errors shown represent Feingold to the left and Voinovich, Murkowski, and Lugar in the center. The errors in the center are close to the cutting line, indicating that the senators were nearly indifferent on the bill. Feingold's error is far more substantial.

financial firms to pay for the costs of financial regulation. This provision was quickly dubbed a "bank tax." As a result, Brown, who had supported the earlier Senate version, began to waver. The provision not only ran counter to his ideological opposition to anything resembling a tax increase, but would have been costly to large financial firms in Brown's home state.

In the aftermath of Byrd's death, a defection by Brown would necessitate picking up the two Democrats who had opposed the original Senate bill, Feingold of Wisconsin and Maria Cantwell

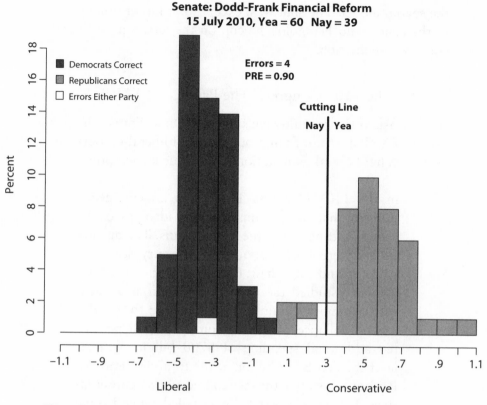

Figure 7.5. (*cont.*)

of Washington. Cantwell did switch her vote, but Feingold did not, necessitating the removal of the bank tax. This shifted $19 billion in costs from the banks to taxpayers. Feingold performed the legislative equivalent of a liberal voting for Ralph Nader in Florida in the 2000 presidential election: standing on principle only to get an outcome he couldn't possibly have wanted.[51]

The other three errors shown in figure 7.5 are trivial exceptions. Republican senators George Voinovich (OH), Lisa Murkowski (AK), and Richard Lugar (IN) voted against the bill when their ideology score called for a vote in favor. Their ideal points are so close to the cutting line that these are very minor errors for the spatial model. The split was, except for a tad of randomness in the center and Feingold's hiccup on the left, a pure liberal-conservative division.

The 110th Congress: The Passage of TARP

In contrast to the stimulus package and Dodd-Frank, the passage of TARP does not fit into our model of liberal-conservative voting. Why? Several explanations complement each other.

1. In the 110th Congress TARP was an emergency measure that went against the core ideology of the agenda-setting party, the Republicans. The agenda setters were Bush appointees, Treasury secretary Paulson and Fed chair Bernanke. Bernanke, who intensely studied the Great Depression as an academic, almost certainly was motivated to avoid a second collapse of the economy. The bill permitted additional spending of $700 billion, with at least the first $350 billion at the total discretion of Paulson—a slap in the face to free market conservatives. The week before Lehman failed, when Fannie and Freddie were effectively nationalized, "Doctor Doom," Nouriel Roubini, keying off economist Willem Buiter, wrote of "comrades Bush, Paulson, and Bernanke."[52] The absence of support in core ideology is a factor that led TARP not to fit into the standard pivotal politics story.

2. Presidential leadership was absent; Paulson and Bernanke, not Bush, were the agenda setters. Following Lehman's collapse and the AIG bailout, Bush's job approval fell into the low 20s.[53] Presidential candidate McCain and Republican congressional candidates were loath to mention Bush's name. In fact, McCain undercut the White House; following the AIG bailout, he announced that he was suspending

his campaign to return to Washington to work on the financial crisis. Two days later, Paulson proposed TARP. Bush's appeals to congressional Republicans to support TARP in the national interest fell on deaf ears in the context of his failed presidency.

3. With elections only weeks away, legislators in close races feared a populist backlash were they to vote for the bailout.

4. Support for the bailout reflected the local interests of representatives from New York and campaign contributions.

These four factors combined to fracture the usual ideological splits. Before we indicate the nature of this fracture, we will show that, before Lehman, the 110th Congress did vote on financial services matters along ideological lines. Post-TARP, Congress also voted ideologically on the bailout of the auto industry. The force of ideology before and after TARP indicates that the TARP episode was a deviation that arose in dire circumstances, starting with the collapse of the housing market.

The housing market meltdown began in 2006, and Washington was unresponsive to the fall in housing prices. Fed chair Alan Greenspan had indicated that the Fed would not intervene in asset market bubbles. Bush appointed Bernanke to succeed Greenspan near the start of the meltdown. At Bernanke's Senate confirmation hearing on November 15, 2005, he said what the Republican-controlled Congress wanted to hear: "I will make continuity with the policies and policy strategies of the Greenspan Fed a top priority."[54] In the summer of 2007, a St. Louis Fed document claimed, "The [Bernanke] Fed has been successful in preserving continuity with the Greenspan era."[55] Neither the Fed nor the executive branch nor Congress was eager to address the consequences of the bursting housing bubble.

The Democrats, having won the 2006 midterm elections, were in control of Congress for the first time since 1994. They made some attempt to control the worst practices of the subprime market. In the House, Representative Brad Miller, a North Carolina Democrat, introduced the Mortgage Reform and Anti-Predatory Lending Act of 2007.[56] Patterned after similar legislation in Miller's state that had been enacted in 1999, this bill strengthened the Home Ownership and Equity Protection Act of 1994 (HOEPA). By 2007, some thirty states and the District of Columbia had enacted their own legislation. Miller's bill was aimed at a federal strengthening of consumer protection in the mortgage market. It passed the House on November 15, 2007, by a vote of 291–127, with all Democrats and 64 Republicans in favor. The vote was highly ideological, with the more moderate Republicans joining the Democrats. There were, as shown in figure 2.5, only thirty-two prediction errors, all Republicans close to indifference, as shown by the cutting line. At that time, less than a year before the political pop, the Senate failed to act on a bill. The bill was reintroduced in the 111th Congress and passed, on May 7, 2009, by a vote of 300–114, with only 3 Democrats voting against it. Again, Republican moderates split from conservatives. And again the Senate failed to act. Miller's bill would eventually become legislation as Title XIV of Dodd-Frank.

The previous antipredatory lending statute was extremely weak. The interest rates and fees that would trigger HOEPA protection were so extreme that they would apply only to 1 percent of subprime loans.[57] Presidents of both political parties preempted the more stringent state regulations. In 1996, under Clinton, the Office of Thrift Supervision, that weak regulator created by FIRREA, exempted all federally chartered savings and loans from state regulation. In 2004, under Bush, the Office of the Comptroller of the Currency (OCC) exempted all national banks. Representatives Bob Ney (R-OH) and Paul Kanjorski (D-PA) tried to go one step further in 2005 by introducing a bill that would preempt all state regulation. The bill never made it to the floor, perhaps because Ney got caught up in the Jack Abramoff scandal and eventually served seventeen months in prison.

The Supreme Court, regulators, and legislators also addressed the issue of federal preemption of state regulations. The OCC

had fought state level prosecutions of national banks for violating state fair-lending laws. This led to the *Cuomo v. Clearing
House* Supreme Court case discussed earlier in this chapter. In a
surprise decision, Justice Antonin Scalia voted with court liberals to strengthen state intervention.[58] The role of the states was
reinforced only after the pop, not only by the court but also
by Dodd-Frank, which set federal regulations in this area, like
minimum wages, as a floor rather than a ceiling.

If the predatory lending issue failed to gain political traction
before the pop, the fall in housing prices created political pressure in the 110th Congress to provide relief to homeowners who
were being forced into foreclosure. Some homeowners engaged
in strategic default, but others simply lacked the resources to
make their monthly payments, either because they had become
unemployed or because their mortgages had reset from a teaser
rate to a higher rate or because they had never from the start had
enough income to make payments.

Former Treasury official Phillip Swagel observed that there was
no spike in mortgage defaults around the reset dates of specific
types of adjustable rate mortgages (the so-called 2-28 and 3-27
mortgages.)[59] He thus concluded that the problem was the initial
lack of income and credit worthiness of the borrowers.[60] Some
of these borrowers had been led into the loans by shady originators. Regardless, just as Wall Street and the automobile industry
expected a bailout, households in foreclosure were looking for
government assistance. Many borrowers were in the low-income
minority electorate that supported the Democrats.

A limited response to foreclosures finally took place in the
summer of 2008. On July 30, President Bush, withdrawing an
earlier veto threat, signed the Housing and Economic Recovery
Act. The bill is better known by its House title, the American
Housing Rescue and Foreclosure Prevention Act (AHRFPA), a
measure designed to reduce foreclosures by securing reductions
both in the principal amount of a home mortgage and in penalties. Because lender participation in the program was voluntary,
the bill packed little punch. The bill also opened a blank check

extending credit to Fannie, Freddie, and other federal housing institutions and it contained legislation designed to improve mortgage disclosure and to license mortgage originators.

At the time AHRFPA passed, a foreclosure relief program with sharp government mandates and haircuts imposed on lenders was unthinkable, particularly because President Bush was pivotal. Also unthinkable was that the credit subsidies to the privatized GSEs would be small potatoes in a government takeover of Fannie and Freddie, an event less than two months away.

Because AHRFPA was both pre-Lehman and prior to the 2008 elections, any options were limited to tweaks that were consistent with the free market conservative perspective. Before the financial crisis, the mortgage market was almost entirely privatized. The activity of the government was reduced, as we explained in chapter 5, to subsidizing the private sector off budget. Through the regulatory implementation of the Community Redevelopment Act, the government also pushed private firms into targeting more loans to the poor and minorities. All of these government policies were indirect, and nearly all mortgage contracts were written by for-profit financial intermediaries. Depression Era–style moratoriums or government takeovers of the servicing of these privately held mortgages were off the table. The proposed legislation continued to rely on the private market. Nonetheless, Bush opposed the bill when it was introduced in April.

The agenda for foreclosure relief was set by the Democrats, who held majorities in both the House and the Senate. In April 2007, the Senate transformed what originally had been an energy bill, HR 3221, into a foreclosure prevention act. Throughout the legislative process, the Senate always voted for passage by large margins. The bill passed the Senate by an 84–12 vote on April 10. After the amended bill had been returned by the House, the Senate, between June 25 and July 11, acted and returned the bill to the House with votes that were no closer than 79–16. The Senate then passed the final bill by a 72–13 margin and sent it to the president for signature on July 26. In April 2007 Senator Richard Durbin (D-IL) had proposed an amendment directed at

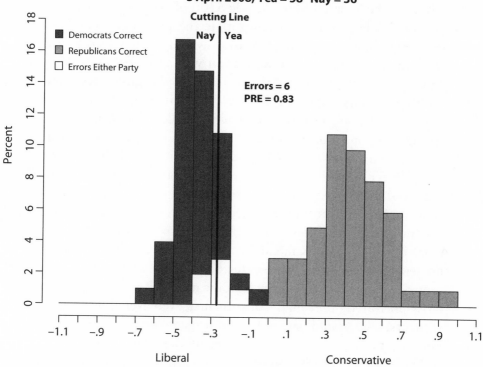

Figure 7.6. The Senate vote on the Durbin Amendment to allow bankruptcy judges to block foreclosures. The vote is liberal-conservative, with the errors symmetric about the cutting line. The vote is a further indication that Congress divided ideologically on financial reform before the failure of Lehman Brothers. The vote also indicates that Democrats would not be a solid majority in favor of progressive financial reforms.

allowing bankruptcy judges to prevent foreclosure. This measure, which was much more than a tweak on free market conservatism, might have kept many homes from foreclosure, but it was opposed by all Republicans. The amendment was tabled in a 58–36 vote in which 11 Democratic moderates voted with the Republicans (see figure 7.6). The versions of the bill accepted by the Senate, however, always drew large, bipartisan support with limited Republican opposition. Only a minority of Senate Republicans opposed the bill.

The House was far more divided. On May 8, 2007, the House modified the Senate bill to include $300 billion in loan guarantees for lenders willing to renegotiate the principal amount of mortgages. The House modification was met by a veto threat from the president. The modification was approved on a 266–154 vote, with all Democrats voting for the guarantees and the Republicans opposing, 154–39. Atif Mian, Amir Sufi, and Francesco Trebbi have shown that Republican opposition was stronger among conservatives,[61] where conservatism is measured by our DW-NOMINATE scores. As indicated above, DW-NOMINATE makes some errors on the AHRFPA vote. Mian, Sufi, and Trebbi explain that Republicans were more likely to support AHRFPA if they were from districts with high foreclosure rates, especially if foreclosure rates were high in Republican parts of the district. Roll call voting by the Democrats showed no sensitivity to foreclosure rates because ideology alone promoted support for mortgage modifications. Republicans were cross-pressured; they had constituents, even Republican constituents, who would benefit from mortgage resets, but a federal program ran against the grain of free market conservatism.

The voting patterns present on the May 2007 vote were repeated on the final vote in the House on July 23. The vote was 272–152, with only 3 Democrats voting against it and only 45 Republicans in favor. When the roll was called, fidelity to free market conservatism dominated. Fewer than one-fourth of House Republicans voted for AHRFPA. (The vote is illustrated in figure 2.6.) Even though it took place less than two months before the fall of Lehman Brothers, the vote remains highly ideological but contains somewhat more error than earlier votes. The increased voting prediction errors relate, as shown by Mian, Sufi, and Trebbi, to increased foreclosure rates in congressional districts. For a few, constituent interests trumped ideology.

In contrast to Obama and the Democrats with the stimulus and Dodd-Frank, George W. Bush was not part of the agenda-setting process on foreclosure legislation. The demand to change the status quo came from the Democrats. A Senate filibuster was not in the cards, perhaps because many constituents in most senators' states had problems with foreclosure. Because the Democrats were not even close to a veto override majority, the president's support, not that of the sixtieth senator, was pivotal. Bush appears to have come on board for two reasons. First, between April and July 2008 the housing crisis worsened considerably. Presidents, as well as Republican House members, can be sensitive to foreclosure rates. In September 2008, Fed chair Ben Bernanke was reported to have said, "There are no atheists in foxholes and no ideologues in financial crises."[62] The Republican supporters of AHRFPA are indicative of Bernanke's claim. Second, as indicated earlier in this chapter, AHRFPA had no bite. The president's support was largely a symbolic acknowledgment of the foreclosure crisis. Even with the loan guarantees in place, Senate Republicans did not make a fuss and Bush signed the bill. When real money was on the line, as was the case with TARP, Republican ideologues in Congress would not be helpful to Bernanke.

After Bush signed, in a rare sign of media bipartisanship, both the *New York Times* and the *Wall Street Journal* touted it as the most significant housing legislation since the New Deal. That the elite media failed to see that the legislation would do little about foreclosures is indicative of how uninformed most of the nation was about the impending collapse of Wall Street. By 2011, Washington was still unable to solve the foreclosures problem, in part because of the complexity of securitization and servicing that had doomed the shadow banking system.[63] People in homes facing foreclosure are stuck between a rock and a hard place. If banks were to take haircuts and reduce the principal amount of large numbers of mortgages quickly, they would have to take a huge accounting hit, which would reveal that they were badly wounded paper tigers. Foreclosing in dribs and drabs spreads out the accounting losses. If the government were to pay for a haircut it would have to raise the revenue or increase the deficit. In chapter 8 we show that bailing out homeowners had become politically unthinkable.

Although the pop of financial markets is often identified as the Panic of 2007,[64] the political pop—delayed, of course—occurred only in September 2008. The pop resulted in the rather chaotic voting on TARP, which we discuss below. To complete our story of the force of ideology in the 110th Congress, however, we first jump to the bailout of the automobile industry. This episode shows how quickly the standard liberal-conservative conflict reasserted itself after TARP. When the lame-duck House passed a bailout bill for the automobile industry on December 10, 2008, the vote was more normally liberal-conservative, with only fifty-four prediction errors. The vote was largely along party lines. Salvatore Nunnari has shown that the location and ownership of automobile manufacturing plants was important to this vote.[65] Nonetheless, ideology is the primary determinant of roll call voting behavior. The Senate cloture vote failed by a 52–35 margin, with only eleven prediction errors. With a lame-duck president, Congress could not develop a coalition capable of supporting the auto industry. Gridlock forced a Republican president to turn against the foxhole ideologues in his own party and prop up Detroit on a short-run basis with TARP funds. The reappearance of a liberal-conservative split in the 110th Congress foreshadowed the legislative history of the 111th Congress.

Between AHRFPA in July 2008 and the auto bailout votes in December, the standard liberal-conservative division fell apart over TARP. After Lehman failed on September 15 and AIG was bailed out a day later, Congress had to be dragged, kicking and screaming, with both liberal and conservative ideologues objecting, into approving the Emergency Economic Stabilization Act (EESA), which included the Troubled Asset Relief Program fund.

President Bush was largely absent. Liberals were reluctant to bail out the too-big-to-fail firms on Wall Street. Conservatives, even in a financial crisis, were reluctant to support government intervention in the economy. (The word *nationalization* became taboo in describing both the takeovers of Fannie and Freddie and the considerable government investment in AIG, Citigroup, General Motors, and other firms.) Populist outrage made legislators reluctant to support EESA, with the $700 billion TARP fund. Moreover, congressional elections were only weeks away. Indeed, the initial September 29 vote on TARP failed. On that day, the Dow lost nearly 800 points.

The votes on TARP were only weakly related to the liberal-conservative scale. The House votes, shown in figure 7.7, indicate that a liberal-conservative cutting line model fails to discriminate between supporters and opponents. There are 197 prediction errors on the failed September 29 vote and 151 on the October 3 passage vote, in contrast to only 9 on the stimulus plan, 21 on Dodd-Frank, and 47 on AHRFPA. In the Senate, there were 23 errors on passage on October 1, as against 1 on the stimulus, 4 on Dodd-Frank, and 6 on the Durbin amendment to AHRFPA.

The breakdown of the typical liberal-conservative alignment is nicely illustrated in the graph shown as figure 7.8. The graph plots the probability of House members voting for the bailout (TARP) as a function of the DW-NOMINATE score. There are three curves: one for safe seats, another for vulnerable seats, and another for seats where the representative had previously announced retirement. Those with vulnerable seats tended to cave in to populism and were the most likely to oppose the bill. Those with safe seats and especially those retiring were more likely to support the bill.

Why weren't the Republicans running for reelection especially likely to vote for TARP? Would they have not wanted the party to escape the blame for an economic meltdown on the scale of the Great Depression? The answer is that when TARP was voted on, elections were only thirty-two days away. It might have been difficult to see either the benefits of approving or the costs of disapproving TARP within that time span. After all, even after TARP was enacted, the stock market continued to decline and unemployment rise for months. So it was easy, given the time frame, to cater to populist rage.

Very conservative Republicans voted consistently with their free market conservative ideology. They would have been more comfortable had Andrew Mellon's ghost been Treasury secretary

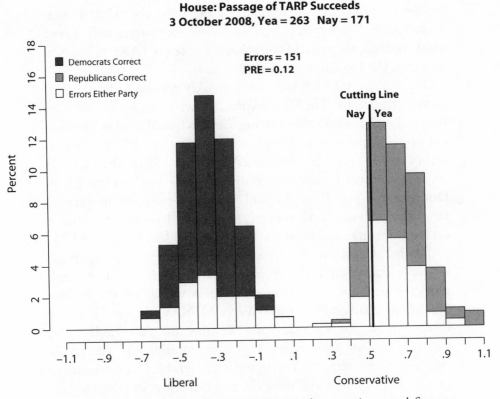

Figure 7.7. The two House votes on TARP. Neither vote is a good fit to a liberal-conservative model. There are almost as many prediction errors as votes on the minority side of each vote.

rather than Henry Paulson. Very liberal Democrats also were more likely to be against than for. Their egalitarian, redistributive ideology made them loath to bail out Wall Street firms, whose executives were royally compensated. There turned out to be more than a few ideologues in financial crises. The bill was supported mainly by moderates in safe seats, and even these members were not solid in their support. More detailed analyses that we and Mian, Sufi, and Trebbi have conducted indicate a small influence for other factors, such as receiving campaign contributions from the financial services industry.[66]

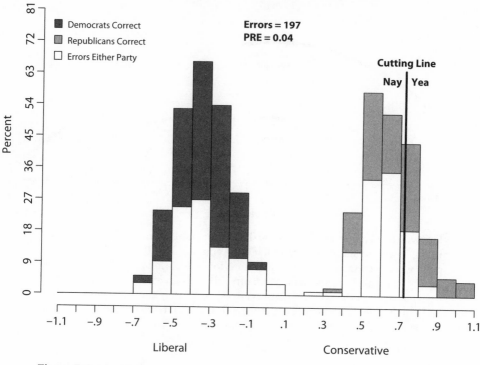

Figure 7.7. (*cont.*)

The rejection and subsequent passage of TARP reflected, in summary, several forces. The most conservative Republican members played ideologues, even in a financial crisis. So did the most liberal Democrats. The Right was unwilling to go against its beliefs that government intervention in the economy was bad per se, particularly so if it confirmed moral hazard. The Left was unwilling to support an upward redistribution to financial firms and their executives. Past campaign contributions of the financial sector were associated with just a slight marginal willingness to favor the bailout.[67] Thus, ideological extremism trumped the supposed "capture" of Washington by Wall Street. On the other hand, members were more likely to help Paulson and Bernanke

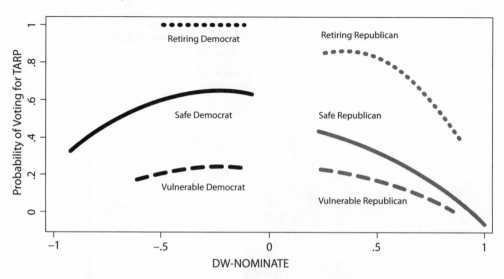

Figure 7.8. The first House vote on TARP. Incumbents running for reelection in vulnerable seats were very unlikely to vote for TARP. Incumbents in safe seats were somewhat more likely to vote for it. Retiring incumbents were by far the most likely supporters. Moderates showed greater support than either extreme liberals or extreme conservatives. Note that the curves for retiring and vulnerable incumbents do not extend to the extremist ends of the graph (−1 and +1). This is because extremists are found only in safe seats.

avoid a meltdown if they were not facing a reelection challenge in November.

One might have been wary that the TARP vote indicated political instability, such as that which preceded the Civil War after the Compromise of 1850 unraveled. Alternatively, there may have been a permanent political realignment similar to the replacement of the Whig-Democrat system with the Republican-Democrat system around the time of the Civil War.[68] The Civil War events, as Nobel Prize Laureate Robert Fogel has stressed, were not ones of economics but ones in which, in the North, a moral aversion to slavery emerged.[69] Financial panics are different. Not even the Great Depression led to realignment in congressional ideology. So it is not surprising that congressional Democrats and the Obama administration would be forced to form coalitions along the liberal-conservative dimension.

Conclusion

In this chapter we have argued that ideology largely reduces to one dimension. This ideology, with the exception of the turmoil in the wake of the collapse of Lehman Brothers, proved very stable. On particular issues, specific economic interests can run counter to ideology. The influence of interest groups on roll call voting, however, does not generate a systematic second dimension. Mortgage foreclosures were significant to votes on AHRFPA but not on TARP or on the auto industry bailout. Similarly, financial services contributions affected only the TARP vote. Domestic auto manufacturer employment mattered only on the auto bailout. Currently, there is not an important, systematic second dimension in American politics beyond the liberal-conservative continuum. Highly polarized liberal-conservative politics and the power of pivots in American institutions made up the framework that generated the response to the pop of 2008. The configuration within which the president and Congress operate is determined by the influence of campaign contributions, lobbying, and elections.

In the short run, the behavior of financial markets can break the configuration. Intervention in the rotten market of subprime mortgages, bogus collateralizations, overleveraged banks, and incorrectly priced credit default swaps was long delayed because of ideological rigidity and interest-group pressures. After Bear Stearns, bailouts were taboo. Once Lehman went over the cliff, however, AIG was bailed out the very next day. TARP was quickly brought to Congress. Initially, ideology and electoral pressures led the House of Representatives to reject the proposal. The stock market then plunged off another cliff. Days later, Congress acquiesced. Once the worst was avoided, Washington returned to business as usual. Pivots ruled within established liberal-conservative ideology.

CHAPTER 8
"Pop"ulism

This is America! How many of you people want to pay
for your neighbor's mortgage that has an extra bathroom and can't pay their bills?
                    —Rick Santelli, on CNBC

A STRIKING PUZZLE OF THE 2008 financial crisis and the ensuing
Great Recession is the very restrained and short-lived public outrage against the financial sector. The absence of public outrage
explains why we have focused on the *Three I's*—ideology, institutions, and interests—up to this point. The fact that the public
did not press for reforms contributed, in our view, to the failure
of American democracy in the financial crisis. True, outrage was
expressed over the bailouts in 2008. Outrage over his membership in "the friends of Angelo," a group that benefited from very
favorable mortages from Countrywide Financial under then
CEO Angelo Mozilo, played a part in Chris Dodd's announcing
his retirement.[1] (It was a bit of chutzpah for Dodd to coauthor
the "reform" bill.) The outrage was manifest in the difficulty in
passing the TARP legislation, as we discussed in chapter 7.

A small aftershock arose with the Senate vote on Ben Bernanke's reappointment as Federal Reserve chair on January
28, 2010. Bernanke drew thirty votes not to confirm, a record
negative vote for a Fed chair confirmation. Like that of the
Troubled Asset Relief Program (TARP) this vote was not a
liberal-conservative split. The Left was enraged with Bernanke
for his inaction before the collapse of Lehman Brothers, the

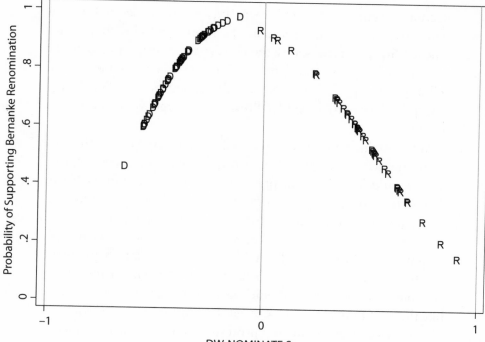

Figure 8.1. Estimated probability of a vote to reappoint Ben Bernanke as Fed chair, January 28, 2010. Each token represents 1 of the 100 senators, with D for Democrats and R for Republicans. Moderates, with scores near zero, were very likely to support Bernanke. Extremists on both sides of the aisle opposed.

Right by his interventionist actions through Fed policies after Lehman fell. Figure 8.1 shows our estimates of a vote to confirm as a function of ideology score.[2] Moderates were virtually certain to vote for Bernanke. Extremists, especially very conservative Republicans, were likely to oppose. But the rage on Capitol Hill in January 2010 had little echo in the American public. By 2009 and certainly by 2010 the outrage had fizzled, to return, via the Occupy Wall Street demonstrations, only in the late summer of 2011.

Where was the outrage in the first years following the crisis? After all, the crisis was associated with dramatic losses to wealth and income. Millions lost their homes. Private retirement accounts went south. Retirement income from defined-benefit pensions became endangered as the fund portfolios took a hit. The low interest rates set by the Fed caused a drop in income for owners of certificates of deposit. Fixed-income investments also fell as corporations were able to call in their bonds. The "ownership society" embraced by President George W. Bush was in shambles.

Who could blame the voters if they had demanded the dismantling and reorganization of the entire financial sector? Who would have been surprised if a Huey Long had emerged, demanding to share the wealth? But the paroxysms of populist rage against the financial sector scarcely materialized. True, the crisis may well have influenced the 2008 elections, as Barack Obama pulled ahead of John McCain only in late September. On the other hand, Obama won only 53 percent of the popular vote when the crisis should have perhaps led to a landslide like those of Franklin D. Roosevelt, Lyndon Johnson, or Richard Nixon. Moreover, organized protests, such as those engendered by the prospect of Obamacare, were largely absent.

Why?

One exception may prove a general observation. In March 2009, it came to light that employees of the financial products division of American International Group (AIG), the unit whose trading caused the firm's collapse, were to receive $165 million in bonuses. The response to this disclosure was swift and fierce. Cable talk shows went crazy, congressional hearings were televised, and the House even voted to tax the bonuses at a rate of 90 percent. Yet the rage did not focus generally on Wall Street's bonus culture but specifically on the AIG bonuses and bonuses to other firms that had received bailouts, including TARP money. The policy response correspondingly focused on ways to undo the relevant AIG compensation contracts and to place limitations on compensation at TARP firms. But general reform to executive compensation was not in the offing. One reason that the response was focused in this way is that the issue quickly became one of "paying bonuses with taxpayers' money." This framing redirected the rage from what Wall Street had done to what the government had done.

In addition to pummeling the ownership society, the crisis resulted in levels of unemployment not seen since the early 1980s. Long-term unemployment, particularly of younger workers, rose. In October 2011 the unemployment rate for Americans ages 20 to 24 was 14.0 percent, compared to 7.8 percent for those 25 and over. People 55 and over had an unemployment rate of 7 percent.[3] The unemployment situation makes Occupy Wall Street understandable, but the movement came late. The occupiers were largely people without a financial stake.

At its heart, the populist impulse, both in the reaction to bonuses and in Occupy Wall Street, arises from mistrust of elites and the institutions they govern. Populism comes in different flavors depending on where that mistrust is directed. As in many other countries, the United States is home to populism of a left-wing variety rooted in a deep distrust of big business, finance, and concentrated economic power. But in contemporary America, that kind of populism runs a distant third to two more common forms: cultural and antistatist populism. Cultural populism, honed by George Wallace and Richard Nixon and perfected by Sarah Palin and Michele Bachmann, is based on distrust of cultural elites in the media, entertainment, and academia. Since this form of populism became disengaged from the left-wing flavor in the 1970s, its adherents have not been particularly hostile to businesses except to those with Hollywood zip codes. Cultural populism has much more in common with the right-wing, antistatist variety that has had a profound impact on American politics over the past thirty years.

Americans don't trust their government. On the eve of the financial crisis "trust in government" was almost as low as it had been at any point since survey researchers started asking about it in the late 1950s.[4] In 2007, only about 20 percent of the American public trusted the government to do what is right "just about always" or "most of the time." Conversely, before the Watergate scandal, strong majorities trusted government.

When the bubble popped in 2008, even voters willing to blame Wall Street for the damage were unable to turn their anger into calls for tighter government regulation and scrutiny. They believed that government was inherently ineffectual, or worse, complicit in a coconspiracy with financiers. So the mantle of "the People" was picked up initially not by the Left but by the Tea Party, which called for a return to "constitutional first principles" to prevent big government from selling out to big finance. Only much later, after the policy decisions outlined in chapter 7 were settled and the Democrats were routed in the midterm elections, did the populist Left occupy Wall Street. But as we discuss below, the Occupy movement combined opposition to Wall Street and concentrated economic power with extreme mistrust in American political institutions and processes. This near-anarchic mix meant that the movement was slow to translate its concerns into concrete policy proposals or to mobilize in the arena of electoral politics.

The undercurrent of mistrust in government helps us to understand the specifics of public opinion toward the crisis. Notably, it helps us to understand why public opinion played such a limited role in shaping the policy response to the pop. It was not because the public was divided, even along partisan lines, over the causes of the crisis or the need to reregulate the financial services industry. Instead, it appears that the public's engagement with the issue was dampened both by skepticism that the government would succeed in restraining the industry and by uncertainty about the best course of action.

These conclusions are based on several observations about public opinion drawn from polls taken during the crisis and during the lead-up to the passage of the Dodd-Frank Wall Street Reform and Consumer Protection Act. A range of opinion surveys reveals the following patterns.

- The public did blame the financial sector for the crisis. This was true across the political spectrum, with Republicans only slightly less likely than

Democrats to believe that Wall Street's behavior was responsible.

- Citizens did believe that deregulation of the financial sector was an important cause. Again, at least during the early part of the crisis, this view was held by self-identified Republicans and conservatives as well as by Democrats and liberals.
- The public was not opposed to government intervention during the crisis. The public initially supported both assistance to financial firms and aid to homeowners facing foreclosure. This support, however, declined as concerns about the government rewarding bad behavior increased. The concerns about moral hazard subsequently polarized the public on partisan and ideological grounds.
- The public generally supported financial reform. But this support was undercut by the belief that the industry itself would be the primary beneficiary.

The Public Blamed the Financial Sector

A *Los Angeles Times*/Bloomberg poll asked voters in September 2008 whether they blamed President George W. Bush, Congress, or Wall Street for the financial crisis. Thirty-two percent blamed Wall Street; only 26 percent pointed to Bush and 11 percent to Congress.[5] Only Democratic respondents were more likely to blame Bush than Wall Street. The difference between Republicans and Democrats here undoubtedly does not reflect favorable views of Wall Street by Democrats but a projection by Democrats of their intense dislike of Bush arising as a result of other issues such as the Iraq War and his inept response to Hurricane Katrina.

The public continued to blame the financial sector well after the worst had passed. As late as February 2010, more voters blamed Wall Street for the bad economy than blamed the Obama administration.[6] In a separate poll that month, only about a quarter of voters indicated that they were confident that bankers and executives at financial institutions would make the right decisions for the economy. Voters were more confident in labor union leaders, the Obama administration, Republicans in Congress, and Democrats in Congress. Only automobile executives inspired less confidence than did financiers.[7]

The Public Blamed Deregulation

Public opinion polls generally show that Americans blame lax regulations for the financial crisis. In a CNN poll taken at the height of the fallout after the collapse of Lehman Brothers, a slim majority said that financial institutions were not regulated enough (only 41 percent said this about business in general).[8] In October 2008, 73 percent in a *Los Angeles Times*/Bloomberg poll agreed that the lack of regulation is partly responsible for the current financial and housing crisis.[9] Even healthy pluralities of Republicans and "very conservative" voters agreed. By December 2008, 87 percent felt that deregulation of the banking and financial institutions had contributed at least somewhat to the crisis.[10]

The Public Was Not Overwhelmingly against Intervention at the Height of the Crisis

It is widely believed that the Treasury's TARP proposal immediately unleashed populist rage. But a closer examination of the polling data suggests a much more ambivalent response. On the eve of the TARP proposal (September 19–21, 2008) a CNN poll asked whether citizens supported the "millions in aid" that had already been provided to financial firms.[11] Almost 55 percent of citizens responded affirmatively. In the same poll, a stronger majority agreed that the government should step in to address the problems in financial markets.

Notably, the public was not exceptionally polarized along party lines. Fifty-eight percent of Democrats and 50 percent of Republicans supported aid for the financial sector. Despite the effect of reelection incentives we found in legislative voting on TARP, only 14 percent of voters said that they would vote against their member of Congress if she had voted for TARP, 17 percent said they were more likely to vote for her if she had supported TARP, and 60 percent said her vote would have no effect.[12] This support was despite the fact that voters were not confident that TARP would work. Slightly more voters were "not too confident" or "not confident" than were very or somewhat confident that TARP would stabilize the market.[13] Moreover, three quarters of respondents reported feeling very or somewhat worried about the "possibility that the people who caused these problems in the first place will benefit if the federal government takes action to address these problems."[14]

So it appears that the initial resistance to TARP was driven not by majoritarian political considerations but by the opposition of vocal minorities on both the right and left (abetted by sectors of the media and the blogosphere). Once the TARP votes were cast, citizens took their cues from the opponents, and soon after the height of the crisis support for intervention began to drop. In a CNN poll taken on October 3–5, 2008, approval of TARP registered at 46 percent. By October 17, support was down to 40 percent.[15] This turn came about as voters began to view TARP as more a "bailout for Wall Street" than a "rescue of the economy." Opposition to further assistance was running better than three to one. CNN asked voters how TARP would work.[16] Their responses are summarized in table 8.1.

The patterns of support and opposition were fairly consistent across the political spectrum. Republicans and Democrats nearly equally supported the program, a pattern that was largely repeated in several polls through the end of 2008. By December, voters preferred letting financial firms fail rather than be rescued by the government by a thirteen-point margin.[17] Support for financial bailouts did not bottom out until early in 2009, after President Obama successfully secured the second tranche of TARP funding. In polls taken in February 2009, support for aid to the financial sector had fallen to the mid-30s. The drop

TABLE 8.1.
Public opinon on TARP

TARP Will . . .	Agreement*
Treat American taxpayers fairly	40%
Make sure that money that is supposed to help the economy doesn't go to the businesses and individuals who caused these problems in the first place	53%
Help ordinary Americans who have mortgage problems keep their homes	51%
Make sure that the government's money is spent properly and not wasted	47%

Note: *"Likely" and "somewhat likely" responses.

corresponds to increased disillusionment with TARP's effectiveness. In January 2009, 85 percent of respondents said TARP has "not done what it was supposed to do to help the economy."[18] It was only after President Obama's inauguration that a partisan gap appeared, with Democrats 20 percentage points more likely than Republicans to support bailouts.[19]

Mistrust of the government's ability to manage the bailouts was a major contributor to the decline in support and the partisan gap. In February 2009, only a bare majority of respondents said that they trusted the federal government more than the financial sector when it came to using TARP money. The partisan gap on this question was large, with Democrats 20 points more likely than Republicans to trust the government more.[20] Poll respondents also strongly tended to subscribe to the belief that financial executives were primarily using government aid to pad their salaries rather than to stabilize their firms before returning to lending.

During the financial crisis, policy makers were obsessed with the problem of moral hazard in the mortgage market. The public was less so. Majorities routinely favored financial assistance to homeowners facing foreclosure, and support grew as the crisis deepened. In December 2007, a slim majority of those polled by CNN had supported "special treatment that would prevent [homeowners] from defaulting on their mortgages."[21] By the end of April 2008, this number had grown to 59 percent. Support for policies against foreclosures expanded even further when the full-blown crisis erupted. In a survey fielded by the *Los Angeles Times* and Bloomberg in October of that year, a strong majority responded favorably to the "federal government providing assistance to individual homeowners who are facing foreclosure."[22] A CNN poll about the same time also found strong support in favor of assistance to homeowners facing foreclosures.[23] Both of these polls revealed substantial partisan gaps. Poll respondents were far more sensitive to inducing moral hazard among banks. An overwhelming majority opposed special treatment for financial institutions that would prevent them from losing money on mortgages.[24]

The Public Supported Financial Regulation but Worried about Capture

Voters generally supported increasing regulation of the financial sector. In an April 2009 CBS/*New York Times* poll, more than 70 percent of respondents, including 60 percent of Republicans, said that they supported increased regulation of banks and financial institutions.[25] But support slipped and polarized over time. By March 2010, a slight majority supported financial reform, but the difference between Democrats and Republicans was more than 30 percent.[26] Overall support rebounded slightly in May with the partisan gap holding firm, possibly in response to the Securities and Exchange Commission filing civil charges against Goldman Sachs over its Abacus collateralized debt obligations.[27] (As we discussed in the introduction to Part I, Goldman Sachs sold long positions to clients who were unaware that the company had permitted the hedge fund manager John Paulson to take a short position.) The level of support for reform and the partisan gap persisted through the passage of Dodd-Frank.[28]

Throughout the pop, support for reform was tempered by concerns about whether government could regulate the financial sector in ways that promoted the public interest. In the same CBS/*New York Times* poll, only 47 percent felt that new regulations would help all Americans. Almost 40 percent said that new regulations would mainly "benefit the bankers." Certainly this degree of mistrust was stoked by the unfolding AIG scandal. A whopping 86 percent of respondents had heard or read about the bonuses lavished on its executives.[29] The public also felt that "big financial institutions such as major banks and insurance companies" had too much influence over decisions made by the Obama administration.[30] Democrats were almost as likely as Republicans to agree.

These concerns about interest-group influence and capture help explain the substantial decline in support for new regulation. By February 2010, support for increased regulation had fallen to 56 percent.[31] Not surprisingly, the biggest drop was among Republicans. By July 2009, only a bare majority thought the government "should exert more control" over the financial system.[32] The partisan gap on this question was almost forty points. Income began to emerge as a predictor of support as well with low-income voters preferring more control 54 percent to 33 percent and high income voters opposing more control 52 percent to 46 percent. Support for financial regulation continued to fluctuate in the mid-50s with large partisan differences.

The polling evidence indicates support for treating the banks and their executives more aggressively than the Obama administration did. About two-thirds of those who proffered an opinion in April 2009 said that financial firms who received government loans should be forced to restructure their management as had the automakers who received loans.[33] This view was shared in equal measures among Democrats and Republicans.

In the lead-up to Dodd-Frank, there was some support for more interventionist measures, although many voters professed ignorance of the specifics. For example, in February 2010, voters supported the administration's bank tax proposal but most said they had not heard enough about it to make a decision.[34] Lack of information by the voters relates to the growing hostility to government intervention. Although by November 2010 more than half of the TARP bailout money had been repaid, more than a quarter of those interviewed responded "don't know" on a repayment question asked by the Pew Research Center, and more than half the respondents incorrectly stated that less than half or none of the money had been repaid.[35] Democrats and Republicans were equally likely to be inaccurate. Public beliefs were clearly more correlated with the messages of antigovernment ideologues than with those of the Obama administration.[36]

As further evidence of the unease about a greater government role, public opinion was downright hostile to more extreme governmental responses. Only 14 percent of those polled (and only 22 percent of self-described liberals) supported government ownership and control of the banks.[37] Not surprisingly, the government had called its takeover of Fannie Mae and Freddie Mac "conservatorship" rather than "nationalization." No one in either the Bush or Obama White House wanted more wake-up calls from Jim Bunning in France.

The Tea Party

The origins of the Tea Party movement can be traced to several events, including those organized by the Ron Paul presidential campaign in 2008 and antistimulus package protests in early 2009.[38] But the birth of the movement is generally thought to be CNBC reporter Rick Santelli's rant from the floor of the Chicago Mercantile Exchange on February 19, 2009. The Obama administration had proposed spending $75 billion to subsidize the refinancing of mortgages for homeowners who had negative equity but were current on their payments. Calling such underwater homeowners "losers," Santelli argued that their homes and cars should go into foreclosure so that they could be bought and used by those "who could carry the water instead of drink the water." When nearby traders began shouting their applause,

Santelli continued "This is America! How many of you people want to pay for your neighbor's mortgage that has an extra bathroom and can't pay their bills?" And then he gave the movement its meme: "We're thinking of having a Chicago Tea Party in July. All you capitalists that want to show up to Lake Michigan, I'm gonna start organizing."

The right-wing populist movement that roiled American politics through the 2010 elections and the August 2011 debate on raising the debt ceiling began in earnest as a diatribe against a government program to refinance underwater mortgages. The setting for the occasion was ironic: the floor of a derivatives exchange before an audience of commodity traders—who Santelli suggested represented "a pretty good statistical cross-section of America, the silent majority." Santelli's screed made no admission of the culpability of the financial sector other than to joke that he would be throwing derivative securities into Lake Michigan.

Santelli's rant hit all of the right-wing populists' hot buttons. First, the government was not to be trusted, and all politicians were compromised.[39] Second, elite policy analysts and academics have crazy ideas.

As Santelli posited at the time, "If the multiplier that all of these Washington economists are selling us is over one . . . we never have to worry about the economy again. The government should spend a trillion dollars an hour because we'll get 1.5 trillion back."[40]

Third and most important, Santelli stressed that the main motivation of government was to take from the "responsible," the "deserving," and the "working" and give it to the "irresponsible," the "underserving," and the "freeloaders." As Theda Skocpol and Vanessa Williamson have demonstrated in their study of the Massachusetts Tea Party, this notion became the unifying theme among the party rank-and-file.

Although born at the Merc, the emergent Tea Party was relatively unengaged on financial reform issues. The hundreds of "Tax Day" protests on April 15, 2009, centered primarily on opposition to taxes and to the stimulus package that Congress had passed in February.[41] By the time Congress went on recess in August, the Tea Party had begun to focus primarily on opposition to health care reform. During that recess, Tea Party activists packed several town hall meetings held by members of Congress to discuss health care reform. In several instances, the protesters shouted down the legislator. By the time consideration of Dodd-Frank rolled around, the Tea Party was fully engaged in electoral politics as it attempted to defeat several incumbents in Republican primaries. Very little effort was exerted either to defeat Dodd-Frank or to push for tougher measures to prevent the risks of "too big to fail" financial institutions. In a further touch of irony, Scott Brown, who owed his Senate election to the mobilization of the Tea Party and other conservative groups, cast the pivotal vote for cloture on Dodd-Frank.

To establish a crude indicator of Tea Party priorities and activities, we conducted Google searches on November 29, 2011 using the terms "Tea Party" paired with other search terms including "financial reform," "stimulus," and "immigration." Table 8.2 shows the number of hits for each search.

TABLE 8.2.
Google hits on selected topics

Topic	Hits (millions) Joint with Tea Party
Immigration	96
Unions	78
Welfare	64
Stimulus	42
Bailout	33
Health care reform	20
Obamacare	18
Budget deficit	8
Public employees	4
Financial reform	3
Dodd-Frank	2

The table clearly demonstrates that on the Internet, the Tea Party was far less often associated with words related to the financial crisis and reform than with words related to other parts of their agenda such as immigration, welfare, public sector unionization, and health care reform.

Given that the Tea Party was born of the anger and anxiety of the financial crisis and recession, why did it play such a muted role in the politics of financial reform? The first factor is that certain political and ideological entrepreneurs who channeled the Tea Party movement were hostile to reform. Initially, after Santelli's rant went viral, the Tea Party membership was a legitimate grassroots movement, and many of its activists had never been involved in politics before. But well-heeled conservative and libertarian organizations and donors provided plenty of Astroturf to fill in the bare patches. Elite *ideology and interests* worked hard to point the Tea Party in the "right" direction.

One of the most important of these elite benefactors was FreedomWorks, a libertarian group that was spun off from Citizens for a Sound Economy, founded by the libertarian billionaire brothers Charles and David Koch in the 1980s. FreedomWorks is led by former House majority leader Richard Armey, a conservative Republican (with a DW-NOMINATE score of 0.601 in the 107th Congress). Armey passionately crusaded against corporate welfare and crony capitalism while in Congress but worked as a pharmaceutical lobbyist until the conflict between being a Washington lobbyist and populist crusader became untenable. Also undermining his bona fides as a populist, Armey was crucial for the passage of the Commodity Futures Modernization Act and its inclusion of the "Enron loophole." So Armey and FreedomWorks were never likely to try to move the Tea Party in the direction of reforming Wall Street. Indeed, in April 2010, three months before Dodd-Frank passed, Armey said that FreedomWorks had not "had a chance to study it."[42] The other groups who took up leadership and coordinating roles were equally hostile or uninterested in financial market reform.

Of course, these groups might have mobilized the Tea Party against Dodd-Frank with the same ferocity that they turned on Obamacare. But other than the dubious notion that Dodd-Frank was a "bailout bill," there were few populist memes that could rally the movement in the same way that "death panels," "government takeover," and "individual mandates" generated passion on health care reform.

Public opinion surveys of Tea Party supporters and sympathizers underscore the lack of engagement and interest in financial reform on the part of the rank and file. In April 2010, *CBS News* and the *New York Times* conducted a poll with a large oversample of Tea Party supporters. Reflecting the ambivalence of the movement to financial reform, there were no direct questions about Dodd-Frank or other proposals for reform. The only question related to finance was a question about whether TARP and other bailouts of financial reform were necessary for the economy's health. An overwhelming majority—74 percent of Tea Party supporters—felt that the economy would have improved on its own without bailouts of financial firms, whereas only 51 percent of all respondents answered this way.

The survey did ask several questions that provide clues to the relative inactivity of the movement on financial issues.

- Eighty-nine percent thought Obama had expanded government too much (37 percent of all respondents thought so).
- Nineteen percent of Tea Party supporters said government never does the right thing. Only 6 percent of the supporters said government would do the right thing always or most of the time. Among all respondents to the poll only 8 percent said government never does the right thing, whereas 20 percent said that it always or mostly does the right thing.
- Tea Party supporters were no less confident in the Federal Reserve's ability to promote financial stability than were other respondents.

- Tea Party supporters were no more likely to feel
  that Obama supported the rich but were twice as
  likely to believe he favored the poor. This response
  suggests the movement was considerably less concerned about upward redistribution than it was
  about redistribution to the poor.

Although the survey results clearly reflect the overwhelming antigovernment sentiment of the Tea Party, it appears that
two of the conservative arguments about financial reform failed
to resonate. The first is the culpability of the Federal Reserve's
monetary policies and its bailouts of banks. The second is that
Dodd-Frank was the Democrats' attempt to expand government
for the benefit of rich Wall Street bankers. The echo here is that
repeal of Obamacare was a far more strident theme in the 2012
Republican nomination contest than was repeal of Dodd-Frank.
In summary, the Tea Party was mainly concerned about preventing an expansion of government to favor the poor.

But there is another, even more troubling, view. The Tea Party
largely represented people who benefited little from government
policy and who objected to those who did benefit. For example,
in his essay on the Tea Party in the *New Yorker*, Ben McGrath
interviewed a party supporter who had lost his Chrysler dealer-
ship and was not benefiting from the auto industry bailout.[43]
The people who would benefit were those who had bought
speculatively and were underwater or those who were ill-advised
(or were the victims of predatory lending) and did not have the
income to make their monthly payments. Although they were
not the poorest of the poor, these mortgagees were poorer than
average Americans. In addition to opposing foreclosure relief,
the Tea Party objected to the stimulus package, much of which
was aimed at maintaining government employment at the state
and local levels. Public sector employees have had, on the whole,
decent jobs and benefits and are not the poorest of the poor.
But they are, unlike the traders who applauded Santelli, disproportionately African American.[44] Those who would benefit from

Obamacare were at the tail end of the income distribution but they were also disproportionately African American and Hispanic citizens, and disproportionately immigrants. In contrast, the Tea Party is disproportionately made up of white citizens. So the Tea Party not only attracted people with principled objections to big government but also drew support from those motivated by racial and ethnic animus. Given its primary focus on limiting redistributive social policy, the Tea Party was not an active player in the writing of the Dodd-Frank Bill.

The Tea Party was, however, a large factor in the midterm elections, and its supporters were decisive in many Republican primary contests. The movement forced Arlen Specter to switch parties, defeated Senator Robert Bennett in Utah, and denied a Senate nomination to longtime Delaware House member Michael Castle. Pushing the party far to the right undoubtedly cost the Republicans some seats, but these losses were hardly a ripple in the "shellacking" given to President Obama and the Democrats. The Tea Party's impact is apparent in that seventeen of the eighty-four House Republican freshmen were affiliated with the movement. These seventeen plus forty-three returning Republican incumbents formed the Tea Party Caucus. As table 8.3 shows, the Tea Party affiliates are overrepresented in the conservative wing of the party and have discernibly moved the party to the right. The Tea Party freshmen are considerably more conservative than the other first-term Republicans, and the returning members who identify with the movement are much less likely to be in the moderate wing of the party. So even if the grassroots movement was not directly engaged on Dodd-Frank, the election of so many more Republican conservatives will undoubtedly shape implementation even if Republican attempts to repeal fail.

After the passage of Dodd-Frank and the midterm elections of 2010, there were some efforts to mobilize the movement in support of repeal. Tea Party caucus chair Representative Michele Bachmann (R-MN) and member senator Jim DeMint (R-SC) introduced repeal bills in Congress in 2011. (DeMint's 2010 campaign drew heavy support from the Club for Growth,

Table 8.3.
Ideology of House Republicans

	Tea Party First Term	Other First Term	Tea Party Returning	Other Returning
Moderate DW-NOMINATE less than .33	1 (6%)	13 (19%)	0 (0%)	29 (26%)
Conservative DW-NOMINATE between .33 and .67	12 (70%)	44 (64%)	36 (84%)	61 (55%)
Extreme DW-NOMINATE greater than .67	4 (23%)	12 (17%)	7 (16%)	21 (19%)

a fundamentalist free market conservative group whose former president was Senator Pat Toomey [R-PA]. DeMint had endorsed the Tea Party candidate Christine O'Donnell against Michael Castle in Delaware.)

A new group called Dodd-Frank Exposed was created by Robert Bork Jr. (the son of the failed Supreme Court nominee) and Gary Marx, a vice president at Ralph Reed's lobbying firm. (Reed is best known as former executive director of the Christian Coalition.) In February 2011, representatives of this organization attended the Tea Party Patriots American Policy Summit and conducted a poll of the attendees about Dodd-Frank. According to the survey, 42 percent indicated that they had heard little about Dodd-Frank or were not at all familiar with it. Of those who were familiar with it, nine out of ten supported repeal. Dodd-Frank Exposed did not disclose their survey instrument, but their press release leads one to believe that the survey was conducted after the group provided attendees with one-sided information against Dodd-Frank.

Occupy Wall Street

Following the collapse of Lehman, the populist left led a number of anti–Wall Street protests. This burst of street activism was sporadic and short-lived. By Inauguration Day, it had almost petered out. Throughout the course of the development and passage of financial reform legislation, left-wing populists and unions were relatively quiet. Most of the progressive criticism of the administration's approach to financial reform came from elites such as the *New York Times, Vanity Fair,* George Soros, Paul Krugman, Joseph Stiglitz, and Simon Johnson.

It was over a year after the passage of Dodd-Frank before this quiescence would end. In the summer of 2011, Kalle Lasn, the publisher of the anticonsumerist and proenvironmentalist magazine *Adbusters,* devised a marketing campaign for an anti–Wall Street protest movement that would make the ad executives on TV's *Mad Men* happy. A simple one-page advertisement announced a protest in lower Manhattan with a simple premise: Occupy Wall Street and bring a tent.[45]

Unlike the Tea Party, which mobilized in opposition to specific policy proposals (stimulus spending and Obamacare) and on symbolic dates (Tax Day, the Fourth of July), the Occupy Wall Street protests were not targeted at any policy agenda, and the kickoff date of September 17 was selected to coincide with the birthday of Lasn's mother.

The Occupy Wall Street (OWS) movement was unable to coalesce around an agenda. The movement, with its anarchist roots, was unwilling to adopt any form of hierarchical organization or leadership structure. No one, not even Lasn, was to speak on behalf of the movement. Instead, each Occupy encampment was governed by a general assembly composed of all participants. The assemblies made decisions by consensus after open-ended discussion. Any participant could block a decision subject to an override of nine-tenths of those present. As a result many participants, often the most unreasonable ones, filibustered like U.S. senators. Clearly, this requirement precluded the setting of an agenda and the formulation of a common political strategy.[46] Although many ideas floated in OWS circles, ranging from a financial transactions tax to campaign finance reform to student debt relief, no set of official demands emerged.[47]

Whereas Tea Party activists were somewhat amenable to receiving support and direction from existing partisan and ideological groups, the Occupy movement was much more resistant. Some financial and logistical support came from labor unions but there was resistance on both sides to greater cooperation. In November, Occupy Oakland called for a general strike following the shutdown of its encampment that resulted in critical injuries to a protesting Iraq War veteran. But not a single Oakland union local joined in the strike. Relations with the Democratic Party were also at arm's length. Many party leaders endorsed the goals of OWS, but any collaboration was precluded by the strong disappointment of many of the activists in the record of the Obama administration as well as by the opposition of the anarchist fringe to any sort of engagement with electoral or party politics.[48]

Of course, no movement is entirely leaderless, and a leadership cadre did form. But the group maintained few ties to the institutional Left such as the Democratic Party or labor unions.[49] By the end of November 2011, mayors concerned about public sanitation and safety had ordered the closure of the encampments. Because the encampments formed the primary organizational structure, the future political success of the movement is in question. The first anniversary of OWS in New York fizzled.

To assess the future impact of OWS on American politics, it is important to understand the views and motivations of those involved in the movement. But there have been few efforts at systematic opinion surveys of the activists. In one study, pollster Douglas Schoen conducted 198 face-to-face interviews in Zuccotti Park, the site of the OWS encampment in Manhattan, on October 10 and 11, 2011.[50] The Tea Party was overwhelmingly middle-aged and older, whereas Schoen's respondents were quite young, with a near majority under age thirty. Schoen's sample also reveals a very high degree of disengagement with party politics. Although 32 percent identified as Democrats, more (33 percent) identified with no political party, and the remaining third were scattered among anarchists, libertarians, and members of New York's leftist Working Families Party. Only 56 percent had voted in the 2008 presidential election, a rate slightly lower than that of the general population.[51] And 100 percent agreed that they were turned off by the current political system.

Schoen's poll results do contain some suggestion that many activists would like to see the movement more engaged in partisan politics. The respondents were asked an open-ended question about what they would like to see the movement achieve. A strong plurality of 35 percent said that they would like the movement to have the same degree of influence on the Democratic Party that the Tea Party has on the Republicans. The second highest total (11 percent) said that they would like the movement to break the "two-party duopoly," presumably by building a third party.

Just as many Tea Party supporters took positions on issues that belied their reputation as an antigovernment movement, the same may be true about OWS activists. Thirty percent of Schoen's respondents suggested that there should be the same or a lower level of regulation of the financial sector. Moreover, 35 percent disagree that the government has a responsibility to provide health care. The respondents split almost evenly on the financial sector bailouts. Twenty-two percent said the rich already paid their fair share of taxes, and most were against raising taxes for everyone.[52] So it appears that ideological heterogeneity may also be an impediment to further mobilization. OWS is characterized by a lack of structured organization and a common *ideology*, factors that kept elite *interests* away.

Conclusion

It would hardly be an overstatement to say that Occupy Wall Street has increased the salience of inequality and the power of the financial sector as political issues. The movement was remarkably effective in highlighting the divergence between the 1 percent and the 99 percent and has brought attention to the "heads Wall Street wins, tails citizens lose" nature of our financial regulatory regime.

But OWS was better at marketing than at movement. Its slogans are effective, but political change requires mobilization within the political system or overturning it. Americans do not want the latter. The main impediment to the former is that the intellectual origins of the movement are not only deeply suspicious of our existing institutions but also hostile to any hierarchical form of organization that might be necessary to make the movement a political force.[53] This is quite a contrast to the Tea Party movement. The Tea Party shares much of OWS's hostility toward our political elites and institutions as well as some of the anger toward Wall Street. But it does not share the animus toward hierarchical organizations. The Tea Party built organizations and a political infrastructure and were able to influence Republican primary elections and a few general elections.

The contrast between OWS and the Tea Party illustrates how popular outrage can be channeled and built upon by elites. It suggests a different scenario for the Obama administration and the Democrats. After taking office, Obama failed to keep hammering on the regulatory failures of the George W. Bush–Alan Greenspan–Ben Bernanke team from 2001 to 2008. He distanced himself from strong advocates of reform. These included, at least initially, both Paul Volcker and Elizabeth Warren, and—permanently, it appears—the successful but reformist financier George Soros.[54] The White House failed to build support for financial reform when it was hot, and instead chose to move on health care.

Congress had its own problems. The two chairs of the finance committees were compromised by questionable activities during the bubble. This was especially true of Chris Dodd in the Senate, who was tarnished by the disclosure that he had benefited from a "friends of Angelo [Mozillo]" loan, matters related to his acquisition of a country home in Ireland, and ties to AIG. Both Dodd and House chair Barney Frank were avid supporters of Fannie Mae during the subprime loan period; Frank's partner worked at Fannie Mae.[55] So what went on at opposite ends of Pennsylvania Avenue was not a confidence builder for public support for regulatory reform. Public support for regulatory reform was never mobilized.

CHAPTER 9
How to Waste a Crisis

> You never want a serious crisis to go to waste. What I mean by that is that it is an opportunity to do things you think you could not do before.
>
> —Rahm Emanuel, Comments to *Wall Street Journal*'s "CEO Council" Conference, November 19, 2008

RAHM EMANUEL WAS NOT ALONE in believing that the financial crisis of 2008 and the Great Recession would usher in an era of fundamental reform. Liberals were certain that the crisis had proven them right about the inherent dangers of unregulated financial capitalism and that the voters would finally see things their way. A charismatic new leader and progressive legislative majorities would lead the country toward a newer and fairer deal. Not only would the financial system be restructured but the tax system would be made more progressive, there would be health care for all, there would be immigration reform, and the planet would be saved from climate change.

Well, that ain't the way American politics works.

Just as financial markets are not self-regulated by superrational traders who optimally revise their expectations on the basis of new information, politics is not driven by purely rational actors updating beliefs about the best policies. Ideology matters. The crisis did not prove the liberals correct to anyone but liberals. The conservatives believed that their warnings about government intervention in the housing sector were vindicated.

Market-oriented liberals, such as those who led the administration's reform efforts, believed that a little more regulation was needed before the crisis, and that's exactly what they believed afterward.

Of course, preferences may not have shifted because the damage from the crisis, in retrospect, was fairly contained. Within a year after Lehman Brothers had failed, the financial system appeared to have been rescued by the Troubled Asset Relief Program (TARP) and Federal Reserve policies, the National Bureau of Economic Research had declared the recession over, and unemployment had been contained at levels far below those of the Great Depression.

Given the stickiness of ideology, any opportunities afforded by the crisis were those generated in the elections of 2008 that replaced the obstacle of a Republican president and produced an exceptionally liberal Congress.[1] The median member of the House was the most liberal median in the history of Congress. But in our polarized era, the supermajoritarianism of the U.S. Senate radically narrowed those opportunities. Nevertheless, presidents are not completely powerless. Even in such a challenging environment, the president still possessed many advantages that could be used to shape the congressional agenda, to lead his own party, and to mold public opinion.[2] Successfully taking advantage of the crisis to reform the financial sector, therefore, would require focus, leadership, and mobilizing the public.

Unfortunately, the administration of Barack Obama provided none of these ingredients. First, it clearly prioritized the Democratic shibboleth of health care reform over financial market reform. We need not take a position on the merits of Obamacare to see that its passage was not as time-sensitive as financial reform. In addition, given the lack of urgency that might have been applied to financial reform, the nature of pivotal politics guaranteed that any health care bill would be at best a complicated and flawed compromise and that the process would use up valuable time on the agenda. The president signed the health care bill fourteen months after his inauguration. The new administration did not have its Rooseveltian one hundred days. By the time the administration began to focus on financial reform, the banks had returned to profitability, had paid off their TARP loans, and were once again politically potent. Ironically, the bank bailouts engineered by Ben Bernanke and Henry Paulson worked too well, curing the financial sector so quickly that it bounced back strong enough to fight real reform.

The administration was also not predisposed to leading reform efforts. Its primary economic policy makers were the architects of financial deregulation a decade earlier. Their views were likely tempered by the substantial sums they had made on Wall Street in the years between the administration of Bill Clinton and that of Obama, as was true of Larry Summers and Rahm Emanuel, or by future opportunities, as illustrated by Peter Orszag's move from the White House to Citigroup. Not surprisingly, few in the inner circle seemed willing to concede that their previous views were mistaken.

As the Dow Jones Industrial Average continued to plummet in the first months of his administration, Obama chose to reassure Wall Street rather than pursue an aggressive reform agenda. Given the dominance of the ancien régime inside 1600 Pennsylvania Avenue, the early administration proposals avoided major restructuring of financial services and relied primarily on macroprudential supervision of the industry as it existed. Only later, when pressed from the left, did the administration endorse the Volcker Rule against proprietary trading by commercial banks.

Little was done to mobilize the public in favor of reform. As we showed in chapter 8, the public was generally sympathetic to reform, especially in 2009. Even the conservative opposition represented by the Tea Party never mobilized specifically for or against financial regulation. If reform had been a priority, the field was clear for President Obama to rally the public for larger reforms. Early in his administration, at the Pittsburgh G20 summit, Obama failed to address widespread moral, civil, and criminal corruption on Wall Street but spoke out only against a "reckless few." As late as October 2011, President Obama still maintained that "on the issue of prosecutions on Wall Street, one of the biggest problems about the collapse of Lehman's and the subsequent financial crisis and the whole subprime lending fiasco is that a lot of that stuff wasn't necessarily illegal, it was just immoral or inappropriate or reckless."[3] So other than a few toe-dipping explorations of criticism against the financial sector (for which his surrogates immediately apologized), Obama never tried to mobilize public opinion in favor of reform. Much as his predecessor did, he continued to maintain that few if any laws were broken. In December 2011 he told *60 Minutes*, "Some of the most damaging behavior on Wall Street—in some cases some of the least ethical behavior on Wall Street—wasn't illegal."[4]

Claims that few laws were broken just do not stand up to the numerous civil settlements reached since the crisis. Goldman Sachs paid $550 million to settle charges that it misled investors.[5] Bank of America, Wells Fargo, Ally Financial, Citigroup, and JPMorgan Chase entered into a $25 billion agreement to settle mortgage loan servicing and foreclosure abuses.[6] Bank of America agreed to pay $1 billion to settle mortgage fraud charges and $335 million to settle minority discrimination charges.[7] Angelo Mozilo reached a $67.5 civil settlement regarding charges of securities fraud and insider trading while at the helm of Countrywide Financial.[8] The behavior was illegal, just not criminal or at least too difficult or costly to prosecute as criminal.

As of this writing at the end of 2012, there have been no criminal prosecutions of the leading figures in the crisis.[9] A true reform would make criminal prosecutions easier and would turn immoral or unethical behavior into crimes.

Although the Dodd-Frank Wall Street Reform and Consumer Protection Act does contain some important new provisions for regulating the financial services industries, many holes and uncertainties remain.

TOO BIG TO FAIL. Ultimately Dodd-Frank does not eliminate the problem of "too big to fail." In fact, it does almost nothing about "big." Few of its provisions are certain to shrink the largest financial firms. The principal irony of the crisis is that the largest financial firms are even larger now than they were before the crisis. Although there are provisions in Dodd-Frank to slow down mergers, the bill allows major banks to buy struggling banks. Large banks can still grow just as Wachovia, Bank of America, and other banks were allowed to grow before the pop (see chapter 5).

The crisis has received too much of the blame for financial concentration. Concentration took place after it was green-lighted by the Riegle-Neal Bill in 1994, as illustrated by our tracing of the New Jersey National Bank account in chapter 5. In September 2003, the four largest commercial banks held 33 percent of all commercial bank assets. By March 2008, on the eve of the financial meltdown, the figure had already risen to 45 percent. It grew further to 48 percent in March of 2012.[10] Concentration may have been valuable in the crisis. It allowed Secretary Paulson to assemble the largest banks in a Washington meeting and force a coordinated acceptance of TARP funds.[11] But any such ex post advantage in a crisis must be viewed against the disadvantage of the egregious ex ante behavior of the big banks.

The big banks were too big to fail well before the crisis. They were, however, for all intents and purposes allowed to gamble using the public purse. The crisis resulted in nonbank institutions, including Goldman Sachs and Morgan Stanley, being given many of the advantages enjoyed by commercial banks, so the concentration percentages presented above understate the problem. Most perniciously, Dodd-Frank identifies a set of "systemically important" financial institutions that the government would protect in the event of a financial crisis. This implicit government protection will lower these firms' borrowing costs and better allow them to leverage up and grow. In effect, Dodd-Frank turned all of the major financial firms into government-sponsored enterprises (GSEs).

Having banking in the private sector has all the usual pluses that go with market incentives. But because these banks are essentially GSEs, they have a responsibility to stakeholders rather than to their executives, shareholders, and bondholders. This responsibility includes transparency—no Abacus deals by Goldman Sachs for John Paulson, no predatory lending, no "robosigning," no accounting gimmicks about leverage, no bogus ratings, no money laundering, and so forth. At best, Dodd-Frank dealt with these issues in a very limited fashion.

Even if the Dodd-Frank approach of strengthening the regulation of ever larger financial institutions were to reduce the likelihood of future crisis, it still will have done precious little to rein in the political clout of the industry.

THE GOVERNMENT-SPONSORED ENTERPRISES. Although the government spent billions to bail out Fannie Mae and Freddie Mac, these firms remain completely intact. The only difference is that the once implicit guarantees of their debt are now quite explicit. The firms have been nationalized, so the taxpayers will at least enjoy any profits. Given past political manipulation of Fannie and Freddie by Congress and the executive branch, however, we are dubious that taxpayers will see significant returns to the Treasury anytime in the immediate future; in June 2012, they were in hock for $147 billion.[12]

CONSUMER FINANCIAL PROTECTION. Among the most important reforms of Dodd-Frank was the creation of the Consumer Financial Protection Bureau. Political pressure from the Republicans prevented Obama from nominating its architect, Elizabeth Warren, to lead the agency. Senate Republicans were just as adamant in opposing Richard Cordray, who was nominated in place of Warren, and they blocked his nomination. The directorship was filled only through Cordray's controversial recess appointment.

REGULATORY COMPLEXITY AND DISCRETION. The Glass-Steagall Act was a thirty-seven-page document. Dodd-Frank is almost three thousand pages long, and most of the details are still to be worked out in regulatory rule making in various agencies. There is little doubt that these regulatory processes will be dominated by financial lobbyists, and certainly not by anyone from the Occupy Wall Street movement. For example, as of this writing, there is no final rule on credit retention or "skin in the game" covered by Section 941 of Dodd-Frank. Moreover, Section 941 does not apply to GSEs.

On March 29, 2011, the Securities and Exchange Commission (SEC) did issue a draft of rules for comments. Rather than drawing a bright line where, say, the issuer of a mortgage or a mortgage-backed security must retain a 5 percent interest in the security, Dodd-Frank allowed for the exemption of qualified residential mortgages (QRMs). The rules for QRMs, such as the credit score of the borrower or the loan to value, and the like, are to be defined by a regulator. The definition of QRMs and the treatment of mortgage pools that included a mixture of QRMs and non-QRMs immediately drew commentary from financial institutions such as JPMorgan Chase and from legislators. Republican senator Johnny Isakson attacked the SEC proposal as being market unfriendly.[13] As a continued testament to ideology and interests over experience, Isakson represents Georgia, a state that far outpaced every other state in bank failures in the crisis. Although the discretion allowed by Section 941 might make for a more efficient market than a bright-line rule, it opens the door to regulatory forbearance that could eventually lead to the same practices that arose in the subprime mortgage crisis.

A broad summary of the delay in implementing Dodd-Frank has been provided by the law firm Davis Polk:

- As of June 1, 2012, a total of 221 Dodd-Frank rule-making requirement deadlines have passed. This is 55.5 percent of the 398 total rule-making requirements, and 78.9 percent of the 280 rule-making requirements with specified deadlines.
- Of these 221 passed deadlines, 148 (67.0 percent) have been missed and 73 (33.0 percent) have been met with finalized rules. Regulators have not yet released proposals for 21 of the 148 missed rules.

- Of the 398 total rule-making requirements, 110 (27.6 percent) have been met with finalized rules and rules have been proposed that would meet 144 (36.2 percent) more. Rules have not yet been proposed to meet 144 (36.2 percent) rule-making requirements.[14]

Unless there is a spate of rule making in the coming months, the next presidential election occurred, more than four years since the Lehman Brothers bankruptcy, with most of Dodd-Frank unimplemented thanks to complexity, discretion, and the resultant lobbying.

EXECUTIVE COMPENSATION. Almost nothing has been done to modify executive compensation practices that lead to excessive risk taking. Reasonable people can disagree about the extent to which there should be ex ante curbs on executive pay. But the continued limitations on the ability of regulators, shareholders, and courts to claw back compensation from executives who looted their companies and left taxpayers holding the bag are unconscionable.

Perhaps the highest-level financial executive to face civil prosecution was Angelo Mozilo of Countrywide Financial. As previously noted, Mozilo's case was resolved with a penalty of $67.5 million. Mozilo was off the hook for all but $22.5 million of the penalty. The rest was paid, as a contractual obligation, by Bank of America after it acquired Countrywide.[15] And any pension assets of Angelo (and his friends) are fully exempt from civil litigation.

Would it be amiss to limit the ability of corporations to cover damages from suits filed by government agencies? Would it be wrong to protect, say, the first $5 million of pension assets from litigation but to make the rest available for claw back? No and no, but the 0.001 percent won't let the 99.999 percent even think about such a remedy.

COMPLEXITY. The authors of Dodd-Frank ignored one of the central drivers of the financial meltdown: complexity. As the financial sector was steadily deregulated in the 1980s and '90s, complex financial instruments emerged. The creators of these instruments had better information than the rating agencies, the regulatory agencies, and Congress. In addition, the stupefying profits enabled the financial sector to hire the best and the brightest from the Ivy League to devise ever more complex instruments thereby further increasing their information advantage. The rating agencies had the Wall Street securitizers as clients. They were too willing to issue AAA ratings on these securities no matter how complex they were or what their true underlying values were.[16] The SEC and the Fed ignored the warnings, and Congress did nothing.

Dodd-Frank simply creates a dense kudzu of regulations that does not deal with the central issue of asymmetric information. Regulations need to be as straightforward as possible, with bright red lines. The long Glass-Steagall regime may not be economically efficient in theory but it prevented serious banking problems until the deregulation craze of the 1980s and '90s.

So this is the status quo postcrisis. It fits the historical pattern we established in chapter 6. The new regulations came with a transition in power, were further delayed (while the party base was rewarded with Obamacare), were limited, and now risk being at least partly reversed with a new transition to Republican control.

The return to normal, noncrisis politics is unlikely to improve the situation. As the famous political scientist E. E. Schattschneider once observed, it is the "moneyed interests" that dominate politics when the public is not aroused.[17] Perhaps the Occupy movement will keep the public focused on these issues, but will it direct it to arcane regulatory rule-making procedures?

For much of the past hundred years, the notion that "what's good for General Motors is good for the country" has been an important, if controversial, part of America's public philosophy. Unfortunately, it appears that over the past thirty years Goldman Sachs and other financial firms have supplanted GM at the core of that creed. But at least when GM was the exemplar of American economic might, we were celebrating a firm and an industry that helped generate broad prosperity responsible for pulling millions of Americans into a steadily expanding middle class. But in the thirty years that financialization has replaced industrialization, America has seen prosperity, but it has not been widely shared. And as we know all too well, the "what's good for Goldman Sachs" philosophy has wrought financial insecurity for millions.

American prosperity requires deep, liquid, and active capital markets, but these markets should be a means and not an end. How to restore financial services to its proper place in the political economy is not simply a question of economics. An increasingly dysfunctional politics lies at the heart of the problem. No regulatory regime can succeed without the underlying support of elected officials. As long as American politics remains polarized, such support seems unlikely. New bubbles will continue to effervesce.

The First Sign of a Wasted Crisis: MF Global

In fact, it did not take long for the reappearance of the type of shenanigans that went on before the financial crisis. MF Global failed in October 2011. Somehow $2.1 billion of clients' money was missing and, as of mid-2012, had yet to be recovered. MF Global was headed by Jon Corzine, who went through the revolving door from Goldman Sachs on Wall Street to the Senate and the governorship of New Jersey and back out again to MF Global.

Dodd-Frank might have provided a bright-line rule for the handling of client funds. The rule might have included substantial criminal penalties for malfeasance. Instead Dodd-Frank left enormous discretion to the Commodity Futures Trading Commission (CFTC), which was headed by Gary Gensler—like Corzine a Democrat and Goldman Sachs alum. Although Gensler has generally been well regarded as an active regulator, he allowed himself to be lobbied by Corzine. As reported in a *Wall Street Journal* editorial, their postpop interaction was facilitated by Ivy League connections when Gensler guest-lectured for a

Princeton University course taught by Corzine.[18] The ethical action would have been for Gensler to recuse himself from contact with Corzine.

MF Global failed because the firm made bad bets on European securities. If sophisticated investors were making the same bets through MF Global, their losses would just be part of the give and take of capitalist markets. MF Global was too small to pose systemic risk. And at the time that Corzine was betting his ranch and those of many others, most financial institutions were conservative after the pop. But MF Global's clients were not making bets that had gone belly up. Someone at MF Global stole their money to do so.

A fundamentalist free market conservative might simply say *caveat emptor*: if you don't trust Jon Corzine with your money, don't invest in MF Global. Markets work better, however, with rules that aim to guarantee transparency, reduce the risk of embezzlement, and produce a level playing field for investors at an informational disadvantage and without connections to the best and the brightest, such as Gary Gensler. Ideology and interests combined, within the context of institutions—particularly the filibuster rule in the Senate, to make Dodd-Frank too weak to put a firewall between the interaction of interests that brought Corzine and Gensler together. Moreover, given limitations free market conservatives have placed on staffing regulatory agencies (see figure 5.3), it was cheap for Gensler to take Corzine's call, and costly for him to monitor MF Global's books. MF Global is a symptom of potential problems that we seek to confront with our broader recommendations.

Recommendations

At the core of our analysis is our belief that boom-and-bust cycles are endemic to democratic capitalism. But certain reforms can deflate the bubbles a bit without forgoing the benefits of modern finance. Few if any of these recommendations originate with us, and many other good ideas are floating around. We focus on the ones below because of their linkages to the political foundations of modern finance. We start with economic reforms that could be implemented. We then turn to political reforms that might make the economic reforms possible.

Use Simple Regulatory Rules

When Paul Volcker first unveiled his eponymous rule, it was a short bright-line rule: commercial banks shall not trade securities on their own account. But after Dodd-Frank let regulators formulate rules that would allow for "legitimate trading activities," the Volcker Rule became anything but simple. The initial proposed rule came in at more than three hundred pages and solicited input on 1,347 different questions.

Of course, the simple bright-line rule would impose economic costs. It would limit the products that commercial banks could offer their customers, and limitation might lead to less diversification and some lost economies of scope. Yet the political benefits outweigh the costs. Enforcement and compliance monitoring of the simple rule is much easier than that for a three-hundred-page rule. Legal and regulatory complexity always works in the favor of the industry that can devote significant resources into turning loopholes into tunnels.

Simple rules also act as important ex ante brakes on financial excesses. They leave less room for financial firms to lobby later to weaken reform. But the overarching principle of Dodd-Frank is the reliance on ex post mitigation—that is, let the market operate freely, monitor for systemic risks, and then intervene. We remain skeptical that regulators have either the technical capacity or the political will to intervene when the necessity arises.

Set Rules That Account for Political Risk

As we mentioned in chapter 5, Joseph Stiglitz, Peter Orszag, and Jon Orszag placed the odds of a Fannie Mae collapse at 1 in 500,000 given the capital standards of that time. So what happened? It could have been one unbelievably unlucky draw. After all, even low probability events can occur. But more likely it was the failure of their analysis to account for all of the things that Fannie could do to subvert the enforcement of that capital standard. It failed to account for the fact that Fannie's accountants could make their accounting capital look bigger than their true capital—and that they would do this precisely when the probability of collapse increased. It failed to account for the fact that big firms like Fannie could press ratings agencies for favorable risk assessments of their assets (which in turn lowers their capital requirements). It failed to account for the fact that Fannie and Freddie used their political leverage to intimidate their regulators and Congress into turning a blind eye.

In our view, political risks grow proportionately (if not exponentially) with the size of financial firms. The modern financial megafirm is a magnificent collection of conflicts of interest housed under one roof. Self-regulation of these conflicts through the creation of internal controls and "Chinese walls" is not likely to succeed. In July 2012, both the chairman and the CEO of Barclays were forced to resign after it was revealed that employees in the bank's treasury department were manipulating the London Interbank Offered Rate and sharing that information with traders who profited from it.[19] A more segmented financial sector would certainly lose economies of scale and scope, but it would also certainly be less prone to such flagrant fraud.

In general, when policies for the financial sector are established, it must be assumed that they will not be perfectly enforced. Consequently, the standards must be set so that the outcomes are satisfactory even with less than perfect compliance. Think about speed limits. When she evaluates a change in speed limit from 55 to 65 miles per hour on an interstate highway, a regulator should not assume that drivers adjust by going from 55 to 65. A better assumption would be that drivers are already going 65 and that they will go 75 after the change.

Our argument about compliance goes further. Automotive innovation evolves relatively slowly. If anything, government regulations made cars safer, something that might argue for higher speed limits. Finance is different. In chapter 4, we quoted Henry Paulson as arguing that it was a good thing that regulators could not keep up, because the lag in regulation allowed financial innovation to proceed. Paulson was dead wrong. The past decade has witnessed a lot of harm and very little good that has come from such "innovation." The innovation did not produce strong growth in the economy, except in the financial sector. Compare the twenty-first century to the 1950s, a time of high growth and the peak of regulation of financial markets.[20] What's worse, the innovation of the 1980s and beyond occurred during a period of rising income inequality. Virtually nothing trickled down to the bottom half of the income distribution (again, see figure 5.2). Foreclosures led to a decline in the fraction of households in owner-occupied housing. To paraphrase Ronald Reagan, "Are you better off than you were before financial markets were deregulated?"

Limit the Activities of Taxpayer-Insured Financial Firms

With federal deposit insurance, commercial banks gamble with house money. For this reason, it is especially important to treat insured commercial banks as public utilities. Just as rates of the local power utilities were regulated in exchange for a monopoly franchise, insured commercial banks should be subject to more restrictions because of the implicit subsidy on their deposits. Although it appears that reerecting the firewalls of Glass-Steagall is not in the political cards, a stronger Volcker Rule would go a long way toward getting commercial banks to focus on their core function.

Reform Compensation Practices

High compensation to financial executives and traders is often justified as compensation for risk. But as we now know, the risks they took were very asymmetric: the potential for gain was always much, much greater than the threatened losses. Limits on personal and corporate liability always create these asymmetries. The asymmetries are compounded when financial firms own the equivalent of a put by which the government picks up some losses in order to avoid a crash. It was disheartening to see so many people walk away after destroying their companies with their bubble gains bolstered by their boom-time severance contracts and pensions.

To prevent a bonanza for malfeasance from happening again, legal and regulatory mechanisms must be established to ensure that financial gamblers have to cover a larger share of their own losses. Courts and regulators should be able to claw back bonuses and compensation obtained when the bad bets looked good. Notably, executives should not be able to shield these gains by having them appear as pension benefits. The pension exemption for civil liability should be capped.

There is an ongoing debate about the extent to which current compensation practices contributed to the bubble. Many executives with the largest stakes in their own companies made the biggest bets. This suggests that the common proposal of forcing executives to hold their companies' stock over longer periods may have little effect. Richard Fuld let his Lehman Brothers shares go down with the ship. But even if compensation reform is not a silver bullet for bubble avoidance, standard notions of fairness and equity require it.

Prevent "Too Big to Fail" by Preventing "Big"

Dodd-Frank deals with the notion of "too big to fail" by subjecting large firms to greater regulatory scrutiny along with the requirement to create a "living will" that will facilitate orderly resolution in case of failure. Of course, this approach is at odds with our plea for simple, ex ante, politically feasible rules. To us, the only approach to "too big to fail" that meets these criteria are limits on the size or autonomy of financial firms. Even Alan Greenspan has expressed concern about the size of financial institutions.[21] Mervyn King, the governor of the Bank of

England, and Joseph Stiglitz have argued that "a bank that is too big to fail is too big to exist."[22] We may not go that far, but at the very least, large financial institutions should be heavily and effectively regulated. A living will is great as long as the taxpayers don't have to pay for the coffin and the funeral. Moreover, the federal government and regulatory agencies should not act in a way that encourages ever-increasing bigness. One example is the acquisition of Wachovia by Wells Fargo. Another is the acquisition of National City by PNC, which we discussed in chapter 4. Both the Wachovia and National City acquisitions were determined by government policies.

Increase Regulatory and Prosecutorial Capacity

Even if simple and tough rules were to be promulgated, regulators and prosecutors must have the tools and resources necessary to enforce them. As we discussed in chapter 5, regulatory resources were drawn down just as the bubble was expanding. This should not happen again. To riff on an old Warren Buffett line, bubbles occur when more people are swimming naked. That's the time to either beef up the beach patrol or drain the pool.

There are some other aspects to regulatory capacity beyond simple resources. Financial regulators are often disadvantaged by extreme informational asymmetries with respect to the industry. First, regulators should be given more power to obtain information about financial products as well as to enforce greater levels of transparency. Second, financial regulatory agencies should strive to develop more independent expertise about the financial marketplace so that they are less dependent on the Wall Street in-and-outers.

Third, we should strengthen not just federal regulatory capacity but also that of state governments. During deregulation, state laws and regulations were regularly preempted by federal statute in the name of creating a uniform national marketplace. But federalism still has a place in financial regulation. Just as the federal minimum wage is a floor and not a ceiling, states should be able to regulate activities such as insurance and mortgage lending more strenuously than the federal minimums dictate. Although financial firms would like the economy of scale inherent in uniform national regulatory standards, the political benefits of intervention by the states, given the influence of Wall Street in Washington, outweigh the economic costs.

Having better enforcement and monitoring would be great, but we realize that it may be a chimerical goal. Taxpayers and free market conservatives are reluctant to pony up the funds needed for enforcement. Financial firms, as we saw in Scott Brown's opposition to the bank tax, are unwilling to support a tax on their industry for enforcement. Taxpayers and firms are also reluctant to pay bureaucrats the salaries needed to attract top talent. Therefore the door will not stop revolving. Five years in Washington is just a career investment.

In addition to the economics of government careers, another factor rightfully restrains regulatory capacity. This is Americans' reluctance to have Big Brother looking over their shoulder. Power does corrupt and can easily be abused. But the answer is not laissez-faire and caveat emptor; it is transparency and public accountability for regulators. These are best achieved by simple rules and limited discretion.

Political Reforms

There is now a cottage industry of would-be reformers who offer solutions to America's dysfunctional politics. Their pet projects range from public financing of campaigns to banning gerrymanders, instituting open or nonpartisan primaries, and creating third parties. But there is little hard evidence to suggest that any of these weapons in the reformers' tool kit will be very effective. After all, polarization was low in the middle of the twentieth century even though campaign finance was mostly unregulated, districts were ruthlessly gerrymandered, party bosses controlled nominations, and serious third-party presidential candidates were on the ballot in 1948, 1968, and 1980.

Reform agendas also run aground because of the political forces they attempt to change. Reforms are never politically neutral and are sure to be challenged by the status quo's winners. Today's winners, fundamentalist free market conservatives, will surely make reform difficult. Moreover, removing the gridlock from which they benefit will be exceptionally difficult because it is deeply embedded in the Constitution.

For example, as we discussed in chapter 4, the difference in preferences induced by a bicameral legislature with alternative forms of apportionment is an important source of gridlock. This feature is the one part of the Constitution that cannot be amended. Moreover, amending other features of the Constitution is incredibly hard. Should a majority of Americans believe that campaign spending should not be protected as free speech and want to reverse Supreme Court rulings, a two-thirds majority would be required in both chambers of Congress, making the gridlock zone much larger than it is for ordinary legislation. Moreover, the requirement for ratification by three-fourths of the states could doom an amendment passed by Congress. Ratification by the states failed for the Equal Rights Amendment. Polarization makes amendment more difficult. We are likely to be stuck indefinitely with the Constitution we have and the court that interprets it.[23]

One aspect of gridlock that could be changed without a constitutional amendment is the cloture rule in the Senate.[24] The cloture rule was certainly constraining, as we showed in chapter 7, to the Obama administration's actions after the pop. But there are risks to changing it in the current era of polarization. A momentarily electoral triumph for free market conservatives could easily move deregulation back to the prepop status quo and beyond.

Another seemingly impervious aspect of American democracy is our two-party system, with the major fault line between Democrats and Republicans that was established with the end of Reconstruction in 1876. Forming new major parties has not succeeded in well over 120 years, despite popular dissatisfaction with the current division. Sentiment against both the Democrats and Republicans is indicated in polling: *Wall Street Journal/ NBC* polls have shown that a majority of Americans prefer divided government to unified control. Divided government may be their best chance of obtaining moderate policies.[25] Sentiment against the major parties was also evident when an oddball candidate, Ross Perot, with an even odder running mate,[26] obtained 19 percent of the vote in the 1992 presidential election. Yet one-off presidential candidacies can only influence the outcome of the current election, not alter the system. The Bull Moose, Theodore Roosevelt, found this out when he was dissatisfied with his successor, William Howard Taft. To alter the system, a new party must have a base that contests congressional as well as presidential elections. The separation of powers in the Constitution creates a huge obstacle to political entry.

Another vehicle for reform is ideological change that is not rooted in narrow self-interest. Such a change occurred when the abolitionist movement initiated the political realignment of the Civil War era.[27] It also occurred with the progressive movement of the turn of the last century, most identified with President Theodore Roosevelt and Robert La Follette in the Senate. This was primarily a middle-class reformist movement that had supporters in both political parties.[28] Progressives were concerned with corruption and injustices issuing from the rise of industrial capitalism in the United States. They supported the Sixteenth Amendment that legalized federal income taxation, direct election of senators with the Seventeenth Amendment, Prohibition with the Eighteenth Amendment, and women suffrage with the Nineteenth Amendment. They were not anticapitalist per se. They viewed themselves as modernizers and reformers.[29] In particular, Theodore Roosevelt was surely a capitalist. When he visited Pittsburgh he stayed at the home of Henry Clay Frick, the man who broke the Homestead Steel Strike. Yet Roosevelt was a trust buster and was not averse to government regulations that he considered in the public interest. And, as the founder of the national park system, he was not averse to public goods.

The progressives contributed to the long arc of moderation of the Republican Party from the early twentieth century to the presidency of Dwight D. Eisenhower, who, credited with the interstate highway system, supported public goods. The Bank Holding Company Act of 1956, which was the apex of financial regulation, was passed during his presidency.[30] Even though Eisenhower signed it, he did not think the act went far enough to constrain the banks and to preserve market competition.[31]

Eisenhower, however, was the last gasp of moderation. Free market conservatism was already incipient, and it found its first national expression in the candidacy of Barry Goldwater in 1964.[32] The ideological pendulum swung back. Although crony capitalists and free market ideologues would later bond, conviction independent of interest was part of the story. Many of the market-oriented ideas developed as an intellectual response to the government failures and economic sluggishness of the 1960s and '70s. Many innovative proposals emerged to use markets and incentives to solve pressing problems such as "cap and trade" environmental regulation and the earned income tax credit.

On the other hand, free market conservatism became as much a matter of near religious conviction, inspired by writers including Ayn Rand, as a matter of policy analysis of the American economy. For more classical conservatives like George H. W. Bush and his economic adviser Paul McAvoy, Reaganomics was "voodoo economics."[33] After Reagan won the 1980 nomination, running mate Bush then kowtowed to the voodoo. Free market conservatism grew in acceptance, and its public philosophy morphed into one in which all taxes were evil, government should be shrunk for the sake of shrinking, all markets should be unregulated, and public goods, including education, should be privatized. Unfortunately, this extreme form of free market conservatism came to be embraced by a sufficiently large segment of the American public that free market conservatives could dominate electoral politics.

The best hope to stabilize our economic system, given the stability of the political system, is to begin to build a new public philosophy for dealing with the challenges of our time, not for those of the 1970s. That philosophy should recognize that, although they are far from perfect, the policies brought about in the years that spanned the Franklin Delano Roosevelt, Harry Truman, and Dwight D. Eisenhower presidencies produced an economic system that, for the first time in history, enjoyed a "Great Moderation," a period of more than sixty years without a major financial crisis.

But this new public philosophy should be much more than a restoration of Great Society liberalism or egalitarianism. Government, too, has its limits. When politicians try to stretch beyond those limits by creating government-sponsored enterprises, sponsoring public-private partnerships, and governing by subsidy, crony capitalism is the result just as surely as it is in the hands of the free market conservatives. Government—federal, state, and local—should be effective, efficient, transparent, and on budget. The concentration of authority in Washington, D.C., has been essential to deal with many important issues, such as civil rights for minorities. But a dose of old-style Jeffersonianism—with more authority in the hands of local and state governments—in many areas would be beneficial and would reduce the influence of powerful rent-seeking national interest groups.

The progressivism of Theodore Roosevelt took root in no small part because new professional and academic elites emerged with views and interests distinct from those of the financial and industrial elites. Unfortunately, such an elite counterbalance to financial interests appears to no longer exist. The meritocracy that has been trusted to run our governmental and financial institutions has failed. Many of the graduates of elite institutions are honest and engaged in productive pursuits in the nonfinancial economy. We cannot help but note, however, what appears to be a dismal record of many who have engaged in politics and finance.

The last four presidents all had Ivy League degrees. The Supreme Court that produced Citizens United is now made up of all Ivy Leaguers. The Harvard Business School has contributed the COO of Enron, two professors who were principals in Long

Term Capital Management, and a Yale University legacy admit who presided over the bubble. Another Harvard MBA was convicted of insider trading after serving as CEO of McKinsey, director of Goldman Sachs, and other corporations, as well as the Bill & Melinda Gates Foundation and many other charitable and educational (including Ivy League) institutions. A future president of Harvard celebrated the Gramm-Leach-Bliley and the Commodity Futures Modernization Acts while ignoring the warnings of the chairwoman of the CFTC. As president of Harvard, he presided over the university's settlement in a federal government civil suit filed for inappropriate behavior in Russian financial markets by a faculty economist.[34] That president also did a rewarding tour of duty on Wall Street. Another Harvard economist sat on the board of American International Group (AIG), alongside a star diplomat, also an Ivy League graduate, and other A-list members. AIG's financial products' risk model was designed by a Yale University professor. A brilliant Harvard undergrad and MBA who served under the future Harvard president in the Treasury Department became the COO of Facebook. She and another Ivy League graduate, the CFO, most likely had a good deal to do with the botched initial public offering of Facebook.[35] The current CFTC chair who interacted with Jon Corzine is a Wharton School MBA. A story, perhaps apocryphal, is that when Michael Milken was sentenced to prison in the 1980s, Wharton students scrawled "Hall of Shame" over the "Hall of Fame" where Milken's name appeared. Our elite universities should stop turning a blind eye to what is going on in the Wall Street casinos. Padding the endowment in the short run can bring national ruin in the long run.

We have subtitled this book "The Failure of American Democracy." By now the reader can see why we chose these words. American democracy has failed the ordinary citizenry in the Great Recession. Neither political party has risen to the occasion and advocated true institutional reform that would reduce the stupefying concentration of money and power in the financial sector. No champion like Theodore Roosevelt has emerged to blast the "Malefactors of Great Wealth" and speak for the devastated communities throughout America. Instead, the elites glower across an ideological divide constructed around the conflicts of the 1960s and '70s and do little toward meaningful reform of institutions and markets that have clearly failed. No, Presidents Bush and Obama; the "reckless" are not those "few." Lest our democracy become a kleptocracy, we need a redo of financial regulation.

Epilogue
Kicking the Can

In the fall of 2012, Americans once again had an opportunity to elect a president and change Congress. But those who hoped that the election would provide an opportunity for the nation and its leaders to engage in a discussion about the unfinished business of financial reform must surely be disappointed.

President Obama and his opponent Mitt Romney avoided the topic of financial regulation. The topic drew just one brief engagement in the three presidential debates. When pressed in the first debate by moderator Jim Lehrer to name examples of excessive regulation, Governor Romney blamed Dodd-Frank for perpetuating banks' too-big-to-fail protection and suggested that the delay in defining a qualified residential mortgage for purposes of securitization made banks reluctant to make loans (see our discussion in chapter 9). When Lehrer asked whether he would repeal Dodd-Frank, Romney said he would "repeal and replace" it. On his turn, Obama defended Dodd-Frank and attacked Romney for wanting to repeal it. The whole exchange lasted about four minutes. Romney never specified exactly what he would replace Dodd-Frank with. Obama never gave any indication of second thoughts or how he might pursue additional reforms were he reelected.

In some ways it is strange that the government's response to a calamity that affected and continues to affect millions of people would have drawn so little attention in an election poised to be a referendum on the president's economic record. It is not as if employment or the housing market had rebounded robustly enough to distract the public from the past four years. It is not as if the financial reform has accomplished its goals. The banking sector is now concentrated among big firms to a level significantly greater than at the onset of the crisis, aided in part by the continuing struggles of small community banks. In particular, the mortgage market has become concentrated, reducing competition for borrowers. In the third quarter of 2012, Wells Fargo originated 29 percent of all mortgages and the top five originators 55 percent.[1]

Our political system just kicked the can down the road when it comes to regulation of mortgage and other important financial markets. Most of the regulations to be promulgated under Dodd-Frank have yet to be written, and several face legal challenges from financial firms. The D.C. Court of Appeals has already struck down the SEC's attempt to implement Dodd-Frank provisions to empower shareholders to oust management. Three challenges to CFTC rules are winding their way through the federal courts.[2] In echoes of the litigation over the Affordable Care Act, the attorneys general of Michigan, Oklahoma, and South Carolina have joined a lawsuit challenging the constitutionality of several provisions of Dodd-Frank.[3] Four years have passed since the crisis of 2008, yet the futures of the GSEs, Fannie and Freddie, are still up in the air. Attempts to reform money market mutual funds, a key source of instability in 2008 when the Reserve Primary fund "broke the buck," gridlocked in the Securities and Exchange Commission.[4] As of January 2, 2013, the law firm of Davis Polk (cited in chapter 9) reported that 142 out of 237 deadlines for rule making have been missed. Four years after the crisis, one-third of the required rules have been proposed but not finalized, and another third have not even been proposed.[5] After the crisis, high-frequency trading (HFT) (chapter 5) became visible as a potentially dangerous financial innovation. While many other countries throughout the world are moving to regulate HFT, Washington has given it a pass.

But most importantly, bad bets by too-big-to-fail banks, financial malfeasance, and scandal have not receded from view. JPMorgan Chase's "London Whale" has grown to $5.8 billion. MF Global's clients still await the return of much of their money as similar thefts of supposedly segregated customer money have come to light at other financial firms.[6]

The banks are now facing as much as $300 billion in losses from civil suits related to the subprime crisis.[7] With their "heads we win, tails you lose" attitude, the banks are arguing that having to pay for bad behavior will cripple the housing market.

Fines of financial institutions have continued. As mentioned in chapter 9, in February 2012, five major banks reached a $25 billion settlement with 49 state attorneys general as a result of fraudulent foreclosure processing practices. The same practices appear likely to generate an additional $10 billion settlement with the federal government from 14 banks.[8] HSBC paid a $1.92 billion fine for money laundering.[9] The Libor rate setting scandal blew open when Barclays paid a fine of $453 million to U.S. and U.K. regulators and its chairman and CEO both resigned. Barclays was let off relatively lightly—regulators even gave Barclays a 20 percent "discount" on its fines in exchange for its cooperation. Total fines over Libor manipulation are expected to be $8.7 billion.[10] As we write, the biggest fine, $1.5 billion, has been levied on UBS. While a couple of lower level employees of UBS's Japanese affiliate have been criminally charged, the big kahunas are so far unscathed. In announcing the supposedly "tough" treatment of UBS, Lanny Breuer, head of the criminal division of the Justice Department, was quoted as proclaiming, "Our goal here is not to destroy a major financial institution."[11] So the approach is the exact opposite of how other forms of organized crime are prosecuted where every effort is made to link each offense to the organization and its leaders. Given that the effects of financial crime are as pernicious as the effects of the sale of illegal drugs, we fail to see how the different approach is warranted. Perhaps UBS should have been the test case for Dodd-Frank's vaunted new resolution authority.

We were not surprised that UBS was central to the Libor scandal. In the introduction, we highlighted both its connections to the Republican Phil Gramm and the Democrat Barack Obama and its $780 million fine for helping a "reckless few" Americans avoid income taxes. In May 2012, the PBS program *Frontline* included claims by UBS executive Robert Wolf that he served as a conduit of information from the Treasury to Obama during the 2008 crisis. So we are also not surprised that the firm is "too big to jail" or to be excluded from doing business in the United States. "Cheat and pay the fines" appears entrenched as a business strategy for UBS and many other financial firms.

This business strategy profits from the lack of regulatory capacity that we discussed in chapter 4. The Libor rate fixing began in 2005. Although the story made it into the media, notably the *Wall Street Journal*, in 2008, national and international regulators were in denial, so no fines were assessed until 2012. Had there been vigorous prosecution in 2008 or 2009, the scandal may have led to a tougher Dodd-Frank. By the time the Libor fuel could have been added to the fire, the fire was out. Public outrage was past. The billion-dollar wrist slaps did not draw attention in the presidential debates.

So the lack of campaign attention was not due to any shortage of headlines.

From the angle of politics, it is easy to see why the candidates spent their time on other issues. President Obama learned very early that there were political costs attached to a populist position. His early attacks on Romney's record as the head of the private equity firm Bain Capital created almost as much division within his party as it hurt Romney. Even Newark's African American Democratic mayor Cory Booker professed to be "nauseated" by the campaign attacks on Bain.[12] Polling analysis suggests that the Bain Capital attacks did not move public opinion.[13]

The combination of the Bain ads and Obama's modest touting of Dodd-Frank appears to have led to a mass exodus of donations to his campaign from the financial sector. Even as late as the 2010 midterm elections, the Democratic Party received about as much financial support from the financial sector as did the Republicans. But that all changed in 2012. Wall Street's money flew to Romney and other Republican candidates. According to data compiled by the Center for Responsive Politics, the Democrats received almost $60 million less from finance, insurance, and real estate interests than did the Republicans (Democrats received $27 million more than Republicans in 2008). The gap among the presidential candidates was even more glaring. Romney outraised Obama from this group by more than 3 to 1 (Obama had outraised McCain almost 2 to 1 in 2008).[14] After such a huge defection by the "money wing," the message was clear: to staunch the outflow, don't talk about Bain and soft-pedal Dodd-Frank. And never suggest going further than Dodd-Frank.

Romney had no stronger incentives to campaign on financial issues. As a candidate who struggled mightily with his plutocratic image, he could scarcely afford to make repealing or even reforming Dodd-Frank an important part of his campaign. As we documented in chapter 8, regulating Wall Street was not an issue that captivated the energized Tea Party segment of his base. Bailouts, a shibboleth of conservative congressional Republicans such as Jim Bunning, had largely been removed as a political issue by substantial repayments of TARP money. The recovery of the auto industry had resulted in Romney's incurring political damage from his earlier criticisms of the auto bailout.

With the elections over, Washington had no time for corrections to Dodd-Frank or solutions for the GSEs. Instead, it struggled to avoid going over the "fiscal cliff": a doomsday device manufactured by our polarized, failed democracy. The cliff was the product of a decades-long failure to settle on an income tax code that is predictable, efficient, and fair. It reflected the inability of our leaders to find a way to stimulate the economy in the short run while paving the way for long-term deficit reductions. It is the victory of gimmicks and position taking over the hard work of genuine policy making and compromise.

The climb to our nefarious precipice began with George W. Bush's tax cuts in 2001 and 2003. As a direct consequence of polarization, these bills had to be passed under reconciliation to avoid a filibuster, resulting in a ten-year limit expiring at the end of 2010. Of course, a smaller, but more durable, tax cut could have passed, had the Bush administration been willing to accommodate the views of moderate Democrats to reach cloture. Bush might have limited his tax initiatives to something similar to what Congress passed in extremis on January 2, 2013—Clinton-era rates on the top 2 percent, cuts for everyone else, and an estate tax only on estates valued greater than $5 million. Such a proposal would now have been a permanent feature of our tax code and would have allowed us avoid the negative economic effects of a decade of tax policy uncertainty. But restraint of this form would have been anathema to both the *ideology* and the *interests* of the contemporary Republican Party. Fiscal policy was too polarized for such a compromise. Following the 2010 elections, with the country economically weak and the Obama administration politically shellacked, there was little choice but to extend the Bush tax cuts for two more years (in exchange for a bit more stimulus).

We reached the edge of the cliff with the Tea Party–inspired battle over raising the federal debt limit in 2011. In order to reach an agreement to raise the debt ceiling and avoid a default, the president and Republican leaders agreed to a sequester of approximately one trillion dollars over 9 years should a "supercommittee" of six Republican and six Democratic legislators fail to agree to a long-term deficit reduction package. The sequester was to be split evenly between defense and domestic spending and was to take effect on January 2, 2013. From the moment the supercommittee failed to reach an agreement, both parties doubleddown on the bet that they could win the 2012 election decisively enough to avoid the cliff on their own terms.

But 2012 was a status quo election putting neither party in full control. Obama's victory and polling numbers favorable to tax increases on high-income earners have put the free market conservatives back on their heels but got their dander up. When push came to shove, the Republicans acquiesced in allowing a House vote on a moderate tax increase—far less than the one Obama campaigned for reelection on. A majority of Republican House members voted against the bill, from either gratuitous ideological posturing or strategic fear of being "primaried" in 2014.[15] And after all of this, Congress and the president scheduled a rematch in two months to deal with the federal debt limit.

While *ideology* and *institutions* combined to put fiscal and entitlement policy at a breaking point, *interests* made any adjustments minor. Income tax rates on the highest 1 or 2 percent of earners will go back only to Clinton rates. No one will wake up in anything remotely close to France and the 75 percent top marginal tax rate advocated by President François Hollande. Similarly the country kicked the can on tough choices on entitlements that will inevitably be forced by changes in birth rates, death rates, and medical technology. Republican plans for privatization of social security (George W. Bush) and Medicare vouchers (Paul Ryan) have proven politically unpopular. Reducing benefits within the current system is anathema for Democrats, nearly to the same extent tax increases are among Republicans. While Bill Clinton could reform "welfare as we knew it" in 1996 with little backlash at the polls, a short-sighted middle class makes dealing with Medicare and Social Security much more difficult.

It is also unthinkable to go back to 1960s regulation of financial markets. The reforms of Dodd-Frank will be located in the gridlock zone for the foreseeable future. The Consumer Financial Protection Bureau is likely to become institutionalized and permanent under a Democratic president for its first five years. The Republicans most likely gave up a Senate seat in Massachusetts because fundamentalist free market capitalism led them to reject Elizabeth Warren as head of the Bureau. She will now be its protector in the Senate. The institutional permanence of the Bureau notwithstanding, its discretionary policies will be subject, like those of the National Labor Relations Board, to an ongoing political tug-of-war. In addition to the Bureau, the old alphabet soup agencies, mainly the FRB, the SEC, the CFTC, the OCC, and the FDIC, have retained so much discretion that Dodd-Frank can be thought of as a gigantic new edifice, built with many revolving doors, for lobbyists and officials. And the FSOC (Financial Stability Oversight Council) has been layered on top of the old structure. Its ability to designate banks as well as non-banks as "Systematically Important Financial Institutions" may end up transforming such institutions into GSEs. New risks in the insurance industry and in state government pension plans will never be addressed proactively but will await a major crisis.

Of course, the continued hold of the Republican Party over the House and the sway of free-market conservatism over its members will remain an obstacle to correcting the many remaining holes in our financial regulatory framework and righting our fiscal ship. But the limited opportunities for financial and fiscal reform also reflect the fact that the Democratic Party is, as we stressed in chapter 3, conflicted between its money wing and its votes wing. Despite all the touting that the 2012 elections empowered everyone except white males and despite the Democratic Party's success in mobilizing turnout among its base, support from wealthy donors remains essential. Those supporters are more likely to favor the Democrats not because they support a sharp increase in regulation and redistribution but because of their concern about global warming, gay rights, abortion, and similar "lifestyle" issues.

Will, then, the financial industry reform itself? Following numerous scandals and exposés about tainted food and medicine around the turn of the twentieth century, the food and drug industry generally backed efforts toward government regulation of the industry in order to restore consumer confidence in its products. The financial sector is also ultimately dependent on the confidence of investors. There are signs that confidence in the sector's products is deteriorating. Since April 2007, ordinary investors have pulled about $380 billion out of U.S. stock mutual funds. Public and private pension funds have also been net sellers over the past five years. Many Americans have adopted the view of a former financial analyst who provides this justification for dumping his stocks: "You have to trust your government. You have to trust other governments. You have to trust Wall Street. And I don't trust any of these."[16] If these trends continue, perhaps the industry will find that its collective self-interest depends not only on reforms that will enhance confidence in markets but also on the government's ability to regulate them in the public interest.

Two related forces work against this hope for internal reform. First, investors have to go somewhere other than under the mattress. Their alternatives have been diminished by increased concentration in the financial sector. The major accounting firms, the ratings agencies, and the banks are all too big to fail. So the industry will have only modest incentives to police itself in the name of promoting investor confidence. It has little motivation to eliminate rent seeking by its largest firms. Second, as we move away from the crisis, bankers and investors will forget "last time" and go back to "this time is different." Financial amnesia was noted a half century ago by the great economists Milton Friedman and Anna Schwartz, cited in the epigraph to chapter 1. Just as Jesus said of the poor, the reckless few are always with us.

Our political leaders wasted a crisis and kicked the can down the road. Democracy has failed ordinary Americans.

Introduction

1. See Dodosh (2008).
2. See Roguski (2008).
3. See Sims (2008).
4. An asset-backed security is one whose value is based on returns from some underlying asset. In the case of mortgage-backed securities, the value is derived from cash flows generated by interest payments on an underlying pool of mortgages.
5. See Foote, Gerardi, and Willen (2012).
6. On Raines's compensation, see Bebchuk and Fried (2005).
7. In a research article, Steven Levitt (coauthor of *Freakonomics*) estimates that personal ideology represented about 50 percent of the mix. See Levitt (1996).
8. Our focus will be on U.S. financial crises, so we are concerned primarily with the particular structure of U.S. policy-making institutions.
9. See "In the Court of Common Pleas of Allegheny County, Pennsylvania, Federal Home Loan Bank of Pittsburgh v. J.P. Morgan Securities Inc., J.P. Morgan Chase & Co., Moody's Corporation, Moody's Investor Services, Inc., and the McGraw-Hill Companies, Inc.," Complaint No. GD 09-016593, filed October 23, 2009. See also "In the State Court of Fulton County, State of Georgia, Federal Home Loan Bank of Atlanta v. Countrywide Financial Corporation (n/k/a Bank of America Home Loans, Inc.); Bank of America Corporation (as successor to the Countrywide Defendants); J.P. Morgan Securities, LLC (f/k/a J.P. Morgan Securities, Inc. and Bear Stearns & Co., Inc.); UBS Securities, LLC; and John Doe defendants 1–50," filed on January 18, 2011.
10. Foote, Gerardi, and Willen (2012) indicate that the ratings problem centered on CDOs constructed from risky tranches. AAA rated MBS were correctly rated.
11. See Faux and Shenn (2011).
12. The Twentieth Amendment changed the presidential inauguration date to January 20 and the starting date of the new Congress to January 3. The amendment was ratified January 23, 1933, but did not take effect until October of that year.
13. See Bruner and Carr (2007).

14. See Hansell (1994); Mallaby (2010); and Partnoy (2009).

15. In another securitization scandal of 1994, Procter and Gamble and other companies successfully sued Banker's Trust for providing customers with inaccurate information about their exposure in interest rate swaps.

16. See Lewis (2010).

17. For example, in the lead-up to the crisis, Lehman Brothers used a questionable accounting practice known as Repo 105 to goose its balance sheet just in time for quarterly earnings reports. Using Repo 105 transactions, Lehman loaned assets collateralized at 105 percent in the overnight repo market. These loans were counted as sales on the firm's balance sheet. See De la Merced and Werdigier (2010).

18. See Berner and Grow (2008).

19. See Reinhart and Rogoff (2009).

20. See chapter 1.

21. See Abelson (2000).

22. *Oxford English Dictionary*, 2nd ed., s.v. "ideology." Although we consider it the most important clause, the third edition of the *OED* drops the final clause. See Benabou (2008) for a formal model of ideological rigidity.

23. See McCarty, Poole, and Rosenthal (2006).

24. See Sorkin (2009: 284, 302, 535–36) and Paulson (2010: 152–53, 285–86). Without congressional pressure, Paulson may well have preferred a bailout for Lehman.

25. See McCarty, Poole and Rosenthal (2006: chap. 6).

26. See Smith (1904) and Mayhew (1974).

27. This provision exempted all over-the-counter electronic trading of energy securities from government regulation. The primary beneficiary of the restriction on regulatory jurisdiction was Enron, which operated the main trading platform for these securities. See Lipton (2008).

28. See Public Citizen's Critical Mass Energy and Environment Program (2001).

29. Ibid.

30. See Morgenson (2012).

31. See Browning (2010).

32. See Shear (2009).

33. To complicate our distinction between ideology and greed a bit more, few advocates of free market conservatism are pure libertarians of the Ron Paul mode. Most are willing to tolerate or support government interventions that benefit business or higher-income voters even when they violate free market or small government principles. For example, many voters who identify with the Tea Party and its support for free market conservatism oppose reductions of Social Security or Medicare benefits for high-income beneficiaries (see chapter 8). So while ideology is more than simply a mask for private interest, the belief systems of politicians and citizens may be shaped by private interest.

34. See Kindleberger and Aliber (2005: 165).

35. Even democracies in which the government is far more engaged in the economy have suffered significant financial crises. Sweden and Japan are notable examples from the 1990s.

36. See Reinhart and Rogoff (2009: 210–13).

37. See Mishkin and Herbertsson (2006).

38. See Halberstam (1969). One of us experienced this failure firsthand. However, the GI Bill may have made him one of "the best and the brightest" after the fact.

39. LTCM was truly elite. Its CEO was a University of Chicago MBA; its partners included two Nobel Prize Laureates, six MIT economics PhDs, and three Harvard professors.

Introduction to Part I

1. See Goldin and Katz (2008).

2. "Robo-signing" is the practice of mortgage company employees signing foreclosure affidavits without reviewing the accuracy of the underlying documentation. Several mortgage lenders were sued over this practice, resulting in a $26 billion settlement. That money was intended to provide relief to struggling homeowners to avoid foreclosure. But the standards for what qualified for such assistance were diluted. See Dewan and Silver-Greenberg (2012).

3. See Mitchell (2007). Another baseball hero, Sandy Koufax, may not have popped pills on the mound, but got scammed by Madoff, through his high school teammate and New York Mets owner Fred Wilpon.

4. Moreover, Paulson's collusion with Goldman Sachs to create MBSs that he could bet against, suggests that this faith in short sellers to correct markets may be naive and entirely misplaced.

5. See Igan, Mishra, and Tressel (2009).

6. Gramlich (2007) summarizes his actions.

7. See Streitfeld and Rudolf (2009).

Chapter 1

1. Economists define the fundamental value of an asset as the net present value of payments (e.g., dividends or interest) over time. Consequently, erroneous beliefs either about the flow of payments or the time value of money can drive a wedge between the price and the fundamentals.

2. For a sampling of the economic arguments about bubbles, see Shiller (2000); Meltzer (2003); and Blanchard and Watson (1982). See also Kindleberger and Aliber (2005).

3. The term *bounded rationality* is usually attributed to Herbert Simon; see Simon (1957).

4. See Nakamoto and Wighton (2007).

5. For empirical evidence on distorted beliefs in the housing market, see Cheng, Raina, and Xiong (2012).

6. See Malkiel (1990: 227).

7. See Buffett (2010). See Benabou (2012) for a formal model of delusion in financial markets.

8. See Clinton (1999).

9. See Greenspan (2005).

10. See Buiter (2008); emphasis in the original. See also Johnson and Kwak (2010).

11. See Jacobe (2008).

12. In May 2005, the Case Shiller Ten City Index was 206 (where an index of 100 equals prices in January 2000). In May 1995, the index was just 77. Data accessed June 5, 2011, at http://www.standardandpoors.com/indices/sp-case-shiller-home-price-indices/en/us/?indexId=spusa-cashpidff--p-us----.

13. See Jacobe (2008).

14. Some government officials, namely Treasury Secretary Geithner, were somewhat sympathetic to this line of argument. See Calmes (2009).

Chapter 2

1. See Malabre (1994: 220).

2. See Dixit and Weibull (2007).

3. See Shamim (2009).

4. See Reuters (2009).

5. Comments on *Fox News Sunday,* July 5, 2009, quoted in Holden (2009).

6. See Brooks (2012).

7. See *The Financial Crisis and the Role of Federal Regulators* (2008).

8. Ibid.

9. Ben S. Bernanke, "Remarks," quoted in Friedman and Schwartz (2008: 243). Mellon also, in an extreme precedent for the current Republican inflation bugaboo, advocated price deflation that would adversely affect nominally denominated industrial and farm debt. In contrast, Franklin Roosevelt, in devaluing the dollar and canceling gold clauses in debt contracts, forced a 31 percent haircut on industrial debt; see Kroszner (1999).

10. See Gramm (1999).

11. See Hill (2008).

12. As we shall see, Greenspan is one of the few free market devotees to publicly adjust their views about the role of regulation.

13. See *The Financial Crisis and the Role of Federal Regulators* (2008).

14. See "Greenspan Pockets $250k for Speech" (2006).

15. Ronald Reagan replaced Paul Volcker with Greenspan in 1987, with only two votes against confirmation in the Senate. When Volcker was appointed by Jimmy Carter in 1979, he was confirmed unanimously. But when reap-

pointed by Reagan in 1983, there were sixteen negative votes. These included the two most liberal Democrats (Howard Metzenbaum and Edward Kennedy) who most likely objected to the Volcker hike in interest rates. Volcker was also opposed by three of the four most conservative Republicans (Jesse Helms, Steven Symms, and Gordon Humphrey), who probably objected to his regulatory stance. Reagan probably concurred with conservative opposition in 1987. In the two Clinton reappointments, Greenspan drew seven negative votes from liberals in 1996 and four in 2000.

16. See Stiglitz (2009a: 51).

17. See Barrett (2008).

18. Ibid. Cuomo's actions may not have been entirely ideologically driven. He also had close political connections with real-estate finance lobbyists who wanted the GSEs to tie up more of their portfolios in subprime mortgages so that they would have to stay out of the high-end market.

19. See Frame (2008).

20. Many analysts agree that ultimately the role of the GSEs in the subprime market played only a limited direct role in the housing and credit crises. Yet the GSEs' participation in that market may well have added legitimacy to the huge expansion of this market and the unsavory practices of mortgage lenders.

21. See Fannie Mae (2003: 18–19).

22. See Slack (2010).

23. See Lucas (2011).

24. See Curry and Shibut (2000).

25. That there are many flavors of liberalism and conservatism and that there is contestation over the meanings of these terms will not detain us here. As we argue below, a single liberal-to-conservative continuum has an ability to explain much of contemporary American politics.

26. See Poole and Rosenthal (1997: chap. 8). Of course, the index of a liberal group will just be a flip of a conservative index. A legislator who gets a 100 score from the Americans for Democratic Action is likely to get a 0 from the National Taxpayers Union.

27. See Poole and Rosenthal (1997) and McCarty, Poole, and Rosenthal (1997). Although many have suspected that this was a Congress-specific artifact, the finding of near one-dimensional politics has been replicated in dozens of national parliaments, the European Union parliament, and American state legislatures. Our historical findings are largely supported by an alternative methodology (Heckman and Snyder 1997). It is fair to say that there is now a professional consensus that current American politics is largely one-dimensional.

28. See Hare, McCarty, Poole, and Rosenthal (2012).

29. On the effects of party discipline, see McCarty, Poole, and Rosenthal (2001).

30. See Poole and Rosenthal (1997, 2007) and McCarty, Poole, and Rosenthal (1997, 2006).

31. For contrary views, see Carmines and Stimson (1989) and Mendelberg (2001).

32. See McCarty, Poole, and Rosenthal (2001) and Nokken and Poole (2004).

33. See Poole (2007).

34. Boxer was elected to Alan Cranston's seat upon his retirement, and Feinstein won a special election to replace Pete Wilson, who had become governor of California.

35. In order of increasing differences, these are Vermont (independent Sanders caucuses as a Democrat), Arizona, South Carolina, and Delaware.

36. See Poole and Romer (1993).

37. The act also created the National Monetary Commission, whose reports became the basis of the Federal Reserve Act.

38. See McCarty, Poole, and Rosenthal (2006).

39. See Schattschneider (1960: 38).

40. See Philippon and Reshef (2009). This financial wage premium is also a major determinant of the overall level of income inequality in the United States; see Kaplan and Rauh (2007).

41. See Philippon and Reshef (2009).

42. See Bakija, Cole, and Heim (2010: tables 2 and 6).

43. See Piketty and Saez (2003).

44. See Abramowitz (2011) and Fiorina, Abrams, and Pope (2010).

45. See Levendusky (2009).

46. The histograms also show the proportionate reduction in error (PRE). If our after-the-fact prediction was that everyone voted with the majority on a roll call, our prediction errors would be the number of votes on the minority side. The minority votes are used, therefore, to benchmark the spatial model. If the spatial model makes no errors, the PRE is 1.0. If the spatial model does no better than the benchmark, the PRE is 0.0. If the spatial model reduces the errors in the benchmark by half, the PRE is 0.5.

47. This bill included federal licensing of mortgage lenders, fines for inappropriate subprime loans, limits on fees and on balloon payments, and liability for firms creating mortgage-backed securities. Many tougher provisions, such as allowing defaulters to use bankruptcy court, were eliminated from the bill.

48. See McCarty, Poole, and Rosenthal (1997). Other techniques include optimal classification (Poole 2000), the factor analytic method (Heckman and Snyder 1997), and Bayesian MCMC (Clinton, Jackman, and Rivers, 2004). DW-NOMINATE scores are used in media reports, as in Stolberg (2009a) and Lizza (2012).

49. For an explanation of the proportionate reduction in error, see note 46, above.

Chapter 3

1. Michael Burry, quoted in Lewis (2010: 55).

2. See Schlesinger (1965: 635).

3. See Lieberman and Asaba (2006).

4. On Enron's lobbying success, see Ismail (2003).

5. See Beckel (2011).

6. See Morgenson (2010).

7. See Igan, Mishra, and Tressel (2009).

8. See Romer and Weingast (1991).

9. Because these data are taken from the 2000 decennial census, they are very likely to understate levels of employment in these sectors at the top of the boom. For example, the National Association of Realtors had its membership grow from 776,580 members in 2000 to 1,338,001 in 2007. See National Association of Realtors (2011).

10. See Bartels (2008: chap. 9). See also Bhatti and Erikson (2011) and Tausanovitch (2011) for more nuanced views of Bartels's claims.

11. Data on industry of employment from the 2008 ANES have not been released as of this writing. Because people routinely lie about voting, both of these are inflated estimates. There is little reason to believe that employees in the financial sector would be any more truthful than the average respondent.

12. Eric Zitzewitz (2006) estimates that late trading costs mutual fund investors $400 million per year.

13. Zitzewitz (2006) finds statistical evidence consistent with late trading for thirty-nine of the sixty-six mutual fund families in his study.

14. See Mian, Sufi, and Trebbi (2010).

15. See Ansolabehere, de Figueiredo, and Snyder (2003). It is also worth pointing out that campaign contributions are only part of the total amount of money spent on politics. Direct lobbying expenditures are also substantial. According to the Center for Responsive Politics, lobbying expenditures for the financial industry since 1998 include $1.3 billion by insurance interests, $746 million by real estate interests, and $636 million by securities and investments firms. See our discussion of lobbying below.

16. Computations provided by Adam Bonica, Stanford University (correspondence with the authors).

17. See Kroszner and Stratmann (1998).

18. See Nuñez and Rosenthal (2004).

19. The data was downloaded from various pages at http://www.open secrets.org/industries; accessed July 11, 2011.

20. Lawyers and law firms contributed $126 million in 2008. A big chunk of these contributors may also have had interests in financial industry regulation.

21. See Philippon and Reshef (2009).

22. The argument is amplified in Toobin (2010: 50–57).

23. In fact, former Goldman CEO and Treasury secretary Henry Paulson is an avid environmentalist. See Sorkin (2009).

24. See Wachtel (2012).

25. On Wall Street's rocket scientists, see Overbye (2009).

26. See Sorkin (2011).

27. See Wilmott (2009) and McGinty and Scannell (2009).

28. See U.S. Commodity Futures Trading Commission and U.S. Securities and Exchange Commission (2010).

29. For a more formal elaboration of these arguments, see McCarty (2013).

30. The insurance industry is omitted, as much of its recent lobbying has been directed at health care rather than financial services.

Chapter 4

1. Parliamentary democracies can in principle hold elections more frequently. The regular term for a parliamentarian is typically five years, but it can be as low as three years (Australia). Presidential systems such as those in East Asia and Latin America have fixed legislative terms, but none elect the entire lower house every two years.

2. See Diermeier and Feddersen (1998).

3. On local interests in the McFadden Act, see Rajan and Ramcharan (2011).

4. See Illinois Department of Financial and Professional Regulation (2013).

5. See Preston (1927).

6. See Bank of Canada (2012).

7. See Hernandez and Labaton (2007).

8. See Romer and Weingast (1991) and McCarty, Poole, Romer, and Rosenthal (2010a).

9. The U.S. Constitution cannot be amended to eliminate equal representation of states in the Senate (Article V). It is permanent. For evidence of its importance for policy outcomes, see Lee (1998) and Lauderdale (2008).

10. See Binder (2003).

11. See Labaton (2005).

12. See Black (1958).

13. For evidence of the responsiveness of politicians and policies to voter preferences, see Erikson, MacKuen, and Stimson (2002).

14. See Cox and McCubbins (2005).

15. Cox and McCubbins (2005) argue that the majority party was able to exercise such agenda control beginning with the establishment of the Reed Rules in the 1890s.

16. A caveat is in order. Because of estimation error in DW-NOMINATE scores, we are more certain that the median is around $-.197$ than we are that Boucher is actually the median.

17. See Sinclair (2002).

18. See Krehbiel (1998).

19. If the bill was too conservative, at least sixty would oppose it and it wouldn't pass even if cloture were obtained.

20. See McCarty (1997); Cameron (2000); and Cameron and McCarty (2004). Presidents' informal agenda-control powers are considerable in their ability to frame issues and originate legislation in executive branch agencies.

21. If the president is sufficiently moderate (i.e., located between the filibuster pivots) the presidential veto does not increase the gridlock interval. If the

president is sufficiently rightist, the gridlock interval ranges from Senator 41's ideal point to the larger of Senator 66 and Congressperson 285's ideal point. The interval for a leftist is the minimum of Senator 34 and Congressperson 146 to Senator 60.

22. See Senate Library (1992).

23. Of course, the House of Representatives affects the veto pivot. But in the current Congress, the veto pivots are senators, and so we refer to them as such.

24. Other Senate personnel changes that occurred before the 2010 elections had no impact on the gridlock intervals.

25. See Wawro and Schickler (2006) for an elaboration of these arguments.

26. See Binder and Smith (1997), Wawro and Schickler (2006), and Koger (2010).

27. McCarty (2007) shows statistically that the width of the gridlock interval can be well accounted for by the degree of polarization and changes to the cloture rule.

28. Senator Long opposed provisions that would allow national banks to open branches, a policy that would threaten small state-chartered banks. Eventually, his objections were accommodated. See Williams (1969) and Kennedy (1973: 72–73).

29. During the first one hundred days of Roosevelt's presidency, Congress passed Glass-Steagall; passed the Economy Act, which cut government salaries; suspended the gold standard; started the Public Works Administration; passed the Farm Security Act to raise farmers' incomes; and established the Tennessee Valley Authority. This is just a partial list. In contrast, President Obama passed his controversial stimulus package.

30. The gold clauses are discussed in more detail in chapter 6.

31. See Gilmour (1995) and Groseclose and McCarty (2000).

32. See Clinton (1995).

33. *Congressional Record* (104th Congress), p. H15219.

34. See Prior (2007, and forthcoming) for a discussion of the relationship between changes in the media environment and polarization.

35. See Sunstein, Schkade, and Ellman (2004); Segal and Spaeth (2002); and Martin and Quinn (2002).

36. See Teles (2008).

37. See Romer and Weingast (1991).

38. *Marquette Nat. Bank of Minneapolis v. First of Omaha Service Corp.*, 439 U.S. 299 (1978).

39. See Ferejohn and Shipan (1990) and Spiller and Gely (1992).

40. *Cuomo v. Clearing House Association, L.L.C.*, 557 U.S. 519 (2009).

41. See Duca, Muellbauer, and Murphy (2012: fig. 1).

42. See Duca, Muellbauer, and Murphy (2012: fig. 2).

43. See Gorton (2010a).

44. See Wooten (2001).

45. See Olshan (2011).

46. The situation was chronicled by Mitchell Martin in the *New York Times* on April 7, 1998:

Sanford Weill, the Travelers chairman, said he expected the Fed to quickly approve his company's application to become a bank holding company and added: "I don't think we have to spin anything off to make this happen." Current law, he said, allows at least two and as many as five years for prohibited assets to be divested. "We are hopeful that over that time the legislation will change," he added. He said the companies had already had talks with the Fed about specific legal impediments and said, "We have had enough discussions to believe this will not be a problem." As well as having had discussions with the Fed and the Treasury, [Citicorp chairman John] Reed said President Bill Clinton was briefed on the announcement Sunday night.

See Martin (1998).
47. See Epstein and O'Halloran (1999) and Huber and Shipan (2002).
48. See Fiorina (1989).
49. See McCubbins and Schwartz (1984).
50. See Lipton and Kirkpatrick (2008).
51. See Kwak (2013).
52. This unfortunate fact is most vividly revealed in Charles Ferguson's documentary film *The Inside Job* (2010). See Zingales (2013) for quantitative evidence.
53. See Huber and McCarty (2004). See also McCarty (2013).
54. On theories of regulatory capture, see Huntington (1952); Bernstein (1955); Noll (1971); and Stigler (1971).

Chapter 5

1. Duca and Saving (2008) have claimed that the increase in equity investments since the 1970s is an explanation of increased support for the Republican Party.
2. See McCarty, Poole, and Rosenthal (2006: chap. 3).
3. A $148 million settlement was paid in 2012 by Wachovia's acquirer, Wells Fargo. See Isidore (2012).
4. See "Wachovia Settlement Checks Real" (2012).
5. For the details of the Wachovia case, see Subramanian and Sharma (2010).
6. Our view about the role of housing policy thus falls in the middle of a debate that has engaged two prominent economists. Chicago professor and former International Monetary Fund chief economist Raghuram Rajan (2010) sees the bubble as part of a political response to rising income inequality. Rajan's position has been critiqued by MIT professor and Clark Medal winner Daron Acemoglu. Acemoglu (2012) emphasizes policy shifts as industry driven.

7. Moreover, unlike most tax deductions, it is not subject to the alternative minimum tax (though the property tax deduction did not receive the same preferential treatment).

8. See Arnold (1990) and Coate and Morris (1995) for discussions of how the lack of transparency facilitates certain types of policy decisions.

9. See Gropp, Scholz, and White (1997) and Bahchieva, Wachter, and Warren (2005).

10. See Acharya et al. (2011: 27–30).

11. Public housing has hardly gone away. More than 600,000 residents of New York City live in public housing. See New York City Housing Authority (2011).

12. See Lemann (1991).

13. Advocates also calculated a political advantage based on their belief that homeowners would be more likely than renters to support conservative policies.

14. See Acharya et al. (2011: 17–19).

15. The Housing and Community Development Act of 1992 (Public Law No. 102-550), Title XIII: Government Sponsored Enterprises, Subtitle A: Supervision and Regulation of Enterprises—Part 3, Miscellaneous Provisions. See Acharya et al (2011: 31–36) for a discussion of the impact of these provisions.

16. See Madrick and Partnoy (2011).

17. From Fannie filings at http://www.sec.gov/cgi-bin/browse-edgar?company=fannie+mae&match=contains&action=getcompany. Capital Research held a much larger stake, averaging 20 percent. AXA, the French insurance giant, was a major investor in Freddie Mac.

18. See Jaffee (2003).

19. See Acharya et al. (2011) for a discussion of how the GSE capital market advantages triggered a regulatory "race to the bottom."

20. See Lichtblau (2012).

21. See Morgenson and Rosner (2011).

22. The SEC complaint was a civil, not criminal, action. Not only does the government fail to take strong action—criminal prosecution—against financial executives involved in the crisis but also the private sector appears to welcome second acts. Mudd, after the disaster at Fannie, was able to recycle himself as the cohead of Fortress Investment Group, a private equity firm. The other cohead was Randal Nardone, who had roots at UBS. When Mudd took a "leave of absence" on December 21, 2011, Fortress, selling on the New York Stock Exchange for over $31 a share in 2007, closed at $3.37. (Share prices accessed September 21, 2012 at Fidelity Investments, http://www.fidelity.com). A predecessor of Mudd, James Johnson, has had his own second acts. He remained (as of September 2012) on the boards of Goldman Sachs and Target; see Goldman Sachs (2012).

23. See Stiglitz, Orszag, and Orszag (2002, 2004).

24. See Morgenson and Rosner (2011: 75–76).

25. See Jaffee (2003).

26. Of course, the political cost of concentration stressed by the Jeffersonian tradition in American politics was the impetus behind traditional antitrust policy developed in the late nineteenth century.

27. See McLean and Elkind (2003: chap. 17).

28. See Glaeser and Scheinkman (1998).

29. See Gerardi, Shapiro, and Willen (2008).

30. Congress passed the Secondary Mortgage Market Enhancement Act in 1984, at a time when 95 percent of the MBS market was in government and GSE issues. Remarkably, Bleckner (1984) accurately anticipated all the problems that would arise with privatization of this market, including the use of private ratings agencies as the source of information that would safeguard investors. The push to deregulate was so strong that the 1984 Act was passed by voice vote in both the House and Senate. See http://thomas.loc.gov/cgi-bin/bdquery/z?d098:SN02040:@@@R (accessed February 8, 2012).

31. See Acharya et al. (2011: 118).

32. See Igan, Mishra, and Tressel (2009).

33. See McNamee (2004).

34. In early 2012, three traders at Credit Suisse were indicted for fraud related to MBSs. The alleged motivation for the fraud was that the traders sought to pump up their annual bonuses. This is again a "skin in the game" problem: the traders' compensation is based on short-run benchmarks and not the long-run performance of the securities. See Lattman and Eavis (2012).

35. See Foote, Gerardi, and Willen (2012).

36. See Tett (2009) and MacKenzie (2009).

37. See Duca, Muellbauer, and Murphy (2011).

38. Some conservative groups, such as the Heritage Foundation, opposed the bill as "fiscally irresponsible." See Utt (2003).

39. See Bush (2003).

40. See Congressional Budget Office (2001).

41. See U.S. Department of Housing and Urban Development (2011).

42. See Commodity Futures Trading Commission (2011: 4).

Introduction to Part II

1. *Citizens United v. Federal Elections Commission*, 558 U.S. 50 (2010).

2. As of July 2012, however, financial firms and other corporations have not extensively used their newfound opportunity to spend corporate treasury money on independent electoral expenditures. By assuming that all undisclosed independent political expenditure was corporate, Adam Bonica estimates an upper bound for corporate independent expenditure in 2010 of $205 million, or just 5.6 percent of the total federal campaign expenditures. See Bonica (2012).

3. Clifford (2009) finds that after the repeal of Glass-Steagall the campaign contributions of various financial industry subsectors became more aligned.

4. See Cooper and Steinhauer (2012). The Constitution allows the president to make appointments to positions that otherwise would require Senate confirmation during periods in which that body is in recess.

Chapter 6

1. See Gerring (1998).
2. Kuhn, Loeb was eventually absorbed by Lehman Brothers.
3. See Tufano (1997).
4. See Warren (1935). See Bolton and Rosenthal (2002) for a theoretical argument that, when debt contracts are incomplete, political intervention in debt contracts is optimal, even when economic agents are fully rational and anticipate that the government will intervene in exceptional circumstances.
5. See Rothbard (1962).
6. *Bronson v. Kinzie*, 41 U.S. 311, 1 How. 311 (1843).
7. See Alston (1983).
8. See Wheelock (2008: 133).
9. See Kroszner (1999).
10. Ibid. The finding is all the more credible because of the author's political affiliations: Randall Kroszner was a member of the Council of Economic Advisors in the George W. Bush administration and a Bush appointee as Federal Reserve governor. His paper finds that cancellation of the gold clauses in industrial bond contracts had widespread economic benefits. After the cancellation was upheld by a 5–4 Supreme Court decision, prices of bonds as well as equities rose. There was a disconnect between the later reaction of markets and ideology in Congress. Republicans in Congress strongly opposed cancellation.
11. See Sorkin (2009: 200).
12. See U.S. House of Representatives (2012).
13. See U.S. Senate (2012).
14. Under the 1974 Budget Act, some budgetary legislation (subject to a few limitations) may be considered under a set of procedures known as reconciliation. The primary benefit of these reconciliation procedures is that the time period for debate is limited, and therefore legislation considered in this way may not be filibustered.
15. See Perino (2010). Of course, there was no shortage of damaging allegations against the industry in 2009 and 2010; the most politically important was the SEC case against Goldman Sachs over its Abacus mortgage-backed CDOs.
16. John J. Raskob, a financial executive and the builder of the Empire State Building, was head of the Democratic National Committee from 1928 to 1932. In the 1928 and 1932 elections, the DNC received nearly 25 percent of its funds from "bankers and brokers." The Republican National Committee received approximately the same share from these sources (Overacker 1932). With retaliation for the New Deal reforms, the Democrats found themselves able to raise only 3.3 percent of their funds from the industry in 1936 (Overacker 1937).
17. See Alston (1983).
18. The mortgage case was *Home Building & Loan Association v. Blaisdell*, 290 U.S. 398 (1934). The gold clause cases were *Norman v. Baltimore and Ohio Railroad*, 294 U.S. 240 (1935); *United States v. Bankers Trust Co.*, 294 U.S. 240 (1935); *Perry v. United States*, 294 U.S. 330 (1935); and *Nortz v. United States*, 294 U.S. 317 (1935).

19. See Kennedy (1973: 73). Although Long claimed to be defending small state banks, Senator Glass charged that Long was doing the bidding of the New York bankers. See "Glass Links Banks to Attack by Long" (1933).

20. See Federal Deposit Insurance Corporation (1984); and "Glass Links Banks to Attack by Long" (1933).

21. Our discussion of the S&L crisis reflects McCarty, Poole, Romer, and Rosenthal (2010a), which draws on Romer and Weingast (1991).

22. The Thrift Industry Recovery Act was Title IV of the Competitive Banking Equality Act. See http://thomas.loc.gov/cgi-bin/bdquery/z?d100:HR00027:@@@D&summ2=m& (accessed June 12, 2012).

23. See Pyle (1995).

24. The RTC is now generally thought to have done a good job, though it had some rocky years. In disposing of the assets of failed thrifts, the RTC faced conflicting political mandates (including social policy objectives such as minority contracting and affordable housing, as well as getting the highest value for the assets). See Davison (2006).

25. See Federal Home Loan Banks (2012) and see Standard & Poor's (2011).

26. See Schaefer (2010).

27. See Rappaport and Rapoport (2010). Hurtado and Sandler (2012) report that in 2009, Ernst and Young "paid $109 million to settle investor claims that it failed to find a $2.7 billion fraud at HealthSouth Corp."

28. See Skeel (2001) and Warren (1935).

29. See Mann (2001) and Berglöf and Rosenthal (2006: 396–414).

30. See Skeel (2001).

31. On the meeting, see Whitehouse (1989) and Wicker (2005).

32. Before the financial crisis, Fuld was named number one CEO by *Institutional Investor*; see Prince (2007). After Lehman failed, he was named the worst CEO of all time by CNBC; see "The Worst American CEOs of All Time" (2009).

33. See Bruner and Carr (2007: 67).

34. On the role of the SEC in corporate bankruptcy, see Skeel (2001).

35. See Weingast (1984). Notably, the end of monopoly profits in the trading of stocks is said to be a factor in Wall Street's gravitation toward excess risk taking in collateralized debt. See Gapper (2008).

36. See Lowenstein (2000: 37).

37. The automatic stay prevents creditors from seizing assets of the bankrupt firm.

38. See Edwards and Morrison (2005).

39. Ibid .

40. See Morgan (2008).

41. See Skeel (2011).

42. See New Generation Research (2012).

43. Populists and Silverites served alongside the major parties.

44. See Hansen (1996).

45. See Berglöf and Rosenthal (2005).

46. On the Interstate Commerce Act, see Poole and Rosenthal (1994).

47. See Balleisen (1996).

48. See Brady, Canes-Wrone, and Cogan (2000).

49. There are cases of widespread public protest against a law. The Medicare Catastrophic Coverage Act, passed in June 1988, resulted in protests over increased premiums for middle- to high-income seniors. The headliner was the pounding on the car of Dan Rostenkowski, the Ways and Means Committee chair, by members of the "Gray Panthers." Yet repeal was voted on only by a new Congress in November 1989. More recently, a firestorm of protests was set off by a provision in the 2009 health care law mandating IRS form 1099 reporting of business expenditures over $600. The provision was repealed in April 2011. Neither of these examples pertains to financial markets.

Chapter 7

1. See Sorkin (2009).

2. See "The Rubin Connection" (2008).

3. *Cuomo v. Clearing House Association, L.L.C.*, 557 U.S. 519 (2009). See Stohr (2009).

4. The proposed rules will implement Dodd-Frank, Section 941. These delays may have had adverse effects on the mortgage market. The definition of "qualifying residential mortgages" that would be exempted from the retention requirement is an example of this. The uncertainty about which loans are the easiest to securitize may have impeded home lending.

5. See Davis Polk (2012).

6. See U.S. Department of the Treasury (2011).

7. See Barofsky (2011). Prominent Yale economist John Geanakoplos made a very public push to get the administration to push harder on mortgage relief but was largely unsuccessful. See Geanakoplos and Koniak (2008, 2009).

8. See Milbank (2010).

9. See Collins (2011).

10. See "Banks Are Off the Hook Again" (2011).

11. See Elmer (2012).

12. See Sussman (2012).

13. See Posner (2009).

14. Technical note: these scores were computed with W-NOMINATE. See http://voteview.com/wnominate_in_R.htm for details.

15. We estimate these measures on all roll call votes rather than just ones related to financial measures. Below we detail specifically that, with the exception of TARP, voting on financial measures was largely unaffected by the crisis.

16. Comparisons are made only for those legislators who voted on at least twenty-five roll calls pre-Lehman and at least twenty-five post-Lehman. This choice implies the exclusion of legislators who served only in the 111th Congress and not in the 110th.

17. They were 0.544 in 2009 and 0.536 in 2007.

18. See Obama (2008).

19. Obama's early overtures toward bipartisanship might possibly have been strategic. Consistent with the blame-game bargaining described in chapter 4, he may have been attempting to out the Republicans as extremists by offering compromises that he knew they would not accept. But if this was the strategy, the outcome of the 2010 elections suggests that it did not work. See McCarty (2009).

20. See Weisman and Herszenhorn (2008). "Pay as you go" rules require that any new expenditure be matched with a spending cut somewhere else.

21. Another fissure within the Democratic Party is that it is home to both committed environmentalists and to coal-state "porkers." State senator and U.S. senator Barack Obama was a strong supporter of coal. See Dilanian (2008).

22. See Herszenhorn (2008b). Some observers suggested that Senate Majority Leader Harry Reid's main rationale for pushing the bigger program was to put Republican senators on record as opposing specific provisions in an election year.

23. See Herszenhorn (2008a).

24. See Cooper (2010). By contrast, the personal tax cuts in the 2009 stimulus package were implemented through changes in the withholding schedule. But this mechanism seems to have denied President Obama political credit for the cuts.

25. See Weisman and Andrews (2008).

26. This delay resulted in the United States implementing a stimulus program several months after most other nations had done so.

27. See Lizza (2012).

28. See Baker and Herszenhorn (2009).

29. Six members did not vote.

30. We do not have 111th Congress ideology estimates for two Democrats who voted in favor.

31. When Specter switched parties, his ideology score went from +0.11 to −0.39—from the moderate center to the right flank of the Democrats.

32. A perceptive reader will see that we could eliminate the Voinovich "error" by moving the cutting line to the left. This would be cheating. For technical details, see Poole and Rosenthal (1997: appendix A).

33. See Stolberg (2009b).

34. CBS News poll, February 2–4, 2009; available at the Roper Center Poll Archive, http://www.ropercenter.uconn.edu/.

35. Ibid. In response to "In your opinion which will do more to get the U.S. out of the current recession: increasing government spending, or reducing taxes?" only 16 percent said increase spending, whereas 63 percent favored lower taxes.

36. CBS News/*New York Times* poll, July 24–28, 2009 available at the Roper Center Poll Archive, http://www.ropercenter.uconn.edu/.

37. See Chan (2010a).

38. See Stolberg (2010) and Calmes (2010a; 2010b).

39. See Ansell (2011).

40. Hall (2010) calculates that by the first quarter of 2010, total purchasing by federal, state, and local governments had fallen around $25 billion below its trend level.

41. See Baker (2010). Of course, other countries' packages may be overstated in a variety of ways as well.

42. See Hall (2010). Estimates by the Congressional Budget Office are in the same ball park; see Congressional Budget Office (2010).

43. Amendments dealing with credit card practices were proposed by Senate Democrats as the Senate passed a bankruptcy bill in 2001. See Nuñez and Rosenthal (2004).

44. *Central clearing* refers to a requirement that derivatives counterparties engage a clearing house that would guarantee each party's performance on the contract.

45. Seventeen such Republicans voted against the reconfirmation of Chairman Bernanke in January 2010. See chapter 8.

46. In the final legislation, the Consumer Financial Protection Agency became the Consumer Financial Protection Bureau.

47. See Dennis (2010b); Chan (2010b); and Appelbaum (2010b).

48. See Dennis (2010a); Appelbaum (2010a); and Wyatt (2010).

49. Cao and Jones were also errors on the stimulus package conference report, but in an opposite sense. They voted against the stimulus package when they were predicted to have voted for it.

50. Castle's primary loss appears not to be closely linked to his vote on Dodd-Frank but to be more a matter of a Tea Party purge—supported by conservative Republican senators such as Jim DeMint—of moderate members of Congress.

51. The Feingold story is elaborated in McCarty, Poole, Romer, and Rosenthal (2010b).

52. See Roubini (2008).

53. See "President Bush Overall Job Rating" (2012).

54. See Bernanke (2005).

55. See Hauke and Nelson (2007).

56. Our analysis of predatory lending draws heavily on DeBold (2010).

57. See Bostic et al. (2008).

58. Conservative jurists often argue that states should be afforded a high degree of deference. Scalia's vote is consistent with that position. The votes of the other conservative justices appear to have accommodated the interests of the financial sector at the expense of ideological purity.

59. A 2-28 is a thirty-year adjustable-rate mortgage with a fixed interest rate for the first two years. A 3-27 resets after three years.

60. See Swagel (2009). See also Foote, Gerardi, and Willen (2012).

61. See Mian, Sufi, and Trebbi (2010).

62. See Baker (2008). Another piece of evidence echoes Mian, Sufi, and Trebbi's (2010) findings. On a vote just prior to the AHRFPA votes in May, the House passed the Neighborhood Stabilization Act of 2008, introduced by liberal representative Maxine Waters (D-CA). This program would have done little for Republican voters; only eleven Republicans voted for passage. The Senate never considered the bill.

63. Piskorski, Seru, and Vig (2010) found that foreclosure was substantially less likely on loans that were held directly by banks than on loans that had been securitized.

64. See Gorton (2010b).

65. See Nunnari (2011).

66. See Mian, Sufi, and Trebbi (2010).

67. Indeed, among Republicans, those receiving the most financial industry cash were more likely to vote against the bill. This indicates that precrisis financial firms often supported free market conservatives with commitments against government intervention of any form. But when the industry needed intervention, its hand was bit by the ideology that it had been promoting.

68. See Poole and Rosenthal (2007).

69. See Fogel (1989).

Chapter 8

1. See Cilliza (2012).

2. These probabilities were estimated using probit separately for each party.

3. See Bureau of Labor Statistics (2011).

4. See Pew Research Center (2011).

5. *Los Angeles Times*/Bloomberg poll, September 19–22 and 26–28, 2008. All polls cited in this chapter's notes are available at the Roper Center Poll Archive, http://www.ropercenter.uconn.edu/.

6. CBS/*New York Times* poll, February 5–10, 2010. Twenty-three percent blamed Wall Street and 6 percent Obama. A plurality blamed President Bush (31 percent). However, 13 percent blamed Congress.

7. CNN poll, February 18–19, 2009. The exact numbers are: labor leaders, 47 percent; Obama, 73 percent; Republicans in Congress, 53 percent; Democrats in Congress, 66 percent; auto executives, 25 percent.

8. CNN poll, September 19–21 2008.

9. *Los Angeles Times*/Bloomberg poll, October 10–13, 2008.

10. *Los Angeles Times*/Bloomberg News, December 6–8, 2008.

11. Because the survey was in the field when TARP was announced, responses probably reflect attitudes about TARP as well as prior bailouts (e.g., Bear Stearns).

12. *Los Angeles Times*/Bloomberg poll, October 10–13, 2008. Even among Republican voters, only 18 percent said they would vote to punish a TARP supporter.

13. *Los Angeles Times*/Bloomberg poll, October 10–13, 2008.

14. CNN poll, September 19–21, 2008.

15. CNN poll, October 17–19, 2008.

16. CNN poll, October 3–5, 2008.

17. *Los Angeles Times*/Bloomberg poll, December 6–8, 2008.

18. CNN poll, January 12–15, 2009.

19. CNN poll, February 18, 2009.

20. CBS News poll, February 2–4, 2009.

21. CNN poll, December 6–9, 2007. Slightly more than 50 percent blamed the homeowners for their problems; only 45 percent blamed predatory lending, however.

22. *Los Angeles Times*/Bloomberg poll, October 10–13.

23. Seventy-one percent of Democrats, but only 43 percent of Republicans, supported such assistance. CNN poll, October 17–19, 2008.

24. The margin was 72–26 percent. CNN poll, December 6–9, 2007.

25. CBS News/*New York Times* poll, April 1–5, 2009. The *Los Angeles Times*/Bloomberg poll from December 6–8, 2008, provides almost identical results.

26. CNN poll, March 19–21, 2010.

27. CNN poll, May 21–23, 2010.

28. CNN poll, July 16–21, 2010. Overall support ran 58 to 39 percent. Democrats favored at 78 percent and Republicans at 42 percent.

29. CNN poll, March 19–21, 2010.

30. The gap was 61 percent to 35 percent. CNN poll, December 16–19, 2009.

31. Support depended on how questions were framed. When asked "Do you favor or oppose Congress passing a law that would give the federal government new powers to regulate large banks and major financial institutions?" support fell as low as 46 percent. Gallup poll, April 17–18, 2010.

32. CBS News poll, July 9–12, 2009.

33. CBS News/*New York Times* poll, April 1–5, 2009. Forty-one percent supported restructuring, but 31 percent answered "don't know." In the same survey, a third of the respondents agreed that financial firms were treated better than the auto manufacturers; only 6 percent said the automakers got a better deal.

34. Twenty-seven percent favored, 14 percent opposed, 56 percent had not heard enough. CBS News/*New York Times* poll, February 5–10, 2010.

35. Pew Research Center for the People and the Press poll, November 11–14, 2010.

36. As of June 18, 2012, 65 percent of all bailout funds had been returned or paid back as interest. Most of the funds outstanding represent the bailout of Fannie and Freddie. See Kiel and Nguyen (2012).

37. CBS News poll, February 2–4, 2009. In December 2008, however, 50 percent thought "government's partial ownership of banks and other industries is a necessary step to save the private sector" *Los Angeles Times*/Bloomberg poll, December 6–8, 2008.

38. The history and background of the Tea Party Movement is detailed in Rasmussen and Schoen (2010); Zernike (2010); and Skocpol and Williamson (2011).

39. When one of the producers suggested that Santelli run for Senate, he retorted, "Do you think I want to take a shower every hour? The last place I'm ever gonna live or work is D.C." For a transcript of Santelli's remarks, see "Rick Santelli, Tea Party" (2009).

40. "Rick Santelli, Tea Party" (2009).

41. See Robbins (2009) and Fox News (2009).

42. See Sarlin (2010). Up to that point the only observed Tea Party action was directed at Republican Senator Bob Corker for cooperating with the Democrats. See also Weigel (2010).

43. See McGrath (2010).

44. See Williams (2011).

45. See Schwartz (2011).

46. As an experiment for the forms of "deliberative democracy" advocated by many political scientists, OWS was a failure.

47. Lasn and *Adbusters* senior editor Micah White drafted a letter to President Obama specifying demands including greater financial regulation, a ban on high-frequency trading, and stepped-up prosecution of those responsible for the financial crisis, but the letter was not adopted by the General Assembly. Instead, the General Assembly drafted a "Declaration of Occupation" that Schwartz (2011) describes as "more worldview than a list of demands." Instead of policy goals, the document contains a long laundry list of grievances and a brief in favor of deliberative and participatory democracy.

48. See Heilemann (2011).

49. Ibid.

50. This study was controversial. It had a relatively small sample size, and the details of how the poll was conducted and the sample was generated have not been released.

51. Generally, poll respondents overreport voting, but it is possible in this context of a protest against the political system that voting may have been underreported.

52. Somewhat surprisingly, Schoen (2011) uses these same data to conclude that OWS "comprises an unrepresentative segment of the electorate that believes in radical redistribution of wealth."

53. Heilemann (2011) reports the frustration of one of the more reformist activists: "I don't want to live in a fucking commune. I don't want to blow shit up. I want to get stuff done."

54. See Soros (2010).

55. See Morgenson (2011).

Chapter 9

1. Other Congresses have had larger Democratic majorities, but the conservative and moderate blocks of the Democratic Party were much larger. See McCarty (2008).

2. For a discussion of these other presidential strategies, see Beckmann (2010).

3. See Tapper (2011).

4. See "Obama's Take on Wall Street Prosecutions" (2011).

5. See U.S. Securities and Exchange Commission (2010b).

6. See U.S. Department of Justice (2012).

7. See U.S. Attorney, Eastern District (2012) and Pelofsky and Vicini (2011).

8. See U.S. Securities and Exchange Commission (2010a).

9. Recently, a federal judge admonished the SEC for its practice of quickly reaching no admission of fault in out-of-court settlements with banks instead of vigorous prosecution; see Lattman (2011). Perhaps this rebuke finally motivated the SEC to go after six Fannie Mae and Freddie Mac executives for lying to investors about the amount of their subprime holdings in the lead up to the meltdown. See "SEC Brings Crisis-Era Suits" (2011).

10. The percentages pertain to banks with more than $300 million in assets. For the top ten banks, the corresponding percentages are 50 percent, 60 percent, and 62 percent. Authors' computations from data available at http://www.federalreserve.gov/releases/lbr/, accessed June 16, 2012.

11. See Sorkin (2009: chap. 20) and Paulson (2010: 362–68).

12. See Kiel and Nguyen (2012).

13. This discussion draws from Chao (2011).

14. See Davis Polk (2012).

15. See Morgenson (2011).

16. See Lowenstein (2008); Lewis (2010: chaps. 4 and 6); and Morgenson and Rosner (2011: chap. 15, esp. 279–89).

17. See Schattschneider (1960).

18. See "The Talented Mr. Gensler" (2011).

19. See Scott and De la Merced (2012).

20. Per the financial regulation index in Philippon and Reshef (2009).

21. See McKee and Lanman (2009).

22. See Stiglitz (2009b) and Treanor (2009).

23. And even if campaign contributions lost free speech protections, what about money spent on lobbying and issue advocacy?

24. Many scholars have concluded that the cloture rule is unconstitutional and have urged the courts to intervene. We think that it is highly unlikely that the courts would do so. Other scholars have argued that a sufficiently determined majority could change the cloture rules by a simple majority vote. But because a party's moderates benefit from the current rules, such an attempt might engender intraparty conflict. See Wawro and Schickler (2006).

25. See Alesina and Rosenthal (1995).

26. Rear Admiral James B. Stockdale won the medal of honor for his heroism as a prisoner of war in Vietnam. His exemplary military service did not translate into politics very well.

27. See Fogel (1989).

28. The movement began to fade after 1920 and should not be confused with current liberals who also use the "progressive" label.

29. On the progressives, see Hofstadter (1955, chap. 4) and Hofstadter, Miller, and Aaron (1959, chap. 32).

30. See Philippon and Reshef (2009).

31. See Eisenhower (1956).

32. See Perlstein (2001) and Kabaservice (2012).

33. See "Faculty Profile of Paul MacAvoy" (2012).

34. See McClintick (2006).

35. See Bates, Zennie, and Durante (2012) and Reuters (2012).

Epilogue

1. See Maxfield (2012).

2. See Protess (2012).

3. See *State National Bank of Big Spring et al. v. Geithner et al.* (2012) and Stephenson (2012).

4. Money market mutual funds (MMFs) generally try to sustain a net asset value (NAV) of $1 to provide security to investors. A run on the Reserve Primary Fund, triggered by its exposure to Lehman Brothers, left it unable to redeem its shares at that price. This forced the Treasury to insure $1 NAV for MMFs. To prevent a replay, the SEC considered new rules that would force MMFs to "float" (i.e., not guarantee $1 NAV) or to hold a larger capital buffer. These proposals failed to generate support from a majority of commissioners and were then tabled by Chair Mary Schapiro.

5. See Davis Polk (2013).

6. See McKenna (2012).

7. See Silver-Greenberg (2012a).

8. See Silver-Greenberg (2012b).

9. See Comfort (2012).

10. Ibid.

11. Puzzanghera (2012).

12. See Hernandez (2012).

13. See Sides (2012).

14. Not many Wall Streeters who contributed to Obama in 2008 switched to Romney in 2012. Typically these donors decreased their contributions in 2012 or sat out the election. Romney's money came largely from those who had not contributed to Obama in 2008. Many who had contributed to Republicans in the past increased their contributions in 2012, to Romney's benefit. (Personal communication from Adam Bonica, Stanford University.)

15. The gratuitous posturing hypothesis is supported by the fact that almost all House Republicans who voted against the tax increase voted in favor of the rule that brought the legislation to the floor.

16. See Condon (2012).

BIBLIOGRAPHY

Abelson, Reed. 2000. "Pets.com, Sock Puppet's Home, Will Close." *New York Times*, November 8.

Abramowitz, Alan. 2011. *The Disappearing Center: Engaged Citizens, Polarization, and American Democracy*. New Haven, CT: Yale University Press.

Acemoglu, Daron. 2012. "Thoughts on Inequality and the Financial Crisis." Accessed February 7, 2012, at http://econ-www.mit.edu/files/6348.

Acharya, Viral V., Matthew Richardson, Stijn Van Nieuwerburgh, and Lawrence J. White. 2011. *Guaranteed to Fail: Fannie Mae, Freddie Mac and the Debacle of Mortgage Finance*. Princeton, NJ: Princeton University Press.

Alesina, Alberto, and Howard Rosenthal. 1995. *Partisan Politics, Divided Government, and the Economy*. New York: Cambridge University Press.

Alston, Lee J. 1983. "Farm Foreclosure Moratorium Legislation: A Lesson from the Past." *American Economic Review* 74: 445–57.

Ansell, Ben. 2011. "The Political Economy of Ownership: Housing Markets and the Welfare State." Unpublished manuscript, University of Minnesota.

Ansolabehere, Stephen, John M. de Figueiredo, and James Snyder. 2003. "Why Is There So Little Money in Politics?" *Journal of Economic Perspectives* 17(1): 105–30.

Appelbaum, Binyamin. 2010a. "Lawmakers at Impasse on Trading." *New York Times*, June 23.

Appelbaum, Binyamin. 2010b. "Six Key Points of the Financial Regulation Legislation." *Washington Post*, March 16.

Arnold, R. Douglas. 1990. *The Logic of Congressional Action*. New Haven, CT: Yale University Press.

Atlas, John. 2007. "The Conservative Origins of the Subprime Mortgage Crisis." *American Prospect*, December 17. Accessed January 22, 2012, at http://prospect.org/article/conservative-origins-sub-prime-mortgage-crisis-0.

Bahchieva, Raisa, Susan M. Wachter, and Elizabeth Warren. 2005. "Mortgage Debt, Bankruptcy, and the Sustainability of Homeownership." In *Credit Markets for the Poor*, ed. Patrick Bolton and Howard Rosenthal. New York: Russell Sage Foundation.

Baker, Peter. 2008. "Administration Is Seeking $700 Billion for Wall St.; Bailout Could Set Record." *New York Times*, September 21.

Baker, Peter. 2010. "Education of a President." *New York Times Magazine*, October 12.

Baker, Peter, and David M. Herszenhorn. 2009. "Senate Allies Fault Obama on Stimulus." *New York Times*, January 8.

Bakija, Jon, Adam Cole, and Bradley Heim. 2010. "Jobs and Income Growth of Top Earners and the Causes of Changing Income Inequality: Evidence from U.S. Tax Return Data." Unpublished manuscript, Williams College.

Balleisen, Edward. 1996. "Vulture Capitalism in Antebellum America: The 1841 Federal Bankruptcy Act and the Exploitation of Financial Distress." *Business History Review* 70: 473–516.

Bank of Canada. 2012. "History." Accessed September 20, 2012, at http://www.bankofcanada.ca/about/who-we-are/history/.

"Banks Are Off the Hook Again." 2011. Editorial. *New York Times*, April 9.

Barofsky, Neil M. 2011. "Where the Bailout Went Wrong." Op-ed, *New York Times*, March 29.

Barrett, Wayne. 2008. "Andrew Cuomo and Fannie and Freddie." *Village Voice*, August 5.

Bartels, Larry. 2008. *Unequal Democracy: The Political Economy of the New Gilded Age*. Princeton, NJ: Princeton University Press.

Bates, Daniel, Michael Zennie, and Thomas Durante. 2012. "Facebook Chief Operating Officer Begs Students to 'Click an Ad or Two' on Social Network as IPO Woes Continue." *Daily Mail*, May 24. Accessed June 17, 2012, at http://www.dailymail.co.uk/news/article-2149443/Facebook-IPO-Sheryl-Sandberg-asks-Harvard-students-click-ads.html#ixzz1y3fs4Lz8.

Bebchuk, Lucian A., and Jesse M. Fried. 2005. "Executive Compensation at Fannie Mae: A Case Study of Perverse Incentives, Nonperformance Pay and Camouflage." *Journal of Corporation Law* 30: 807–22.

Beckel, Michael. 2011. "Ex-Countrywide Chairman Angelo Mozilo, Namesake of Controversial VIP Mortgage Program, Once Aided Pols." Accessed September 20, 2012, at http://www.opensecrets.org/news/2011/02/ex-countrywide-chairman-angelo-mozilo.html.

Beckmann, Matthew N. 2010. *Pushing the Agenda: Presidential Leadership in U.S. Lawmaking 1953–2004*. New York: Cambridge University Press.

Benabou, Roland. 2008. "Ideology." *Journal of the European Economic Association* 6(2–3): 321–52.

Benabou, Roland. 2012. "Groupthink: Collective Delusions in Markets and Organization." Unpublished Manuscript, Princeton University.

Berglöf, Erik, and Howard Rosenthal. 2005. "The Political Origin of Finance: The Case of U.S. Bankruptcy Law." Unpublished manuscript.

Berglöf, Erik, and Howard Rosenthal. 2006. "Power Rejected: Congress and Bankruptcy in the Early Republic." In *Process, Party, and Policy Making*, vol. 2: *Further New Perspectives on the History of Congress*, ed. David W. Brady and Mathew D. McCubbins. Stanford, CA: Stanford University Press.

Bernanke, Ben S. 2005. "Testimony of Ben S. Bernanke." Accessed on September 20, 2012, at http://www.federalreserve.gov/boarddocs/testimony/2005/20051115/default.htm.

Berner, Robert, and Brian Grow. 2008. "They Warned Us about the Mortgage Crisis." *Bloomberg Businessweek*, October 8. Accessed June 28, 2012, at http://www.businessweek.com/magazine/content/08_42/b4104036827981.htm.

Bernstein, Marver. 1955. *Regulating Business by Independent Commission.* Princeton, NJ: Princeton University Press.

Bhatti, Yousef, and Robert Erikson. 2011. "How Poorly Are the Poor Represented in the U.S. Senate?" In *Who Gets Represented?* ed. Peter Enns and Christopher Wlezian. New York: Russell Sage Foundation.

Binder, Sarah A. 2003. *Stalemate: The Causes and Consequences of Legislative Gridlock.* Washington, DC: Brookings Institution Press.

Binder, Sarah A., and Steven S. Smith. 1997. *Politics or Principle: Filibustering in the U.S. Senate.* Washington, DC: Brookings Institution Press.

Black, Duncan. 1958. *The Theory of Committees and Elections.* Cambridge: Cambridge University Press.

Blanchard, Olivier J., and Mark W. Watson. 1982. "Bubbles, Rational Expectations, and Speculative Markets." In *Crisis in Economic and Financial Structure: Bubbles, Bursts, and Shocks*, ed. Paul Wachtel. Lexington, MA: Lexington Books.

Bleckner, David J. 1984. "Section 106 of the Secondary Mortgage Market Enhancement Act of 1984 and the Need for Overriding State Legislation." *Fordham Urban Law Journal* 13: 681–721.

Bolton, Patrick, and Howard Rosenthal. 2002. "Political Intervention in Debt Contracts." *Journal of Political Economy* 110(5): 1103–34.

Bonica, Adam. 2012. "Data on Money Flows." Accessed September 20, 2012 at http://www.ssireview.org/pdf/bonica_cu_data.pdf.

Bostic, Raphael W., Kathleen C. Engel, Patricia A. McCoy, Anthony Pennington-Cross, and Susan M. Wachter. 2008. "State and Local Anti-predatory Lending Laws: The Effect of Legal Enforcement Mechanisms." *Journal of Economics and Business* 60(1–2): 47–66.

Brady, David W., Brandice Canes-Wrone, and John F. Cogan. 2000. "Differences in Legislative Voting Behavior between Winning and Losing House Incumbents." In *Continuity and Change in House Elections*, ed. David W. Brady, John F. Cogan, and Morris P. Fiorina. Stanford, CA: Stanford University Press.

Brooks, David. 2012. "Is Our Adults Learning?" *New York Times*, April 26.

Browning, Lynnley. 2010. "U.S. Drops Criminal Charges against UBS." *New York Times*, October 22.

Bruner, Robert F., and Sean D. Carr. 2007. *The Panic of 1907: Lessons Learned from the Market's Perfect Storm.* Hoboken, NJ: Wiley.

Buffett, Warren E. 2010. "Pretty Good for Government Work." *New York Times*, November 16.

Buiter, Willem H. 2008. "Lessons from the North Atlantic Financial Crisis." Paper presented at the conference The Role of Money Markets, Federal Reserve Bank of New York, May 29–30, 2008.

"Bum Rap For Rahm." 2011. Accessed on September 20, 2012, at http://www
.factcheck.org/2011/01/bum-rap-for-rahm/.

Bureau of Labor Statistics. 2011. "Labor Force Statistics from the Current Population Survey." Accessed November 25, 2011, at http://bls.gov/web/empsit
/cpseea10.htm.

Bush, George W. 2003. "Remarks on Signing the American Dream Downpayment Act." *The American Presidency Project*, December 16. Accessed September 20, 2012, at http://www.presidency.ucsb.edu/ws/index.php?pid
=64935.

Calmes, Jackie. 2009. "AIG Uproar a Test for Geithner." *New York Times*, March 18.

Calmes, Jackie. 2010a. "Obama to Propose Tax Write-off for Business." *New York Times*, September 6.

Calmes, Jackie. 2010b. "Obama Pushes Transportation Spending." *New York Times*, October 11.

Cameron, Charles. 2000. *Veto Bargaining: Presidents and the Politics of Negative Power*. New York: Cambridge University Press.

Cameron, Charles, and Nolan McCarty. 2004. "Models of Vetoes and Veto Bargaining." *Annual Review of Political Science* 7: 409–35.

Carmines, Edward J., and James A. Stimson. 1989. *Issue Evolution: Race and the Transformation of American Politics*. Princeton, NJ: Princeton University Press.

Chan, Sewell. 2010a. "Democrats Are at Odds on Relevance of Keynes." *New York Times*, October 18.

Chan, Sewell. 2010b. "Reform Bill Adds Layers of Oversight." *New York Times*, March 16.

Chao, Justine. 2011. "The Dodd Frank Act: Section 941: Improvements to the Asset-backed Securitization Process: Credit Risk Retention." Unpublished manuscript, New York University. Accessed September 7, 2012, at http://
voteview.com/ChaoCRR_Final_Paper.pdf.

Cheng, Ing-Hae, Sahil Raina, and Wei Xiong. 2012. "Wall Street and the Housing Bubble: Bad Incentives, Bad Models, or Bad Luck." Unpublished manuscript, University of Michigan. Accessed September 24, 2012 at http://aida
.econ.yale.edu/~shiller/behfin/2012-04-11/Cheng_Raina_Xiong.pdf.

Cilliza, Chris. 2012. "Connecticut Sen. Christopher Dodd Won't Seek Reelection, Will Retire at End of Term." *Washington Post*, January 6.

Clifford, Matthew P. 2009. "Congress and the Financial Services Industry 1989–2008." Masters thesis, Department of Political Science, Massachusetts Institute of Technology.

Clinton, Joshua D., Simon D. Jackman, and Douglas Rivers. 2004. "The Statistical Analysis of Roll Call Data: A Unified Approach." *American Political Science Review* 98: 355–70.

Clinton, William J. 1995. "Veto Message Re Private Securities Litigation Reform Act." Accessed September 20, 2012, at http://www.lectlaw.com/files
/leg22.htm.

Clinton, William J. 1999. "Statement on Signing the Gramm-Leach-Bliley Act, November 12, 1999." Accessed June 15, 2011, at http://www.presidency.ucsb.edu/ws/index.php?pid=56922#axzz1PMR0bS3f.

Coate, Stephen, and Stephen Morris. 1995. "On the Form of Transfers to Special Interests." *Journal of Political Economy* 103(6): 1210–35.

Collins, Brian. 2011. "Servicers Sign 'Watered Down' Consent Agreements." *American Banker*, April 7. Accessed December 6, 2011, at http://www.americanbanker.com/news/servicer-settlement-1035663-1.html.

Comfort, Nicholas. 2012. "UBS Fine Brings European Bank Levies to $6.1 Billion." *Bloomberg*, December 18. Accessed December 23, 2012, http://www.bloomberg.com/news/2012-12-19/ubs-fine-brings-european-bank-levies-to-6-1-billion.html.

Commodity Futures Trading Commission. 2011. *President's Budget and Performance Plan, Fiscal Year 2012.* Washington, DC: Commodity Futures Trading Commission.

Condon, Bernard. 2012. "Ordinary Folks Losing Faith in Stocks." *Associated Press*, December 27. Accessed December 28, 2012, http://news.yahoo.com/ap-impact-ordinary-folks-losing-faith-stocks-181042940--finance.html.

Congressional Budget Office. 2001. "Pay-As-You-Go Estimate, H.R. 5640: American Homeownership and Economic Opportunity Act of 2000." Accessed September 20, 2012, at http://www.cbo.gov/sites/default/files/cbofiles/ftpdocs/27xx/doc2722/hr5640.pdf.

Congressional Budget Office. 2010. "Estimated Impact of the Stimulus Package on Employment and Economic Output." Accessed September 20, 2012, at http://www.cbo.gov/publication/25099.

Cooper, Helen, and Jennifer Steinhauer. 2012. "Bucking Senate, Obama Appoints Consumer Chief." *New York Times*, January 4.

Cooper, Michael. 2010. "From Obama, the Tax Cut Nobody Heard Of." *New York Times*, October 18.

Cox, Gary, and Mathew D. McCubbins. 2005. *Setting the Agenda: Responsible Party Government in the U.S. House of Representatives.* New York: Cambridge University Press.

Curry, Timothy, and Lynn Shibut. 2000. "The Cost of the Savings and Loan Crisis: Truth and Consequences." *FDIC Banking Review* 13(2): 26–35.

Davis Polk. 2012. "Dodd-Frank Progress Report." Accessed September 20, 2012, at http://www.davispolk.com/files/Publication/867cc356-a624-49e9-b1fc-529db6946e6e/Presentation/PublicationAttachment/97a3eb90-7d31-41fe-a2a7-815c28e874f5/Jun2012_Dodd.Frank.Progress.Report.pdf.

Davis Polk. 2013. "Dodd Frank Progress Report." January. Accessed January 2, 2013, http://www.davispolk.com/files/uploads/FIG/Jan2013_Dodd.Frank.Progress.Report.pdf.

Davison, Lee. 2006. "The Resolution Trust Corporation and Congress, 1989–1993. Part II: 1991–1993." Accessed November 24, 2011, at http://www.fdic.gov/bank/analytical/banking/2007apr/article1/index.html.

DeBold, Elizabeth. 2010. "Title XIV—The Mortgage Reform and Anti-predatory Lending Act: The Past, Present, and Future of Anti-predatory Lending Protections." Unpublished manuscript, New York University. Accessed September 7, 2012, at http://voteview.com/DeBold_Predatory_Lending.pdf.

Diermeier, Daniel, and Timothy Feddersen. 1998. "Cohesion in Legislatures and the Vote of Confidence Procedure." *American Political Science Review* 92(3): 611–21.

De la Merced, Michael J., and Julia Werdigier. 2010. "The Origins of Lehman's 'Repo 105.'" *New York Times*, March 12.

Dennis, Brady. 2010a. "Sen. Blanche Lincoln's Derivatives-spinoff Plan Gains Support in Congress." *Washington Post*, June 15.

Dennis, Brady. 2010b. "Sen. Dodd to Introduce Plan to Overhaul Financial Regulatory System." *Washington Post*, March 15.

Dewan, Shaila, and Jessica Silver-Greenberg. 2012. "Foreclosure Deal Credits Banks for Routine Efforts." *New York Times*, March 27.

Dilanian, Ken. 2000. "Obama Shifts Stance on Environmental Issues." *USA Today*, July 18.

Dixit, Avinash K., and Jorgen W. Weibull. 2007. "Political Polarization." *Proceedings of the National Academy of Sciences* 104: 7351–56.

Dodosh, Mark. 2008. "National City's Failed Strategy Threatens Fate: Woes That May Lead to Bank's Takeover Rooted in Decisions Nearly a Decade Old." Crain's Cleveland Business. Accessed September 7, 2012, at http://www.crainscleveland.com/apps/pbcs.dll/article?AID=/20080317/FREE/590006312/1099#.

Duca, John V., John Muellbauer, and Anthony Murphy. 2011. *Shifting Credit Standards and the Boom and Bust in U.S. House Prices*. Federal Reserve Bank of Dallas Working Paper no. 1104. Dallas: Federal Reserve Bank of Dallas.

Duca, John V., John Muellbauer, and Anthony Murphy. 2012. "Shifting Credit Standards and the Boom and Bust in U.S. House Prices: Time Series Evidence from the Past Three Decades." Unpublished manuscript, Southern Methodist University.

Duca, John V., and Jason L. Saving. 2008. "Stock Ownership and Congressional Elections: The Political Economy of the Mutual Fund Revolution." *Economic Inquiry* 46(3): 454–79.

Edwards, Franklin R., and Edward R. Morrison. 2005. "Derivatives and the Bankruptcy Code: Why the Special Treatment?" *Yale Journal of Regulation* 22: 91–122.

Eisenhower, Dwight D. 1956. "Statement by the President upon Signing the Bank Holding Company Act of 1956." Accessed September 20, 2012, at http://www.presidency.ucsb.edu/ws/index.php?pid=10799#axzz1xyK2NNY8.

Elmer, Vickie. 2012. "Increased Interest in Expanded HARP." *New York Times*, June 21.

Epstein, David, and Sharyn O'Halloran. 1999. *Delegating Powers: A Transaction Cost Politics Approach to Policy Making under Separate Powers*. New York: Cambridge University Press.

Erikson, Robert S., Michael B. MacKuen, and James A. Stimson. 2002. *The Macro Polity*. New York: Cambridge University Press.

"Faculty Profile of Paul MacAvoy." 2012. Accessed September 20, 2012 at http://mba.yale.edu/faculty/profiles/macavoy.shtml.

Fannie Mae. 2003. *Fannie May Annual Report 2003*. Accessed June 20, 2011, at http://www.fanniemae.com/ir/pdf/annualreport/2003/2003annualreport.pdf.

Federal Deposit Insurance Corporation. 1984. *The First Fifty: A History of the FDIC 1933–1983*. Accessed January 27, 2011, at http://www.fdic.gov/bank/analytical/firstfifty/.

Federal Home Loan Banks. 2012. "The Federal Home Loan Banks." Accessed September 20, 2012, at http://www.fhlbanks.com/assets/pdfs/sidebar/FHL BanksWhitePaper.pdf.

Ferejohn, John, and Charles R. Shipan. 1990. "Congressional Influence on Bureaucracy." *Journal of Law, Economics, and Organization* 6: 1–20.

The Financial Crisis and the Role of Federal Regulators. 2008. Hearing before the Committee on Oversight and Government Reform, House of Representatives 110th Congress, Second Session, October 23, 2008. Serial No. 110-209. Washington, DC: Government Printing Office.

Fiorina, Morris P. 1989. *Congress: Keystone of the Washington Establishment*. New Haven, CT: Yale University Press.

Fiorina, Morris P., with Samuel J. Abrams and Jeremy C. Pope. 2010. *Culture War? The Myth of a Polarized America*. 3rd ed. Boston: Longman.

Fogel, Robert. 1989. *Without Consent or Contract: The Rise and Fall of American Slavery*. New York: Norton.

Foote, Christopher L., Kristopher S. Gerardi, and Paul S. Willen. 2012. *Why Did so Many People Make so Many Ex Post Bad Decisions? The Causes of the Foreclosure Crisis*. NBER Working Paper 18082. Cambridge, MA: National Bureau of Economic Research.

Fox News. 2009. "Thousands of Anti-Tax 'Tea Party' Protesters Turn Out in U.S. Cities." Foxnews.com, April 15. Accessed September 7, 2012, at http://www.foxnews.com/politics/2009/04/15/thousands-anti-tax-tea-party -protesters-turn-cities/.

Frame, W. Scott. 2008. "The 2008 Federal Intervention to Stabilize Fannie Mae and Freddie Mac." *Journal of Applied Finance* 18: 124–36.

Friedman, Milton J., and Anna J. Schwartz. 1963. *A Monetary History of the United States, 1867–1960*. Princeton, NJ: Princeton University Press.

Friedman, Milton J., and Anna J. Schwartz. 2008. *The Great Contraction, 1929–1933*. Princeton, NJ: Princeton University Press.

Gapper, John. 2008. "After 73 Years: The Last Gasp of the Broker-Dealer." *Financial Times*, September 15.

Geanakoplos, John D., and Susan P. Koniak. 2008. "Mortgage Justice Is Blind." *New York Times*, October 29.

Geanakoplos, John D., and Susan P. Koniak. 2009. "Matters of Principal." *New York Times*, March 4.

Gerardi, Kristopher S., Adam Hale Shapiro, and Paul S. Willen. 2008. *Subprime Outcomes: Risky Mortgages, Homeownership Experiences, and*

Foreclosures. Federal Reserve Bank of Boston Working Paper 07-15. Boston: Federal Reserve Bank of Boston.

Gerring, John. 1998. *Party Ideologies in America, 1822–1996*. Cambridge: Cambridge University Press.

Gilmour, John. 1995. *Strategic Disagreement: Stalemate in American Politics*. Pittsburgh: University of Pittsburgh Press.

Glaeser, Edward L., and Jose Scheinkman. 1998. "Neither a Lender nor a Borrower Be: An Economic Analysis of Interest Restrictions and Usury Laws." *Journal of Law and Economics* 41: 1–36.

"Glass Links Banks to Attack by Long." 1933. *New York Times*, December 6.

Goldin, Claudia, and Lawrence F. Katz. 2008. *The Race between Education and Technology*. Cambridge, MA: Belknap Press of Harvard University Press.

Goldman Sachs. 2012. "Board of Directors: James A. Johnson." Accessed September 20, 2012, at http://www.goldmansachs.com/who-we-are/leadership /board-of-directors/07-james-a-johnson.html.

Gorton, Gary B. 2010a. "Questions and Answers about the Financial Crisis." Unpublished manuscript, Yale University, prepared for the U.S. Financial Crisis Inquiry Commission.

Gorton, Gary B. 2010b. *Slapped by the Invisible Hand: The Panic of 2007*. New York NY: Oxford University Press.

Gramlich, Edward M. 2007. *Subprime Mortgages: America's Latest Boom and Bust*. Washington, DC: Urban Institute Press.

Gramm, Phil. 1999. "Gramm's Statement at Signing Ceremony for Gramm-Leach-Bliley Act." Accessed January 2, 2011, at http://banking.senate.gov /prel99/1112gbl.htm.

Greenspan, Alan. 2005. "Remarks by Chairman Alan Greenspan at the Federal Reserve System's Fourth Annual Community Affairs Research Conference, Washington, D.C." Accessed September 20, 2012, at http://www.federal reserve.gov/boarddocs/speeches/2005/20050408/default.htm.

"Greenspan Pockets $250K for Speech." 2006. Accessed September 20, 2012, at http://archive.newsmax.com/archives/articles/2006/2/13/211758.shtml.

Gropp, Reint, John Karl Scholz, and Michelle J. White. 1997. "Personal Bankruptcy and Credit Supply and Demand." *Quarterly Journal of Economics* 112: 217–51.

Groseclose, Tim, and Nolan McCarty. 2000. "The Politics of Blame: Bargaining before an Audience." *American Journal of Political Science* 45(1): 100–19.

Halberstam, David. 1969. *The Best and the Brightest*. New York: Random House.

Hall, Robert E. 2010. "Fiscal Stimulus." *Daedalus* 139: 83–94.

Hansell, Saul. 1994. "Markets in Turmoil: Investors Undone: How $600 Million Evaporated—A Special Report; Fund Manager Caught Short By Crude and Brutal Market." *New York Times*, April 5.

Hansen, Bradley. 1996. "Commercial Associations and the Creation of a National Economy: The Demand for a Federal Bankruptcy Law." *Business History Review* 72: 86–113.

Hare, Christopher, Nolan McCarty, Keith T. Poole, and Howard Rosenthal. 2012. "Polarization Is Real (and Asymmetric)." Accessed September 7, 2012, at http://voteview.com/blog/?p=494.

Hauke, Justin P., and Edward Nelson. 2007. "Recalling Ben Bernanke's First Year as Fed Chairman." *Central Banker*, Summer 2007. Accessed March 31, 2011, at http://www.stlouisfed.org/publications/cb/articles/?id=743.

Heckman, James, and James Snyder. 1997. "Linear Probability Models of the Demand for Attributes with an Empirical Application to Estimating the Preferences of Legislators." *Rand Journal of Economics*, special issue, S142-89.

Heilemann, John. 2011. "2012 = 1968?" *New York Magazine*, November 27, 2011. Accessed December 14, 2011, at http://nymag.com/print/?/news/politics/occupy-wall-street-2011-12/.

Hernandez, Raymond, and Stephen Labaton. 2007. "In Opposing Tax Plan, Schumer Breaks with Party." *New York Times*, July 30.

Hernandez, Raymond. 2012. "Surrogate for Obama Denounces Anti-Romney Ad." *New York Times*, May 20.

Herszenhorn, David M. 2008a. "Congress Votes for a Stimulus of $168 Billion." *New York Times*, February 7.

Herszenhorn, David M. 2008b. "Senate G.O.P. Blocks Additions to Stimulus Bill," *New York Times*, February 7.

Hill, Patrice. 2008. "McCain Advisor Talks of Mental Recession." *Washington Times*, July 9.

Hofstadter, Richard. 1955. *Age of Reform: From Bryan to FDR*. New York: Knopf.

Hofstadter, Richard, William Miller, and Daniel Aaron. 1959. *The American Republic*, vol. 2. Englewood Cliffs, NJ: Prentice-Hall.

Holden, Jeremy. 2009. "Wallace Let Boehner Falsely Claim No Stimulus Contracts Awarded in Ohio." Accessed July 3, 2011, at http://mediamatters.org/mobile/research/200907050004.

Huber, John D., and Nolan McCarty. 2004. "Bureaucratic Capacity, Delegation, and Political Reform." *American Political Science Review* 98: 481–94.

Huber, John D., and Charles R. Shipan. 2002. *Deliberate Discretion: The Institutional Foundations of Bureaucratic Autonomy*. Cambridge: Cambridge University Press.

Huntington, Samuel. 1952. "The Marasmus of the ICC: The Commission, the Railroads, and the Public." *Yale Law Journal* 61(4): 467–509.

Hurtado, Patricia, and Linda Sandler. 2012. "Ernst & Young Suit over Lehman Fees Sent to N.Y. State Court." Bloomberg News, March 22. Accessed June 21, 2012, at http://www.bloomberg.com/news/2012-03-22/ernst-young-suit-over-lehman-fees-sent-to-n-y-state-court-1-.html.

Igan, Deniz, Prachi Mishra, and Thierry Tressel. 2009. *A Fistful of Dollars: Lobbying and the Financial Crisis*. Paper presented at the Tenth Jacques Polak Annual Research Conference, Washington, DC, November 5–6, 2009. Accessed September 7, 2012, at http://www.imf.org/external/np/res/seminars/2009/arc/pdf/igan.pdf.

Illinois Department of Financial and Professional Regulation. 2012. "Illinois Bank Branching History." Accessed September 20, 2012, at http://www.idfpr .com/Banks/cbt/STATS/BR-HIST.ASP.

Isidore, Chris. 2012. "Wells Fargo to Pay 148M Fine for Wachovia Misdeeds." CNN Money, January 6. Accessed September 20, 2012, at http://money.cnn .com/2011/12/08/news/companies/wells_fargo_settlement/index.htm.

Ismail, M. Asif. 2003. "A Most Favored Corporation: Enron Prevailed in Federal, State Lobbying Efforts 49 Times." Accessed September 20, 2012, at http://www.publicintegrity.org/2003/01/06/3160/most-favored-corporation -enron-prevailed-federal-state-lobbying-efforts-49-times.

Jacobe, Dennis. 2008. "Pessimism Clouds Housing Market: Most Americans No Longer Assume Local Housing Prices Will Increase." Gallup Organization, February 11. Accessed September 7, 2012, at http://www.gallup.com /poll/104287/pessimism-clouds-housing-market.aspx.

Jaffee, Dwight. 2003. "The Interest Rate Risk of Fannie Mae and Freddie Mac." *Journal of Financial Services Research* 24(1): 5–29.

Johnson, Simon, and James Kwak. 2010. *13 Bankers: the Wall Street Takeover and the Next Financial Meltdown.* New York: Pantheon Books.

Kabaservice, Geoffrey A. 2012. *Rule and Ruin: The Downfall of Moderation and the Destruction of the Republican Party from Eisenhower to the Tea Party.* New York: Oxford University Press.

Kaplan, Steven N., and Joshua Rauh. 2007. *Wall Street and Main Street: What Contributes to the Rise in High Incomes?* NBER Working Paper 13270. Cambridge, MA: National Bureau of Economic Research.

Kennedy, Susan Estabrook. 1973. *The Banking Crisis of 1933.* Lexington: University of Kentucky Press.

Kiel, Paul, and Dan Nguyen. 2012. "Bailout Tracker." Accessed September 20, 2012, at http://projects.propublica.org/bailout/main/summary.

Kindleberger, Charles P., and Robert Aliber. 2005. *Manias, Panics, and Crashes: A History of Financial Crises.* 5th ed. New York: Wiley.

Koger, Gregory. 2010. *Filibustering: A Political History of Obstruction in the House and Senate.* Chicago: University of Chicago Press.

Krehbiel, Keith. 1998. *Pivotal Politics: A Theory of U.S. Lawmaking.* Chicago: University of Chicago Press.

Kroszner, Randall S. 1999. "Is It Better to Forgive Than to Receive? Repudiation of the Gold Indexation Clause in Long-Term Debt during the Great Depression." Unpublished manuscript, University of Chicago.

Kroszner, Randall S., and Thomas Stratmann. 1998. "Interest Group Competition and the Organization of Congress: Theory and Evidence from Financial Services Political Action Committees." *American Economic Review* 88: 1163–87.

Kwak, James. 2013. "Cultural Capital in the Financial Crisis." In *Preventing Capture: Special Interest Influence and How to Limit It*, ed. Daniel Carpenter and David Moss. New York: Cambridge University Press.

Labaton, Stephen. 2005. "Bankruptcy Bill Set for Passage; Victory for Bush." *New York Times*, March 9.

Lattman, Peter. 2011. "Judge in Citigroup Mortgage Settlement Criticizes S.E.C.'s Enforcement." *New York Times*, November 9.

Lattman, Peter, and Peter Eavis. 2012. "3 Former Credit Suisse Traders Charged with Bond Fraud." *New York Times*, February 1.

Lauderdale, Benjamin E. 2008. "Pass the Pork: Measuring Legislator Shares in Congress." *Political Analysis* 16(3): 235–49.

Lee, Frances E. 1998. "Representation and Public Policy: The Consequences of Senate Apportionment for the Geographic Distribution of Federal Funds." *Journal of Politics* 60: 34–62.

Lemann, Nicholas. 1991. *The Promised Land: The Great Black Migration and How It Changed America*. New York: Knopf.

Levendusky, Matthew. 2009. *The Partisan Sort: How Liberals Became Democrats and Conservatives Became Republicans*. Chicago: University of Chicago Press.

Levitt, Steven D. 1996. "How Do Senators Vote? Disentangling the Role of Voter Preferences, Party Affiliation, and Senator Ideology." *American Economic Review* 86(3): 425–41.

Lewis, Michael. 2010. *The Big Short: Inside the Doomsday Machine*. New York: Norton.

Lichtblau, Eric. 2012. "Gingrich's Deep Ties to Fannie Mae and Freddie Mac." *New York Times*, February 3.

Lieberman, Marvin B., and Shigeru Asaba. 2006. "Why Do Firms Imitate Each Other?" *Academy of Management Review* 31(2):366–85.

Lipton, Eric. 2008. "Gramm and the 'Enron Loophole.'" *New York Times*, November 14.

Lipton, Eric, and David D. Kirkpatrick. 2008. "Veterans of '90s Bailout Hope for Profit in New One." *New York Times*, December 28.

Lizza, Ryan. 2012. "The Obama Memos: The Making of a Post-post-partisan Presidency." *New Yorker*, January 30.

Lowenstein, Roger. 2000. *When Genius Failed: The Rise and Fall of Long-Term Capital Management*. New York: Random House.

Lowenstein, Roger. 2008. "Triple-A Failure." *New York Times Magazine*, April 27. Accessed September 7, 2012, at http://www.nytimes.com/2008/04/27/magazine/27Credit-t.html?adxnnl=1&adxnnlx=1347048185-Q9s2X/MCvVd+sW/aUif/QQ.

Lucas, Deborah. 2011. *The Budgetary Cost of Fannie Mae and Freddie Mac and Options for the Future Federal Role in the Secondary Mortgage Market*. Washington, DC: Congressional Budget Office.

MacKenzie, Donald. 2009. "All Those Arrows." *London Review of Books* 31(12): 20–22.

Madrick, Jeff, and Frank Partnoy. 2011. "Did Fannie Cause the Disaster?" *New York Review of Books* 58(16): 48–52.

Malabre, Alfred L. 1994. *Lost Prophets: An Insider's History of the Modern Economists.* Boston: Harvard Business School Press.

Malkiel, Burton G. 1990. *A Random Walk Down Wall Street: Including a Life-cycle Guide to Investing.* 5th ed. New York: Norton.

Mallaby, Sebastian. 2010. *More Money than God: Hedge Funds and the Making of a New Elite.* New York: Penguin.

Mann, Bruce. 2001. *Republic of Debtors: Bankruptcy in the Age of American Independence.* Cambridge MA: Harvard University Press.

Martin, Andrew D., and Kevin M. Quinn. 2002. "Dynamic Ideal Point Estimation via Markov Chain Monte Carlo for the U.S. Supreme Court, 1953–1999." *Political Analysis* 10: 134–55.

Martin, Mitchell. 1998. "Citicorp and Travelers Plan to Merge in Record $70 Billion Deal: A New No. 1: Financial Giants Unite," *New York Times,* April 7.

Maxfield, John. 2012. "The 5 Biggest Mortgage Originators in 3Q 2012." *The Motley Fool,* November 28. Accessed December 21, 2012, http://www.fool.com/investing/general/2012/11/28/the-5-biggest-mortgage-originators-in-3q12.aspx.

Mayhew, David. 1974. *Congress: The Electoral Connection.* New Haven, CT: Yale University Press.

McCarty, Nolan. 1997. "Presidential Reputation and the Veto." *Economics and Politics* 9: 1–26.

McCarty, Nolan. 2007. "The Policy Effects of Political Polarization." In *The Transformation of American Politics: Activist Government and the Rise of Conservatism,* ed. Paul Pierson and Theda Skocpol. Princeton, NJ: Princeton University Press.

McCarty, Nolan. 2008. "The Most Liberal Congress in History." Accessed September 20, 2012, at http://blogs.princeton.edu/mccarty/2008/12/the_most_liberal_congress_in_history.html.

McCarty, Nolan. 2009. "On the Virtues of Strategic Bipartisanship." Accessed September 20, 2012, at http://blogs.princeton.edu/mccarty/2009/02/on_the_virtues_of_strategic_bipartisanship.html.

McCarty, Nolan. 2013. "Complexity, Capacity and Capture." In *Preventing Capture: Special Interest Influence and How to Limit It,* ed. Daniel Carpenter and David Moss. New York: Cambridge University Press.

McCarty, Nolan, Keith T. Poole, Thomas Romer, and Howard Rosenthal. 2010a. "Political Fortunes: On Finance and Its Regulation." *Daedalus* 139 (4): 61–73.

McCarty, Nolan, Keith T. Poole, Thomas Romer, and Howard Rosenthal. 2010b. "The Price of Principle," *Huffington Post,* July 20. Accessed December 5, 2011, et http://www.huffingtonpost.com/nolan-mccarty/the-price-of-principle_b_652606.html.

McCarty, Nolan, Keith T. Poole, and Howard Rosenthal. 1997. *Income Redistribution and the Realignment of American Politics.* Washington, DC: AEI Press.

McCarty, Nolan, Keith T. Poole, and Howard Rosenthal. 2001. "The Hunt for Party Discipline in Congress." *American Political Science Review* 95(3): 673–87.

McCarty, Nolan, Keith T. Poole, and Howard Rosenthal. 2006. *Polarized America: The Dance of Ideology and Unequal Riches*. Cambridge, MA: MIT Press.

McClintick, David. 2006. "How Harvard Lost Russia." *Institutional Investor*, January 24.

McCubbins, Mathew D., and Thomas Schwartz. 1984. "Oversight Overlooked: Police Patrols versus Fire Alarms." *American Journal of Political Science* 28(1): 165–79.

McGinty, Tom, and Kara Scannell. 2009. "SEC Plays Keep-up in High-Tech Race." *Wall Street Journal*, August 20.

McGrath, Ben. 2010. "The Movement: The Rise of Tea Party Activism," *New Yorker*, February 1.

McKee, Michael, and Scott Lanman. 2009. "Greenspan Says U.S. Should Consider Breaking Up Large Banks." Bloomberg News, October 15. Accessed June 27, 2012, at http://www.bloomberg.com/apps/news?pid=newsarchive&sid=aJ8HPmNUfchg.

McKenna, Francine. 2012. "Auditors All Fall Down; PFGBest and MF Global Frauds Reveal Weak Watchdogs." *Forbes*, July 16. Accessed December 28, 2012, http://www.forbes.com/sites/francinemckenna/2012/07/16/auditors-all-fall-down-pfgbest-and-mf-global-frauds-reveal-weak-watchdogs/.

McLean, Bethany, and Peter Elkind. 2003. *The Smartest Guys in the Room: The Amazing Rise and Scandalous Fall of Enron*. New York: Portfolio.

McNamee, Mike. 2004. "Lewis S. Ranieri: Your Mortgage Was His Bond," *Business Week*, November 29.

Meltzer, Allan H. 2003. "Rational and Nonrational Bubbles." In *Asset Price Bubbles: The Implications for Monetary, Regulatory, and International Policies*, ed. W. C. Hunter, George G. Kaufman, and Michael Pomerleano. Cambridge, MA: MIT Press.

Mendelberg, Tali. 2001. *The Race Card: Campaign Strategy, Implicit Messages, and the Norm of Equality*. Princeton, NJ: Princeton University Press.

Mian, Atif, Amir Sufi, and Francesco Trebbi. 2010. "The Political Economy of the U.S. Mortgage Default Crisis." *American Economic Review* 100: 1967–98.

Milbank, Dana. 2010. "Behind the Foreclosure Crisis, Big Banks' Reign of Error." *Washington Post*, March 6.

Mishkin, Frederic S., and Tryggvi Thor Herbertsson. 2006. *Financial Stability in Iceland*. Reykjavik: Iceland Chamber of Commerce.

Mitchell, George J. 2007. "Report to the Commissioner of Baseball of an Independent Investigation into the Illegal Use of Steroids and Other Performance Enhancing Substances by Players in Major League Baseball." Accessed September 20, 2012, at http://mlb.mlb.com/mlb/news/mitchell/report.jsp.

Morgan, Glen. 2008. "Market Formation and Governance in International Financial Markets: The Case of OTC Derivatives." *Human Relations* 61: 637.

Morgenson, Gretchen. 2010. "Leading Magnate Settles Fraud Case." *New York Times*, October 10.

Morgenson, Gretchen. 2011. "Case on Mortgage Official Is Said to be Dropped." *New York Times*, February 19.

Morgenson, Gretchen. 2012. "Is Insider Trading Part of the Fabric?" *New York Times*, May 20.

Morgenson, Gretchen, with Joshua Rosner. 2011. *Reckless Endangerment: How Outsized Ambition, Greed, and Corruption Led to Economic Armageddon*. New York: Times Books/Henry Holt.

Morison, Elting E., ed. 1952. *The Letters of Theodore Roosevelt*. Vols. 1–8. Cambridge, MA: Harvard University Press.

Nakamoto, Michiyo, and David Wighton. 2007. "Citigroup Chief Stays Bullish on Buy-outs." *Financial Times*, July 9.

National Association of Realtors. 2012. "Membership: Historic Report." Accessed September 20, 2012, at http://www.realtor.org/membership/historic-report.

New Generation Research, Inc. 2012. *20 Largest Public Company Bankruptcy Filings 1980–Present*. Accessed September 20, 2012, at http://www.bankruptcydata.com/Research/Largest_Overall_All-Time.pdf.

New York City Housing Authority. 2012. "About NYCHA: Fact Sheet." Accessed September 20, 2012, at http://www.nyc.gov/html/nycha/html/about/factsheet.shtml.

Newsome, Sunsierre, Matthew Albrecht, and Daniel E. Teclaw. 2011. "Federal Home Loan Banks." Accessed September 20, 2012, at http://www.fhlb-of.com/ofweb_userWeb/resources/SandPCreditReport071911.pdf.

Nokken, Timothy P., and Keith T. Poole. 2004. "Congressional Party Defection in American History." *Legislative Studies Quarterly* 29: 545–68.

Noll, Roger G. 1971. *Reforming Regulation: An Evaluation of the Ash Council Proposal*. Washington, DC: Brookings Institution.

Nuñez, Stephen, and Howard Rosenthal. 2004. "Bankruptcy 'Reform' in Congress." *Journal of Law Economics and Organization* 20: 527–57.

Nunnari, Salvatore. 2011. "The Political Economy of the U.S. Auto Industry Crisis." Unpublished manuscript, California Institute of Technology.

Obama, Barack. 2008. "One Week to Go: Speech in Ohio." Accessed September 20, 2012, at http://www.presidentialrhetoric.com/campaign2008/obama/10.27.08.html.

"Obama's Take on Wall Street Prosecutions." 2011. *New York Times*, December 12. Accessed September 20, 2012, at http://dealbook.nytimes.com/2011/12/12/president-obamas-take-on-wall-street-prosecutions/.

Olshan, Jeremy. 2011. "'Father' of the 401(k)s Tough Love." Accessed June 5, 2012, at http://blogs.smartmoney.com/encore/2011/11/22/father-of-the-401ks-tough-love/.

Overacker, Louise. 1932. *Money in Elections*. New York: Macmillan.

Overacker, Louise. 1937. "Campaign Funds in the Presidential Election of 1936." *American Political Science Review* 31: 473–98.

Overbye, Dennis. 2009. "They Tried to Outsmart Wall Street." *New York Times*, March 9.

Partnoy, Frank. 2009. *Infectious Greed: How Deceit and Risk Corrupted the Financial Markets*. New York: Public Affairs Press.

Paulson, Henry M. 2010. *On the Brink: Inside the Race to Stop the Collapse of the Global Financial System.* New York: Business Plan.

Pelofsky, Jeremy, and James Vicini. 2011. "BofA's Countrywide to Pay $335 million over Bias Case." Reuters, December 21. Accessed September 20, 2012, at http://www.reuters.com/article/2011/12/21/us-boa-countrywide-idUSTRE7BK1UW20111221.

Perino, Michael. 2010. *The Hellhound of Wall Street: How Ferdinand Pecora's Investigation of the Great Crash Forever Changed American Finance.* New York: Penguin.

Perlstein, Rick. 2001. *Before the Storm: Barry Goldwater and the Unmaking of the American Consensus.* New York: Hill and Wang.

Pew Research Center for the People and the Press. 2011. *Fewer Are Angry at Government, But Discontent Remains High.* Accessed September 20, 2012, at http://people-press.org/files/2011/03/711.pdf.

Philippon, Thomas, and Ariell Reshef. 2009. *Wages and Human Capital in the U.S. Financial Industry: 1909–2006.* NBER Working Paper 14644. Cambridge, MA: National Bureau of Economic Research.

Piketty, Thomas, and Emmanuel Saez. 2003. "Income Inequality in the United States, 1913–1998." *Quarterly Journal of Economics* 118: 1–39.

Piskorski, Tomasz, Amit Seru, and Vikrant Vig. 2010. "Securitization and Distressed Loan Renegotiation: Evidence from the Subprime Mortgage Crisis." Booth School of Business Research Paper no. 09-02. Chicago: University of Chicago Booth School of Business.

Poole, Keith T. 2000. "Non-parametric Unfolding of Binary Choice Data." *Political Analysis* 8: 211–327.

Poole, Keith T. 2007. "Changing Minds? Not in Congress!" *Public Choice* 131: 435–51.

Poole, Keith T., and Thomas Romer. 1993. "Ideology, 'Shirking' and Representation." *Public Choice* 77: 185–96.

Poole, Keith T., and Howard Rosenthal. 1993. "The Enduring 19th Century Battle for Economic Regulation: The Case of the Interstate Commerce Act Revisited." *Journal of Law and Economics* 26: 837–60.

Poole, Keith T., and Howard Rosenthal. 1994. "Railroad Regulation and Congress, 1847–1887." In *The Regulated Economy: A Historical Approach to Political Economy*, ed. Claudia Goldin and Gary Libecap. Chicago: University of Chicago Press, 1994.

Poole, Keith T., and Howard Rosenthal. 1997. *Congress: A Political-economic History of Roll Call Voting.* New York: Oxford University Press.

Poole, Keith T., and Howard Rosenthal. 2007. *Ideology and Congress.* New Brunswick, NJ: Transaction.

Posner, Richard. 2009. *A Failure of Capitalism: The Crisis of '08 and the Descent into Depression.* Cambridge MA: Harvard University Press.

"President Bush Overall Job Rating." 2012. Accessed September 20, 2012, at http://www.pollingreport.com/BushJob.htm.

Preston, H. H. 1927. "The McFadden Banking Act." *American Economic Review* 17(2): 201–18.

Prince, C. J. 2007. "Staying Power." *Institutional Investor*, January 10. Accessed September 20, 2012, at http://www.institutionalinvestor.com/Article.aspx?ArticleID=1117671&PositionID=11151.

Prior, Markus. 2007. *Post-broadcast Democracy: How Media Choice Increases Inequality in Political Involvement and Polarizes Elections.* New York: Cambridge University Press.

Prior, Markus. Forthcoming. "Media and Political Polarization." *Annual Review of Political Science.*

Protess, Ben. 2012. "As Wall Street Fights Regulation, It Has Backup on the Bench." *New York Times*, December 29.

Public Citizen's Critical Mass Energy and Environment Program. 2001. *Blind Faith: How Deregulation and Enron's Influence over Government Looted Billions from Americans.* Accessed September 20, 2012, at http://www.citizen.org/documents/Blind_Faith.pdf.

Puzzanghera, Jim. 2012. "U.S. Says UBS Was Motivated by 'Sheer Greed' in Libor Rigging." *Los Angeles Times*, December 19. Accessed December 23, 2012, http://www.latimes.com/business/money/la-fi-mo-ubs-libor-fine-justice-20121219,0,4663488.story.

Purdum, Todd. 2009. "Henry Paulson's Longest Night." *Vanity Fair*, October.

Pyle, David H. 1995. "The U.S. Savings and Loan Crisis." In *Handbooks in Operations Research and Management Science*, vol. 9: *Finance*, ed. Robert A. Jarrow. Amsterdam: Elsevier.

Rajan, Raghuram G. 2010. *Fault Lines: How Hidden Fractures Still Threaten the World Economy.* Princeton, NJ: Princeton University Press.

Rajan, Raghuram G., and Rodney Ramcharan. 2011. "Constituencies and Legislation: The Fight over the McFadden Act of 1927." Unpublished manuscript, University of Chicago.

Rappaport, Liz, and Michael Rapoport. 2012. "Auditors Face Fraud Charge: New York Set to Allege Ernst & Young Stood By as Lehman Cooked Its Books." *Wall Street Journal*, December 20.

Rasmussen, Scott, and Douglas Schoen. 2010. *Mad as Hell: How the Tea Party Movement Is Fundamentally Remaking our Two-party System.* New York: HarperCollins.

Reinhart, Carmen M., and Kenneth S. Rogoff. 2009. *This Time Is Different: Eight Centuries of Financial Folly.* Princeton, NJ: Princeton University Press.

Reuters. 2009. "U.S. Should Be Open to Second Stimulus—Congressional Leader." Accessed, April 17, 2012, at http://blogs.reuters.com/financial-regulatory-forum/2009/07/07/us-should-be-open-to-second-stimulus-congressional-leader/.

Reuters. 2012. "Sheryl Sandberg, Facebook COO, Ducks Questions about IPO Debacle." Accessed September 7, 2012, at http://www.huffingtonpost.com/2012/05/24/refile-facebook-exec-duck_n_1543089.html.

"Rick Santelli, Tea Party." 2009. Accessed September 20, 2012, at http://free domeden.blogspot.com/2009/02/rick-santelli-tea-party.html.

Robbins, Liz. 2009. "Tax Day Is Met with Tea Parties." *New York Times*, April 16.

Roguski, Randy. 2008. "Ten Ways National City Could Have Avoided Trouble." *Plain Dealer*, April 20.

Romer, Thomas, and Barry R. Weingast. 1991. "Political Foundations of the Thrift Debacle." In *Politics and Economics in the Eighties*, ed. Alberto Alesina and Geoffrey Carliner. Chicago: University of Chicago Press.

Rothbard, Murray B. 1962. *The Panic of 1819: Reactions and Policies*. New York: Columbia University Press.

Roubini, Nouriel. 2008. "Comrades Bush, Paulson and Bernanke Welcome You to the USSRA (United Socialist State Republic of America)." September 9, 2008. Accessed April 11, 2009, at http://www.roubini.com/roubini-moni tor/253529/comrades_bush_paulson_and_bernanke_welcome_you_to_the _ussra_united_socialist_state_republic_of_america.

"The Rubin Connection." 2008. *New York Times*, November 24.

Santomero, Anthony M. 2001. "The Causes and Effects of Financial Modernization." Federal Reserve Bank of Philadelphia. Accessed January 22, 2012, at http://www.philadelphiafed.org/research-and-data/publications/business -review/2001/q4/brq401as.pdf.

Sarlin, Benjamin. 2010. "Why the Tea Party Isn't Touching Financial Reform." *Daily Beast*, April 20.

Schaefer, Steve. 2010. "Survey Says: Cuomo Should Slap Ernst & Young with Lehman Fraud Charge." *Forbes*, December 21. Accessed September 20, 2012, at http://www.forbes.com/sites/steveschaefer/2010/12/21survey-says-cuomo -should-slap-ernst-young-with-lehman-fraud-charge/.

Schattschneider, E. E. 1960. *The Semi-sovereign People: A Realist's View of American Politics*. New York: Holt, Rinehart and Winston.

Schlesinger, Arthur M., Jr., 1965. *A Thousand Days: John F. Kennedy in the White House*. New York: Houghton Mifflin.

Schoen, Douglas. 2011. "Polling the Occupy Wall Street Crowd." *Wall Street Journal*, October 18.

Schwartz, Matthias. 2011. "Pre-Occupied: the Origins and Future of Occupy Wall Street." *New Yorker*, November 26.

Scott, Mark, and Michael J. De la Merced. 2012. "Chairman of Barclays Resigns." *New York Times*, July 1.

"SEC Brings Crisis-Era Suits." 2011. *Wall Street Journal*, December 17.

Segal, Jeffrey A., and Harold J. Spaeth. 2002. *The Supreme Court and the Attitudinal Model Revisited*. New York: Cambridge University Press.

Senate Library. 2002. *Presidential Vetoes, 1789–1988*. Washington, DC: Government Printing Office.

Shamim, Adam. 2009. "Obama Adviser Says U.S. Should Mull Second Stimulus." Bloomberg News, July 7. Accessed April 17, 2012, at http://www .bloomberg.com/apps/news?pid=newsarchive&sid=aStWHJXsvePA.

Shear, Michael D. 2009. "Senior UBS Official, Key Donor Shares Some of Obama's Down Time." *Washington Post*, August 24.

Shiller, Robert. 2000. *Irrational Exuberance*. Princeton, NJ: University Press, 2000.

Sides, John. 2012. "Were Obama's Early Ads Really the Game Changer?" *Five Thirty Eight*, December 29. Accessed January 2, 2013, http://fivethirtyeight .blogs.nytimes.com/2012/12/29/were-obamas-early-ads-really-the-game -changer/?hp

Silver-Greenberg, Jessica. 2012a. "Mortgage Crisis Presents a New Reckoning to Banks." *New York Times*, December 9.

Silver-Greenberg, Jessica. 2012b. "Settlement Expected on Past Abuses in Home Loans." *New York Times*, December 30.

Sims, Damon. 2008. "PNC-National City Bank Deal Draws Criticism." *Plain Dealer*, November 16.

Simon, Herbert. 1957. "A Behavioral Model of Rational Choice." In *Models of Man, Social and Rational: Mathematical Essays on Rational Human Behavior in a Social Setting*. New York: Wiley, 1957.

Sinclair, Barbara. 2002. "The 60-Vote Senate." In *U.S. Senate Exceptionalism*, ed. Bruce I. Oppenheimer. Columbus: Ohio State University Press.

Skeel, David. 2001. *Debt's Dominion: A History of Bankruptcy Law in America*. Princeton, NJ: Princeton University Press.

Skeel, David. 2011. *The New Financial Deal: Understanding the Dodd-Frank Act and Its (Unintended) Consequences*. Hoboken, NJ: Wiley.

Skocpol, Theda, and Vanessa Williamson. 2011. *The Tea Party and the Remaking of American Conservatism*. New York NY: Oxford University Press.

Slack, Donovan. 2010. "Stance on Fannie and Freddie Dogs Frank." *Boston Globe*, October 14.

Smith, Adam. 1904. *Adam Smith's Wealth of Nations*. New York: T. Y. Cromwell.

Sorkin, Andrew Ross. 2009. *Too Big to Fail: The Inside Story of How Wall Street and Washington Fought to Save the Financial System from Crisis— and Themselves*. New York: Viking.

Sorkin, Andrew Ross. 2011. "Goldman Limits Facebook Investment to Foreign Clients," *New York Times*, January 17.

Sorkin, Andrew Ross. 2012. "The Man Behind Facebook's I.P.O. Debacle." *New York Times*, September 3.

Soros, George. 2010. "The Real Danger to the Economy." *New York Review of Books*, November 11.

Spiller, Pablo T., and Rafael Gely. 1992. "Congressional Control or Judicial Independence: The Determinants of U.S. Supreme Court Labor-Relations Decisions, 1949–1988," *RAND Journal of Economics* 23(4): 463–92.

Standard & Poors. 2011. *Federal Home Loan Banks*. Accessed November 24, 2011 at http://www.fhlb-of.com/ofweb_userWeb/resources/SandPCredit Report071911.pdf.

State National Bank of Big Spring et al. v. Geithner et al. Accessed December 28, 2012, http://cei.org/sites/default/files/Complaint,%20First%20Amended ,%209-20-2012.pdf.

Stephenson, Emily. 2012. "Three States Join Lawsuit Challenging Dodd-Frank Law." *Reuters*, September 9. Accessed December 28, 2012, http://www.reuters .com/article/2012/09/21us-financial-regulation-lawsuit-idUSBRE88K0WA2 0120921.

Stigler, George. 1971. "The Theory of Economic Regulation." *Bell Journal of Economics and Management Science* 2(1): 3–21.

Stiglitz, Joseph E. 2009a. "Capitalist Fools." *Vanity Fair*, January.

Stiglitz, Joseph E. 2009b. "Too Big to Exist." Accessed June 18, 2012, at http:// www.policyinnovations.org/ideas/commentary/data/000158/:pf_printable.

Stiglitz, Joseph E., Jonathan M. Orszag, and Peter Orszag. 2002. "Implications of the New Fannie Mae and Freddie Mac Risk-based Capital Standard." *Housing Matters* 1(2): 1–10.

Stiglitz, Joseph E., Jonathan M. Orszag, and Peter Orszag. 2004. "Implications of the New Fannie Mae and Freddie Mac Risk-based Capital Standard." In *Housing Matters: Issues in American Housing Policy*, ed. Franklin Raines and Sheila Bair. Washington, D.C.: Fannie Mae.

Stohr, Greg. 2009. "Obama Backs Banks, Seeks to Block Fair-lending Probe (Update 1)." Bloomberg News, March 26. Accessed December 5, 2011, at http://www.bloomberg.com/apps/news?pid=newsarchive&sid=aCdEKIwb iPzQ.

Stolberg, Sheryl Gay. 2009a. "Senate Has Changed in Kennedy's Time." *New York Times*, August 27.

Stolberg, Sheryl Gay. 2009b. "Signing Stimulus, Obama Doesn't Rule Out More." *New York Times*, February 17.

Stolberg, Sheryl Gay. 2010. "Obama Calls Jobs Bill a First Step." *New York Times*, March 18.

Strahan, Philip E. 2002. *The Real Effects of U.S. Banking Deregulation*. Accessed September 7, 2012, at http://research.stlouisfed.org/conferences/policy conf/papers/Strahan.pdf.

Streitfeld, David, and John C. Rudolf. 2009. "States Are Pondering Fraud Suits against Banks." *New York Times*, November 3.

Subramanian, Guhan, and Nithyasri Sharma. 2010. "Citigroup–Wachovia–Wells Fargo." Unpublished manuscript, Harvard Law School, Cambridge, MA.

Sunstein, Cass R., David Schkade, and Lisa M. Ellman. 2004. "Ideological Voting on Federal Courts of Appeals: A Preliminary Investigation." *Virginia Law Review* 90: 301.

Sussman, Anna Louie. 2012. "U.S. Foreclosures Up for 2nd Straight Month." Reuters, July 12. Accessed September 20, 2012, at http://in.reuters.com /article/2012/07/12/usa-housing-realtytrac-idINL2E8IBG6F20120712.

Swagel, Phillip. 2009. "The Financial Crisis: An Inside View." *Brookings Papers on Economic Activity* 40(1): 1–78. Accessed December 8, 2011, at http:// www.brookings.edu/~/media/Files/Programs/ES/BPEA/2009_spring_bpea _papers/2009a_bpea_swagel.pdf.

"The Talented Mr. Gensler: Jon Corzine's Regulator Wants You to Know He's Been Very Busy." 2011. *Wall Street Journal*, December 12.

Tapper, Jake. 2011. "Wall Street Corruption, Solyndra, and Fast & Furious: Today's Q's for O." ABC News, October 6. Accessed September 20, 2012, at http://abcnews.go.com/blogs/politics/2011/10/wall-street-corruption-solyndra-and-fast-furious-todays-qs-for-o-1062011/.

Tausanovitch, Chris. 2011. "Income and Representation." Unpublished manuscript, Stanford University.

Teles, Steven M. 2008. *The Rise of the Conservative Legal Movement: The Battle for Control of the Law*. Princeton, NJ: Princeton University Press.

Tett, Gillian. 2009. *Fool's Gold: How Unrestrained Greed Corrupted a Dream, Shattered Global Markets and Unleashed a Catastrophe*. London: Little Brown.

Toobin, Jeffrey. 2010. "The Senator and the Street: Chuck Schumer, His Financial Constituents and the Next Move." *New Yorker*, August 2.

Treanor, Jill. 2009. "King Calls for Banks to Be 'Cut Down to Size.'" *Guardian*, June 17.

Tufano, Peter. 1997. "Business Failure, Judicial Intervention, and Financial Innovation: Restructuring U.S. Railroads in the Nineteenth Century." *Business History Review* 71: 1–40.

U.S. Attorney, Eastern District of New York. 2012. "$1 Billion to Be Paid by Bank of America to United States." Accessed September 20, 2012, at http://www.justice.gov/usao/nye/pr/2012/2012feb09.html.

U.S. Commodity Futures Trading Commission and U.S. Securities and Exchange Commission. 2010. *Findings Regarding the Market Events of May 6, 2010: Report of the Staffs of the CFTC and SEC to the Joint Advisory Commitee on Emerging Regulatory Issues*. Accessed September 16, 2012, at http://www.sec.gov/news/studies/2010/marketevents-report.pdf.

U.S. Department of Housing and Urban Development. 2012. "American Dream Downpayment Initiative." Accessed September 20, 2012, at http://www.hud.gov/offices/cpd/affordablehousing/programs/home/addi/index.cfm.

U.S. Department of Justice. 2012. "Federal Government and State Attorneys General Reach $25 Billion Agreement with Five Largest Mortgage Servicers to Address Mortgage Loan Servicing and Foreclosure Abuses." Accessed September 20, 2012 at http://www.justice.gov/opa/pr/2012/February/12ag-186.html.

U.S. Department of the Treasury. 2011. *Fact Sheet: Notice of Proposed Determination on Foreign Exchange Swaps and Forwards*. Accessed September 20, 2012, at http://www.treasury.gov/initiatives/wsr/Documents/Fact%20Sheet%20-%20Notice%20of%20Proposed%20Determination%20on%20Foreign%20Exchange%20Swaps%20and%20Forwards.pdf.

U.S. House of Representatives, Office of the Clerk. 2012. "Party Divisions of the House of Representatives (1789 to Present)." Accessed September 20, 2012, at http://artandhistory.house.gov/house_history/partydiv.aspx.

U.S. Securities and Exchange Commission. 2010a. "Former Countrywide CEO Angelo Mozilo to Pay SEC's Largest-ever Financial Penalty against a Public Company's Senior Executive." Accessed September 20, 2012, at http://www.sec.gov/news/press/2010/2010-197.htm.

U.S. Securities and Exchange Commission. 2010b. "Goldman Sachs to Pay Record $550 Million to Settle SEC Charges Related to Subprime Mortgage CDO." Accessed September 20, 2012, at http://www.sec.gov/news/press/2010/2010-123.htm.

U.S. Senate. 2012. "Party Division in the Senate, 1789 to Present." Accessed September 20, 2012, at http://www.senate.gov/pagelayout/history/one_item_and_teasers/partydiv.htm.

Utt, Ronald. 2003. "American Dream Downpayment Act: Fiscally Irresponsible and Redundant to Existing Homeownership Programs." Accessed September 20, 2012, at http://www.heritage.org/research/reports/2003/12/american-dream-downpayment-act-fiscally-irresponsible-and-redundant-to-existing-homeownership-programs.

"Wachovia Settlement Checks Real, Better Business Bureau Says." 2008. *CNN.com*, December 28. Accessed September 20, 2012, at http://www.cnn.com/2008/US/12/25/wachovia.checks/index.html#cnnSTCText.

Wachtel, Katya. 2012. "Goldman CEO: Support for Gay Rights 'Not without Price.'" *Reuters*, May 2. Accessed September 20, 2012, at http://www.reuters.com/article/2012/05/02/goldmansachs-blankfein-criticism-idUSL1E8G28NC20120502.

Warren, Charles. 1935. *Bankruptcy in American History*. Cambridge, MA: Harvard University Press.

Wawro, Gregory J., and Eric Schickler. 2006. *Filibuster: Obstruction and Lawmaking in the U.S. Senate*. Princeton, NJ: Princeton University Press.

Weigel, David. 2010. "Tea Party Groups Protest Financial Reform." *Washington Independent*, March 4.

Weingast, Barry R. 1984. "The Congressional-bureaucratic System: A Principal-agent Perspective (with Applications to the SEC)." *Public Choice* 44: 147–77.

Weisman, Steven R., and Edmund L. Andrews. 2008. "Economists Debate the Quickest Cure." *New York Times*, January 19.

Weisman, Steven R., and David M. Herszenhorn. 2008. "Bush and Congress Seen Pushing for Stimulus Plan." *New York Times*, January 12.

Wheelock, David C. 2008. "The Federal Response to Home Mortgage Distress." *Federal Reserve Bank of St. Louis Review*, May–June, 133–48.

Whitehouse, Michael A. 1989. "Paul Warburg's Crusade to Establish a Central Bank in the United States." Accessed June 27, 2012, at http://www.minneapolisfed.org/publications_papers/pub_display.cfm?id=3815.

Wicker, Elmus. 2005. *The Great Debate of Banking Reform: Nelson Aldrich and the Origins of the Fed*. Columbus: Ohio State University Press.

Williams, T. Harry. 1969. *Huey Long*. New York: Knopf.

Williams, Timothy. 2011. "As Public Sector Sheds Jobs, Blacks Are Hit Hardest." *New York Times*, November 28.

Wilmott, Paul. 2009. "Hurrying into the Next Panic?" *New York Times*, July 29.

Wooten, James A. 2001. "'The Most Glorious Story of Failure in Business': The Studebaker-Packard Corporation and the Origins of ERISA." *Buffalo Law Review* 49: 683–39.

"The Worst American CEOs of All Time." 2009. *CNBC.com*, April 30. Accessed September 20, 2012, at http://www.cnbc.com/id/30502091/Portfolio _s_Worst_American_CEOs_of_All_Time.

Wyatt, Edward. 2010. "Veto Threat Raised over Derivatives." *New York Times*, April 16.

Zeke Faux and Jody Shenn. 2011. "Subprime Mortgage Bonds Get AAA Rating S&P Denied to U.S." Bloomberg, August 31. Accessed September 20, 2012, at http://www.bloomberg.com/news/2011-08-31/subprime-mortgage -bonds-getting-aaa-rating-s-p-denies-to-u-s-treasuries.html.

Zernike, Kate. 2010. *Boiling Mad: Inside Tea Party America*. New York: Henry Holt, 2010.

Zingales, Luigi. 2013. "Preventing Economists' Capture." In *Preventing Capture: Special Interest Influence and How to Limit It*, ed. Daniel Carpenter and David Moss. New York: Cambridge University Press.

Zitzewitz, Eric. 2006. "How Widespread Was Late Trading in Mutual Funds?" *American Economic Review (Papers and Proceedings)* 96(2): 284–89.

NAME INDEX

. . . .

Page numbers in italics refer to figures and tables.

SUBJECT INDEX

Page numbers in italics refer to figures and tables.